Maternal Ties.
A Selection of Programs
for Female Offenders

Cynthia L. Blinn, Editor

FOUNDED 1870

American Correctional Association
Lanham, MD

Reginald A. Wilkinson, President
James A. Gondles, Jr. , Executive Director
Gabriella M. Daley, Director, Communications and Publications
Leslie A. Maxam, Assistant Director, Communications and Publications
Alice Fins, Publications Managing Editor
Michael Kelly, Associate Editor
Mike Selby, Production Editor

Cover Design by Mike Selby. Photo: Summit House, Greensboro, NC.

Printed in the United States of America by Kirby Lithographic Company, Inc.,
    Arlington, VA.

ISBN 1-56991-068-5

This publication may be ordered from:
American Correctional Association
4380 Forbes Boulevard
Lanham, Maryland 20706-4322
1-800-222-5646

For information on publications and videos available from ACA, contact our World Wide Web home page at: http://www.corrections.com/aca

Library of Congress Cataloging-in-Publication Data

Maternal ties: a selection of programs for female offenders / edited by Cynthia L. Blinn.
        p. cm.
    Includes bibliographical references.
    ISBN 1-56991-068-5
    1. Women prisoners—Services for—United States. 2. Women prisoners—United States—Family relationships. 3. Children of women prisoners—Services for—United States. I. Blinn, Cynthia L.
HV9304.M28 1997
365'.66'082—dc21   97-12521
                                                                    CIP

Dedication

For my husband,
John B. Blinn,
whose love and support
carry me through each day.

And for his parents,
William J. and Jean T. Blinn,
with eternal gratitude
for enabling our paths to cross.

Acknowledgments

To Christopher Mitchell, Massachusetts Department of Corrections Program Services Director—without his help, I would not be in corrections. To Alice Fins, Publications Managing Editor of ACA, who saw the need for this project. To the wonderful people who submitted chapters and the equally wonderful people who reviewed this book.

Table of Contents

Preface

James A. Gondles, Jr. vii

Foreword

Cynthia L. Blinn ix

Introduction

Mary Q. Hawkes xi

Chapter 1: Developing Services for Incarcerated Mothers

Denise Johnston, M.D. 1

Parenting Education

Chapter 2: The S.A.P.P.O.R.T. Program

Angela D. Ashley 9

Education and Support Services

Chapter 3: The Center for Children of Incarcerated Parents

Denise Johnston, M.D. 15

Visitation for Reunification (Day Visits)

Chapter 4: The Rhode Island Women's Prison

Roberta Richman and Alberta Bacarri 25

Children and Community Partnerships

Chapter 5: Girl Scouts Beyond Bars

Marilyn C. Moses. 35

Chapter 6: The PROGRAM for Female Offenders, Inc.

Tracie M. Haigh 51

The Nation's Oldest Complete Prison Program

Chapter 7: The Children's Center Programs of Bedford Hills Correctional Facility

Kathy Boudin 55

Residential Programs

Chapter 8: Women's and Children's Halfway House Program Model: NEON, Inc.

Lysa K. Judson, Lee Pratt-Beardsley, Dona Ditrio 87

Chapter 9: Summit House

Karen V. Chapple, M.A., E. Paula Cox, Ph.D.,

Jamie Macdonald-Furches 99

Chapter 10: The Neil J. Houston House

Phyllis Buccio-Notaro, Barbara Molla,

Carolyn Stevenson, Carolyn Diane Wood 113

Foster Care Program

Chapter 11: Las Comadres: A Parenting Education/Foster Parenting Program

Gretchen Newby 131

Overnight Visitation

Chapter 12: Camp Dismas

Raymond J. Weis 141

Chapter 13: The Mother Offspring Life Development Program

Mary Alley 151

International Perspective

Chapter 14: A Cross-national Perspective on Residential Programs for Incarcerated Mothers and Their Children

Kelsey Kauffman 159

Index 167

About the Editor 177

Preface

Maternal Ties: A Selection of Programs for Female Offenders provides a look at a variety of approaches to helping incarcerated women keep in touch with their children and learn parenting skills so that when they are released, they will be better able to parent those children. After all, of the women sentenced to prison, more than two-thirds have children, and in the majority of cases the offenders are single parents. So, when they go to prison, their children suffer additional losses.

This is a theme with which ACA has a concern. In 1995, the ACA Delegate Assembly ratified a Public Correctional Policy on Female Offender Services that emphasized these points:

Correctional systems should develop service delivery systems for accused and adjudicated female offenders that are comparable to those provided to males. Additional services also must be provided to meet the unique needs of the female offender population.

Correctional systems should be guided by the principle of parity. Female offenders must receive the equivalent range of services available to male offenders, including opportunities for individualized programming and services that recognize the unique needs of this population. The services should:

A. Ensure access to a range of alternatives to incarceration, including pretrial and post-trial diversion, probation, restitution, treatment for substance abuse, halfway houses, and parole services;

B. Provide acceptable conditions of confinement, including appropriately trained staff and sound operating procedures that address this population's needs in such areas as clothing, personal property, hygiene, exercise, recreation, and visitations with children and family;

C. Provide access to a full range of work and programs designed to expand economic and social roles of women, with emphasis on education; career counseling and exploration of nontraditional vocational training;

relevant life skills, including parenting and social and economic assertiveness; and pre-release and work/education release programs;

D. Facilitate the maintenance and strengthening of family ties, particularly those between parent and child;

E. Deliver appropriate programs and services, including medical, dental, and mental health programs, services to pregnant women, substance abuse programs, child and family services, and provide access to legal services; and

F. Provide access to release programs that include aid in achieving economic stability and the development of supportive family relationships.

This theme is echoed in two recent publications. In *Women Behind Bars*, the offenders discuss being separated from their children as one of the hardest aspects of prison life. In *Parents in Prison: Addressing the Needs of Families*, Dr. James Boudouris describes a variety of programs and legal issues surrounding these programs. We are pleased to provide the current book as another resource that addresses this population, and we welcome hearing about other programs that provide for family reunification.

James A. Gondles, Jr.
Executive Director
American Correctional Association

Foreword

Maternal Ties: A Selection of Programs for Female Offenders provides descriptions of more than a dozen parenting programs in the United States, written by the experts— those who run the programs. Created specifically to assist correctional administrators in determining what programming would best suit their circumstances, this book is meant to be used in the early planning stages of program development or revision. Others who might find this book useful include those concerned with women's issues and those interested in childhood development. *Maternal Ties: A Selection of Programs for Female Offenders* documents the histories of a variety of types of programs. Administrators should consider the experiences shared by the authors when preparing to replicate or improve upon these programs, and contact each for more specific information, as needed.

Children are our future. For them to succeed in our complex world, a strong home-base and family-support system is necessary. I hope this collection will further our nation's efforts to break the intergenerational cycle of crime and to help families splintered by maternal incarceration to reunify successfully.

This book was compiled over the course of two years. During this time, staff and program changes may have occurred which may not be reflected here. Sincere thanks to all the dedicated people who took time to write about their programs for this collection. Regrettably, not all of the remarkable programs I encountered while researching this collection could be included, and many programs were unable to participate when invited.

Cynthia L. Blinn
Editor

Introduction

Female Offenders and Their Children

The programming needs of female offenders differ from those of male offenders, especially with regard to children. Females traditionally are the primary caregivers of their infants and children. In the offender population, the majority of mothers are the sole caregivers.

In the early decades of the nineteenth century, very few females were convicted and sent to jails, workhouses, or penitentiaries. Those who were incarcerated lived congregately in a separate room from the men with little or no supervision from a male keeper. They were physically and sexually abused by both the male keepers and prisoners who were allowed access to them. Children accompanied their mothers to the institutions, and babies were born in them.

By midcentury, with the rise of the suffragist movement and higher education opening up for women, reform movements concerning women and children were incipient. The women's reformatory movement, started by women who were lay visitors to the prisons, was led by Quakers, charity workers, and social feminists. They called for separate reformatories for females to be administered by women.

The first of these opened in the 1870s—Indiana (1873) and Massachusetts (1877). The first annual report, December 31, 1877, of the Massachusetts Reformatory Prison for Women at Framingham lists the total population for the months it was opened as 241 women and 35 children.

Between 1900 and 1933, seventeen reformatories for women were opened, primarily in the northeast and the midwest. Many of these had nurseries for babies born while their mothers were in the institutions. Some accommodated children sent with their mothers. The New York Reformatory at Bedford Hills, opened in 1901, is the only one whose nursery has been in continuous operation since its very early days.

The reformatory nurseries of this era and into the fifties kept the babies in the institutions until they were one to four years old, depending on the facilities and staff available for nursery school programs. There were also "parenting" classes for the mothers, though that term had not yet come into popular use. At one reformatory, they were called "baby hygiene" classes.

In June 1929 and July 1930, national conferences were held on "Care of Infant Children of the Inmates of Correctional Institutions." These conferences were held under the auspices of the National Committee on Prisons and Prison Labor's Subcommittee on the Care of Infant Children of the Inmates of Correctional Institutions.

Major issues revolved around (1) the rights of the mothers to maintain contact with their children while incarcerated and (2) the moral and social attitudes of the extended family and community towards her and her fitness to care for her children upon release. The preferred placement was with extended family members who were willing and able to care for children while their mothers were incarcerated. Otherwise, placement was in a foster home under the state child caring agency.

In terms of long-range planning, the institution's primary concern was for the mother while the state agency's concern was for the children. State workers usually held the attitude that the mother who had committed an offense was not fit to care for her children. They were reluctant to make arrangements for the children to visit the mother and did not consult with her on postincarceration planning. The institution's major concern was the mother, which included planning for her return to the community. Tensions arose particularly for the mother who wanted to be included in planning for her children. Tension between the institution and the state agency was high because the latter failed to communicate with the mother and often the institution, too.

By the end of the forties, thinking began to change as to the appropriateness of a penal institution as a setting for raising babies and young children. Practical concerns compounded the impetus to close the nurseries. Maintaining and running a good nursery program was expensive, and it was often difficult to hire and keep qualified staff. As a result, most of the nurseries were closed by the end of the sixties.

Some institutions kept hospital nurseries open for babies up to six months of age, allowing a short period for bonding. By the midseventies, however, virtually all the nurseries were closed with the exception of Bedford Hills, New York. As a result, the mothers delivered their babies in community hospitals and usually returned to the institution the next day. The babies went to relatives or foster homes as soon as they were ready to leave the hospital. There was no possibility for mother-baby bonding.

Of interest in the 1959 edition of the American Correctional Association's (ACA) *Manual of Correctional Standards* is the statement: "The most scrupulous study should be made as to how these cases should best be handled for the benefit of mother, child and society. . . . The closest scrutiny must be made of foster homes. Many damaged personalities result from a series of unsuccessful foster home placement[s]." The 1966 edition of the manual advises: "It is generally believed that babies should be delivered in community hospitals, and in most cases placed directly in the community . . . either with relatives or in some foster home."

Professionals concerned with the care and treatment of women offenders, combined with the surging women's movement during the seventies, generated programming both inside women's facilities and in the community to enhance contact between offender-mothers and their children. By the mideighties, the incarceration rate of women began to rise at a higher rate than that of men.

New correctional facilities for women have been built, some in states which never had one. Special children's visiting rooms have been incorporated into new and old facilities. Innovative parenting programming has developed. Community agencies have arisen to facilitate transportation of children to visit their mothers and to concentrate on facilitating the mothers' handling of their children's affairs.

Many sources have called for community programs for mothers and children. Women commit relatively few violent crimes and can be handled safely in the community. Facilities for mothers to reunite with their children postincarceration are on the increase. Some jurisdictions provide community programs as alternatives to incarceration. All incorporate creative programming to meet the multiple needs of these women and their children. This book describes some of these programs.

Mary Q. Hawkes, Ph.D.
Professor Emerita
Rhode Island College

Developing Services for Incarcerated Mothers

1

Denise Johnston, M.D.
Director
Center for Children of Incarcerated Parents, Pasadena, California

The majority of adults incarcerated in the United States are parents. In 1993, among the 90,000 women incarcerated in the United States, approximately 67,500 were mothers (Inter-University Consortium 1991, U.S. Department of Justice [USDJ] 1993b); about 37,500 were in prison and about 30,000 were in jail.

The great majority of all prisoners are low-income persons with twelve or fewer years of education and few job skills. They are disproportionately persons of color. Significant numbers have experienced separations from their own parents, parental substance dependency, and/or the incarceration of a family member. Most have been convicted previously; many are multiple recidivists. Incarcerated mothers do not differ from other prisoners in these characteristics.

Differences Between Incarcerated Mothers and Incarcerated Fathers

Some significant differences exist between incarcerated mothers and incarcerated fathers. Jailed and imprisoned mothers are half as likely to be married as incarcerated fathers, three times as likely to have lived with their children prior to arrest, and half as likely to be satisfied with their children's placement. They are visited less often and are usually incarcerated at a greater distance from their children's homes than incarcerated fathers. They have more difficulty in arranging and maintaining secure child placements during incarceration and appear to be far more likely to have child custody problems than their male counterparts. Understanding these and other gender differences between incarcerated parents is important for the planning of appropriate and effective services.

Characteristics and Critical Issues of Incarcerated Mothers

Much of the early research that has been done on women offenders in jails and prisons has examined their perceptions of the maternal role and their maternal concerns. This emphasis reflects the general impression of the public that offenders, and particularly women prisoners, are not good parents. In fact, there is no objective evidence to support that impression. Almost no research has been done on incarcerated offenders, for example, comparing them as parents to similar populations in studies controlled for the effects of race, income, education, employment, and adult or childhood victimization. LeFlore and Holston (1990) compared incarcerated mothers with demographically matched non-criminal mothers and found that parenting attitudes and self-ratings of parenting performance among the two groups were similar. Other studies which did not use matched controls also have found that incarcerated mothers have appropriate maternal behaviors and concerns (Baunach 1979, Bonfanti, et al. 1974, Henriques 1982, McGowan and Blumenthal 1978).

Child Custody Issues

Women offenders appear to be at great risk for loss of their parental rights. This risk is the result of two factors: maternal substance abuse and lack of family reunification services for women prisoners. Other significant issues include shorter statutory timelines for reunification and limited child placement options for families with incarcerated mothers.

No studies specifically examine the extent of loss and retention of parental rights among female offenders; however, some evidence exists that terminations occur disproportionately among women offenders. The Center for Children of Incarcerated Parents has found that about 25 percent of women offenders whose children participate in Center therapeutic programs have lost parental rights to at least one child (Johnston 1992). Also, national samplings of court data on terminations of parental rights in black families have revealed that 12 to 18 percent of all terminations occur among incarcerated parents (National Black Child Development Institute 1989).

The Effects of Maternal Recidivism

Clearly, maternal incarceration has become more damaging to mother/child relationships over the past three decades. Exactly why this is so is not clear. There were far fewer women prisoners and women's prisons thirty years ago, so that a greater proportion of women were imprisoned further from their children's homes, and sentences were longer (Zalba 1964).

The variable that has increased, as contact and visitation between incarcerated mothers and their children have decreased and terminations of parental rights have become more prevalent, is female recidivism. In 1964, Zalba reported that 80 percent of California's women prisoners were serving their first prison term, compared to only one-third of women currently imprisoned in the United States (USDJ 1991). Studies show that the likelihood of mother/child reunification after a mother serves time decreases with each prior maternal incarceration (Gibbs 1971, Hairston 1990, McGowan and Blumenthal

1978). As women increasingly are rearrested, reconvicted, and reincarcerated, the rates at which they are permanently separated from their children also are rising. Although this relationship is neither apparent in their stated concerns, nor in the research literature, it may become the greatest problem facing incarcerated mothers in the future.

Service Needs of Incarcerated Mothers

The earliest studies of incarcerated mothers identified services that would improve the status of these women and their children. Thirty years later, the need for those services remains essentially unmet. Three areas merit special attention:

(1) Retaining Parental Power and Authority

Over half of all women prisoners in the United States were surveyed by McGowan and Blumenthal in 1978. More than 3,000 women identified eight areas of service needs for incarcerated mothers; a mother's ability to make decisions regarding her children was an important factor in each area. Children's placement at the time of arrest; selection of children's caregivers; participation in dependency hearings; and resolution of issues regarding children's schooling, health care, and religion, all have been named as decisions in which incarcerated mothers should participate (Johnston 1994). Without such participation, maternal satisfaction with child placement decreases, parent/child/caregiver conflicts increase, and the mother's parental authority is weakened beyond what is common following parental arrest and incarceration.

(2) Maintaining Mother-Child Contact

Another critical need of incarcerated mothers is contact with their children. Correctional agencies generally have recognized the need for visitation programs. Virtually all women's prisons allow mother-child contact visits. The prevalence of special, extended-contact visitation programs varies by region, from a high of 62.5 percent in the Northeast to a low of 16.7 percent in the Western United States. Nationally, on-site child-care for visitors is available in about one in eight women's prisons (Task Force on the Female Offender 1990).

However, when the National Council on Crime and Delinquency recently reprised McGowan and Blumenthal's study (Bloom and Steinhart 1993), they found mother-child prison visitation had declined from 92 percent in 1978 to less than 50 percent in 1992. Continuing contact between parent and child is perhaps the most significant predictor of family reunification following parental incarceration. The worrisome decline in the ability of women prisoners to maintain contact with their children is due to:

- *restriction of prison telephone privileges* to mutually exclusive systems of collect calls, which burden the children's caregivers, or telephone credits, which severely limit calling by indigent prisoners

- *construction of the majority of larger women's prison facilities in rural and outlying areas* not easily accessible for visits by the children of prisoners, most of whom reside in cities

- *lack of financial and worker support from the child welfare system* for visitation between incarcerated women and their children in foster care

Correctional and social service agencies have been extremely slow to address the needs of incarcerated mothers and their children in these areas.

(3)   Retention of Parental Rights

Women offenders with children in foster care do not receive adequate reunification services (Barry 1985, Beckerman 1989 and 1994, Johnston 1995). In addition to the inability to maintain optimal mother/child contact, incarcerated mothers also do not have access to resources needed to meet other reunification requirements commonly imposed by dependency courts, including parent education, drug treatment, psychological counseling, and employment training.

Designing and Implementing Services for Incarcerated Mothers

Historically, noncustodial correctional services for prisoners have been provided by persons with little professional training or expertise. Recently, this often has been by intent, as correctional systems have been forced to both cut costs and reflect the larger society's philosophy of retribution rather than rehabilitation for crime. These circumstances have been tragic and ironic, since criminal offenders typically have histories of enduring trauma, compulsive behavior problems, and complex developmental issues which require the attention and assistance of persons with the greatest degree of education, training, experience, and competence in their respective fields.

At the same time that a nonprofessional standard of services has characterized noncustodial correctional programs, voters and their representatives have demanded profound results from correctional programming. Virtually all forms of programs for prisoners, even those as basic as visitation, are expected to lead to reduced recidivism. Simple cognitive interventions, like parent education classes, are expected to change behavioral and developmental outcomes for the children of prisoners who participate. Such inappropriate expectations make the development and implementation of high quality correctional programming difficult at best.

Our Center recommends the following steps for creating appropriate, noncustodial, correctional services for incarcerated parents:

(1)   Know the Population

National correctional populations have been well described for three decades. Most correctional facilities maintain enough data on their prisoners to compare their population to the national norms. Correctional programmers should ask: how does this population differ from others? For example, younger prisoner populations typically have a greater prevalence of childhood and adult trauma, higher levels of addiction to drugs, and younger children. Their programming might focus on support groups for abuse survivors, drug treatment, and structured, child-oriented visitation programs and settings.

(2)   Identify Staffing Resources

Good quality parent educators, support group facilitators, drug treatment personnel, and other service providers are educated, trained, and credentialed in their fields. The need for and costs of this type of staffing often present an obstacle to implementation of services at jails and prisons. Correctional programmers should know what expertise is available not only within their facilities and their systems, but also in their extended communities.

(3)   Involve the Community

Partnerships with educational institutions and nonprofit community organizations often can overcome obstacles related to the lack of staffing. While correctional institutions are not eligible for many kinds of public and private funding that would support new services, community-based agencies usually are. In addition, collaborations bring together different perspectives and different forms of knowledge.

(4)   Solicit Input from Potential Clients

High-quality services never are developed without contributions to planning from targeted clients. The clients for correctional services are prisoners, and correctional programmers should solicit prisoner input in selecting the expected outcomes and content of their services.

(5)   Collaborate

The most effective services-planning groups include correctional administrators, correctional custodial staff, professionals from relevant fields, community agency representatives, and prisoners.

(6)   Remember the Children

In all program planning for prisoners who are parents, the outcomes of services always involve prisoners' children in some way. Planners should include in all planning activities persons with expertise in child development, children's emotional and behavioral issues, and family dynamics.

(7)   Know the Field

Collaborative planning should start with a pooling of resources on correctional programming. Where local planning partners do not have a broad expertise, the planning group should consult agencies that provide resources and/or planning expertise.

(8)   Select Outcomes First

Program planning groups should select the outcomes they want from services before they select the content of services. Subsequently, at every stage of planning, planners should ask: "Will the content of this program produce the outcome we want?" If the answer is no, they should put aside the services they are discussing and look for others that will produce the desired outcomes. If planners are wedded to providing specific services, they must be aware of the outcomes, or lack of outcomes, that are possible as a result of those services and be willing to accept them.

(9) Start Small

Planners should identify small target populations for a demonstration of services. There is no guarantee that a well-designed program always will work, even when it has been conducted successfully elsewhere. Starting small allows adjustments in staff and program content to be made before there are costly mistakes.

(10) Remember the Staff

Working with criminal offenders is extremely challenging for many reasons. Not only are they reluctant clients, they may be resistant. They challenge workers' abilities to be nonjudgmental, culturally competent, and professional in conduct. Because prisoners are traumatized persons, those who work with them are subject to compassion fatigue, burnout, and other secondary trauma states. All programming for prisoners should include a staff component that addresses the prevention of secondary trauma through staff support groups, skills training, debriefings, and/or other methods.

Summary

Developing services for jailed and imprisoned mothers requires basic knowledge about their characteristics, concerns, and differences from incarcerated fathers. The range, depth, and complexity of the problems they face demand the greatest degree of knowledge and expertise from those who plan and implement programs serving incarcerated mothers.

References

Adalist-Estrin, A. 1986. Parenting...from Behind Bars. *Family Resource Coalition Report*. 5(1):12-13.

Barry, E. 1985. Reunification Difficult for Incarcerated Parents and Their Children. *Youth Law News*. July/August: 14-16.

————. 1990. *Women in Prison*. In C. Lefcourt, ed. Women & the Law. (6:18.01-18.35). Deerfield, Illinois: Clark, Boardman & Callahan.

Baunach, P. J. 1979, November. Mothering from Behind Prison Walls. Paper presented at the meeting of the American Society of Criminology, Philadelphia, Pennsylvania.

Becker, B. L. 1991. Order in the Court: Challenging Judges Who Incarcerate Pregnant, Substance-dependent Defendants to Protect Fetal Health. *Hastings Constitutional Law Quarterly*. 19:235-259.

Beckerman, A. 1989. Incarcerated Mothers and Their Children in Foster Care: The Dilemma of Visitation. *Children & Youth Services Review*. 11:175-183.

————. 1994. Mothers in Prison: Meeting the Prerequisite Conditions for Permanency Planning. *Social Work*. 39:9-13.

Bloom, B. and D. Steinhart. 1993. *Why Punish the Children: A Reappraisal of the Children of Incarcerated Mothers in America*. San Francisco: National Council on Crime and Delinquency.

Bonfanti, M. A., et al. 1974. Enactment and Perception of Maternal Role of Incarcerated Mothers. Master's thesis, Louisiana State University.

Gabel, K. and D. Johnston. 1995. *Children of Incarcerated Parents*. New York: Lexington Books.

Garcia, S. 1992. Drug Addiction and Mother/child Welfare: Rights, Laws, and Discretionary Decisionmaking. *Journal of Legal Medicine*. 13:129-203.

Gibbs, C. 1971. The Effect of the Imprisonment of Women upon Their Children. *British Journal of Criminology*. 11:113-130.

Hairston, C. F. 1990. Mothers in Jail: Parent-Child Separation and Jail Visitation. *Affilia*. 1:2.

Henriques, Z. W. 1981. *Imprisoned Mothers and Their Children*. Washington, D.C.: University Press of America.

Inter-University Consortium for Political and Social Research. 1991. *Survey of Inmates in Local Jails, 1989*. Ann Arbor, Michigan.

Johnston, D. 1991. *Jailed Mothers*. Pasadena, California: Pacific Oaks Center for Children of Incarcerated Parents.

————. 1992. *Children of Offenders*. Pasadena, California: Pacific Oaks Center for Children of Incarcerated Parents.

————. 1994. *Caregivers of Prisoners' Children*. Pasadena, California: Pacific Oaks Center for Children of Incarcerated Parents.

————. 1995. Child Custody Issues of Women Prisoners. *The Prison Journal*. 75(2):222-239.

Johnston, D. and K. Gabel. 1995. Incarcerated Parents. In D. Johnston and K. Gabel, eds. *Children of Incarcerated Parents*. New York: Lexington Books.

Koban, L. 1983. Parents in Prison: A Comparative Analysis of the Effects of Incarceration on the Families of Men and Women. *Research in Law, Deviance and Social Control*. 5:171-183.

LeFlore, L. and M. A. Holston. 1990. Perceived Importance of Parenting Behaviors as Reported by Inmate Mothers: An Exploratory Study. *Journal of Offender Counseling, Services and Rehabilitation*. 14(1):5-21.

McGowan, B. and K. Blumenthal. 1978. *Why Punish the Children?* San Francisco:National Council on Crime and Delinquency.

National Black Child Development Institute. 1989. *Who Will Care When Parents Can't? A Study of Black Children in Foster Care*. Washington, D.C.

Task Force on the Female Offender. 1990. *The Female Offender: What Does the Future Hold?* Lanham, Maryland: American Correctional Association.

United States Department of Justice. 1991. *Women in Prison.* NCJ-127991. Washington, D.C.: Bureau of Justice Statistics.

————. 1992a. *Correctional Populations in the United States, 1990.* NCJ-134946. Washington, D.C.: Bureau of Justice Statistics.

————. 1992b. *Women in Jail, 1989.* NCJ-134732. Washington, D.C.: Bureau of Justice Statistics.

————. 1992c. *Prisons and Prisoners in the United States.* NCJ-137002. Washington, D.C.: Bureau of Justice Statistics.

————. 1993a. *Correctional Populations in the United States, 1991.* NCJ-142729. Washington, D.C.: Bureau of Justice Statistics.

————. 1993b. *Prisoners in 1992.* NCJ-141874. Washington, D.C.: Bureau of Justice Statistics.

Zalba, S. 1964. *Women Prisoners and Their Families.* Sacramento, California: Department of Social Welfare and Department of Corrections.

The S.A.P.P.O.R.T. Program at Pine Hills County Correctional Center

2

Angela D. Ashley
Correctional Officer Major
Pine Hills County Correctional Center, Orlando, Florida

Background

In 1991, the National Institute on Drug Abuse published their National Household Survey on Drug Use. Analysis of the survey indicated that of the approximately 59.2 million women in the childbearing age group (fifteen to forty-four), over 4.5 million were estimated to have used illicit drugs in the previous month. Especially alarming was the fact that about 601,000 women in this age group appeared to be current users of cocaine.

Unfortunately, with maternal drug use, cocaine is not our only concern. Fetal Alcohol Syndrome (FAS) and Fetal Alcohol Effects (one of the known leading causes of mental retardation in the western world) represent major public health problems, with treatment costs for FAS estimated at nearly a third of a billion dollars per year.

Several interrelated components are involved in maternal drug abuse. Polydrug use (the use of more than one drug) is the norm among drug-abusing women. Research shows that tobacco and marijuana use during pregnancy are associated with low birth weight and decreased gestational age proportionate to the amount smoked. Virtually unheard of before 1981, perinatally acquired immunodeficiency syndrome (AIDS) has risen rapidly as a cause of death among children.

Impact on the Florida Department of Corrections

During fiscal year 1986, 20 percent of female admissions to the Florida Department of Corrections (FDC) were admitted for drug offenses. By fiscal year 1991, the number of drug offenders had increased to 51 percent. Comparatively, male admissions for drug offenses during fiscal year 1991 were much less at 31 percent. According to the Florida Department of Corrections 1991-92 Annual Report, the typical female offender was twenty-nine years old with convictions for either the sale/manufacture of drugs, possession of drugs, or grand theft (related to drug use).

The Florida Department of Corrections increased its admissions of pregnant females, tripling from previous years to fifteen per month, or 6 percent of all female admissions. Studies showed that the rate of substance abuse among the general female population was almost identical to that of pregnant offenders. Fifty-two percent of the pregnant female offenders admitted to heavy alcohol/drug use, both prior to and following their knowledge of the pregnancy. These women had continued to expose their unborn children to alcohol and/or drugs up to the time of incarceration. Only 11 percent of this population had any information regarding the physiological aspects of substance abuse on the fetus, and a mere 3 percent had attended any previous substance abuse programs.

The Florida Department of Corrections had established programs which dealt with the basic principles of addiction and relapse prevention; however, these programs did not specifically address the uniqueness of the female user or the negative impact that substance abuse (and its lifestyle) has on children and the unborn. Recognizing an unmet need, the Florida Department of Corrections pursued appropriate programming.

Proposal for a Healthy Beginning

In January 1992, Harry K. Singletary, the Secretary of the Florida Department of Corrections, submitted an application for funding to the National Institute of Corrections (NIC). The application requested $45,000 to develop and pilot the "Substance Abusing Pregnant and Post-Partum Offenders Receiving Treatment" (S.A.P.P.O.R.T.) program.

In pursuing funding, the Florida Department of Corrections proposed to dedicate a fully staffed, thirty-bed community work release program, and to bear one year's operating cost (totaling $305,407). The Department additionally proposed to seek yearly funding from the Florida legislature to continue the project once developed. With the minimal amount of money requested, it was vital for library, research, and program supplies to be provided through linkage with community service providers such as the March of Dimes, Florida Health and Rehabilitative Services, and other organizations.

The specific objectives of the S.A.P.P.O.R.T. program were identified as follows:

1. To educate the female inmate on the toxic effects of substance abuse on the fetus and the child

2. To reduce substance abuse by program participants

3. To teach the participants to access appropriate aftercare services in the community

4. To focus full facility resources, separate from a major institution, on the total needs of inmates with histories of substance abuse

5. To better prepare participants for family reunification and community reentry

6. To reduce relapse and recidivism rates for program participants

7. To increase cooperation and coordination between appropriate state and local agencies, service providers, and community organizations

8. To gather data to evaluate the program, and, as far as possible, to follow the women's progress after release

9. To gain new experience and resources for use in expanded programs oriented to female inmates

10. To produce written documentation and videotape to assist with program replication

The Birth of S.A.P.P.O.R.T.

In late 1992, the Florida Department of Corrections received funding from NIC for the S.A.P.P.O.R.T. program. The projected period for the program was one year and twelve weeks, to include start-up and evaluation. The period of a S.A.P.P.O.R.T. course was twelve weeks, with a rolling admission and discharge process to ensure that participants had the opportunity to complete the course.

In developing the program, we felt that program participants should be selected with the following guidelines. Participants would:

- Have a history of substance abuse

- Be selected from among inmates currently pregnant or who had delivered within the past year while incarcerated

- Be volunteers in the program, and could choose to discontinue participation at any point in the program

- Have completed at least one of the Florida Department of Corrections' substance abuse programs

Within two months of development, the Department took a proactive stance and expanded the program to include incarcerated women between the ages of eighteen and thirty-five who had histories of substance abuse.

The Program

The twelve-week S.A.P.P.O.R.T. program consists of three four-week modules. Together the modules address issues of pregnancy and prenatal care, the effects of maternal substance abuse on the child, recovery, and life skills necessary for continued sobriety.

Module One Abstract

The objective for the first four-week module of the S.A.P.P.O.R.T. program is to educate and introduce the female offender to information on pregnancy, sexuality, and the effects of substance abuse and high-risk activities on the unborn child during gestation, at birth, and throughout his or her life.

The first week focuses on providing basic information on conception, fetal development, and childbirth to the offender. Participants discuss the importance of good prenatal care and nutrition to a healthy birth experience. Emotional needs of the pregnant and postpartum woman are addressed both to assist in healthy bonding between mother and child, and to avoid chronic postpartum "blues," which could lead to future substance abuse or child abuse.

The second and third weeks focus on the impact substance abuse has on the unborn and how its devastating impact can follow the child for the rest of his or her life. This is a hard topic for the women who already have borne children affected by alcohol and/or drug abuse. The aim of this message is to prevent more children from being born drug/alcohol exposed. A guest speaker from the March of Dimes organization provides education on birth defects and community resources for drug/alcohol exposed children who need special care.

Week four is spent dealing with responsible sexuality and the possible consequences of high-risk activities. Sexually transmitted diseases, especially AIDS, are discussed at length to educate the women about the importance of safe sex and family planning in the nineties. Guest speakers help deliver this message and answer very delicate and personal questions, which need to be addressed with this high-risk group.

Module Two Abstract

The second four-week module is designed to introduce the women to the concept of recovery. The focus of the first module was to show the female offender how substance abuse directly affects her and her children. With this realization, women are ready to examine ways to develop their own personal recovery programs. More critical than merely being educated about the destructive impact of their previous substance abuse and lifestyles, the women need practical guidance on recovery and maintaining a new way of life.

Week five provides basic information on substance abuse and addiction, with the main goal of helping the women to overcome denial mechanisms. By understanding the various defense mechanisms of denial, the women can recognize their own behaviors and realize the importance of the S.A.P.P.O.R.T. program. Understanding why they abused alcohol/drugs, and the importance their family played in enabling the abuse, helps break down the walls of addictive thinking.

During week six, the objective is to assist the women in improving their self-esteem and self-concept. Central to S.A.P.P.O.R.T.'s goals is the ability to instill self-esteem and self-worth within these women. Only then can they feel worthy of recovery and believe in themselves enough to take the "risks" associated with adopting a new lifestyle. Techniques in stress management are taught to help the women adjust to this awkward new way of thinking. The ability to deal constructively with stress also assists these women upon release and helps prevent relapse/recidivism. Ethnic diversity training allows minority women to feel pride in their race and culture, and helps create unity within the program community.

During week seven, communication skills are addressed. Addictive behaviors such as manipulation, aggression, emotional "shutdown," and poor self-expression are discussed. Learning to communicate effectively with their children, family, friends, and employers is crucial to the women's social adjustment in society. The concept of "Johari's Window," shown in Figure 2.1, provides a visual guide for a way to create a balance of privacy and openness with themselves and those around them.

Figure 2.1 Johari's Window

Things you know, but the other person doesn't	Things the other person knows, but you don't
Things neither person knows	Things both have knowledge of

In communicating, one must be aware of the four "panes" of Johari's Window. To communicate effectively, the knowledge both participants have should be widened: only then can one clearly "see."

Finally, in week eight, the second module spotlights relapse prevention. The women learn that relapse occurs long before they ever pick up another drink or drug. They learn to identify physical and psychological signs of impending relapse. Constructive ways to relax and have fun without using alcohol and/or drugs also are discussed, and periodic special outings and events supplement this training.

Module Three Abstract

The third four-week module centers on life skills the women will need to successfully transfer the information and recovery tools they have acquired during the S.A.P.P.O.R.T. program into society. This includes the topics of parenting, surviving economically, future planning, and preparing for graduation.

Week nine addresses becoming a positive parent. By first understanding and recognizing the dysfunction to which these women generally are accustomed, they hopefully may break cycles of addictions and/or abuse. Learning ways to both change their family environments and bond with their children while incarcerated help the women to become better parents. Some of the women have special needs children, and teaching basic parenting skills is vital to easing their already difficult child-rearing task.

Weeks ten and eleven center on learning to set and achieve goals. The women learn to develop a realistic budget, locate community resources, seek assistance, and choose childcare and housing. The bottom line to successful reintegration into society for recovering addicts is the ability to lead balanced lives. This is difficult enough for any working woman today, but for these women, it poses an additional challenge which the program addresses.

During the final week of S.A.P.P.O.R.T., the women work on individual needs assessments. They each write and present an affirmation about what they have learned from the S.A.P.P.O.R.T. program, how they hope to change, and what future goals they hope to attain.

Graduation is the culmination of twelve hard weeks of work, education, counseling, and change. For many of the women, it is one of the first goals they ever have successfully achieved.

Review of the S.A.P.P.O.R.T. Program

In determining the increase of the female offender's knowledge regarding physiological aspects of substance abuse on unborn children, relapse prevention measures, and dysfunctional parental traits, a pre- and post-testing was administered. The results of the post testing revealed an average increase of 85 percent in the offender's awareness. In follow-up with the 120 female offenders who graduated from the program, only three subsequently had relapsed and were returned to incarceration.

In 1995, the Florida Department of Corrections contracted the S.A.P.P.O.R.T. program to an agency that provided substance abuse counseling. Year-end review has been critical. The curriculum veered off the family impact and relied more upon the principal tenet of addiction. The female offenders who were polled stated that they could not develop a bond with the instructors and felt that material was repetitious of previous programs. Documentation was not maintained that could accurately provide information regarding the success of this phase of the program.

In July 1995, the Florida Department of Corrections brought the S.A.P.P.O.R.T. program back under its own direction and intent. The program has been moved from the work release setting to the Florida Correctional Institution, a major institution which is the central processing and housing facility for pregnant female offenders. This move allows women with high-risk pregnancies to participate in the program, and enables a larger number of women to participate. Participants achieve the ability to break the cycle of crime and addiction through our integrated approach which addresses the totality of personal, social, and medical problems and provides a continuum of care through linkages with support agencies.

The Center for Children of Incarcerated Parents: Interventions for Incarcerated Mothers

3

Denise Johnston, M.D.
Director
Center for Children of Incarcerated Parents, Pasadena, California

The Center for Children of Incarcerated Parents was created to address the need for information on and demonstration of model services for children whose parents are incarcerated. The mission of the Center is the prevention of intergenerational crime and incarceration. As part of our program, the Center offers a variety of services for incarcerated mothers.

History of the Center

The Center was founded in January, 1990 with a small grant from a private donor to create a clearinghouse of materials on children of prisoners. Subsequent donations and small grants from private organizations sustained the Center throughout its first two years of operation, during which time key projects were designed and implemented. In the Center's third year of operation, we obtained larger grants from public and private funders. Currently, the Center is supported by its earned income, contracts, private foundation grants, and grants from public agencies.

Services for Incarcerated Mothers

The Center's services for incarcerated mothers are based on a thorough understanding of women prisoners and their needs. This understanding was acquired from our own empirical research, a review of the relevant literature, and extensive staff experience in working with criminal offenders and their families.

Clientele

The Center for Children of Incarcerated Parents has served over 5,500 individual clients since it opened in 1990. The Center serves criminal offenders, members of their families, and individual professionals who work with both of these groups. Within this broad population, several groups comprise the majority of our clients.

Parents Under Correctional Supervision. The Center has served over 3,500 parents under correctional supervision, primarily through our Clearinghouse, educational, and child custody advocacy services projects. These parents have been in jail, in prison, on probation, or on parole in all fifty states, Canada, Great Britain, and Israel. While the majority of Clearinghouse users have been men, the majority of the Center's direct service clients have been women.

Almost all parents under correctional supervision who request the Center's services are seeking ways to reunite with and support their children. They request assistance in maintaining contact with their children, in learning how to parent from prison, in preventing their children from developing behaviors that lead to crime and incarceration, and in understanding the issues that brought them to jail or prison.

As a group, the parents who become clients of the Center are typical of the larger population of criminal offenders in their demographic characteristics. However, compared to other offender populations, Center clients have been charged disproportionately with drug offenses, and about 85 percent have histories of substance dependency. Most have experienced parent-child separations and other traumatic events in their own childhoods. Indeed, throughout their lives, the majority have had what we refer to as "enduring trauma," multiple episodes of different types of traumatic experiences.

Substance-dependent Parents in Recovery. This group of clients is similar to those under correctional supervision; however, these parents are focused on recovery from substance dependency and have somewhat different priorities than those under correctional supervision. The majority of clients in this category have been female residents in California treatment programs.

Clients in drug treatment are less interested in the effects of the justice process and corrections practice on the family and are more interested in the nature and management of intergenerational behaviors. They are demographically different from prisoners, with higher levels of education, more income, and composed of lower numbers of persons of color. Histories of childhood trauma among this client population are almost universal; over 95 percent of females and 65 percent of males in this group report sustained abuse, neglect, molestation, domestic violence, witnessed community violence, and/or multiple parent-child separations in childhood. It is not clear, however, if this finding represents a different incidence of these experiences or merely a different level of reporting than other Center clients.

Persons Who Work with Criminal Offenders and Their Families. The typical Center client in this group is employed as a teacher, social worker, or counselor by a community-based agency that provides services to a correctional population. Persons in this category commonly have had no professional training preparing them to work with criminal offenders, and little current access to training and resources in this area.

These Center clients order materials through the Clearinghouse; request searches of the Center's collection on specific topics; use the Center's "warmline" for immediate information on important topics; and request technical assistance in training themselves, educating their clients, developing parent-child services, and creating customized materials for their service populations.

Other Clients. The Center has a wide variety of clients in this category, including the caregivers of prisoners' children, the partners and adult family members of prisoners, and the children of criminal offenders. Most clients in this category are seeking social or therapeutic services for children of offenders, advice on helping children adjust to parental incarceration, and/or assistance with visiting and maintaining the parent-child relationship.

Program Description

The program of the Center includes four components. Each component conducts several research, educational, and/or direct service projects. In the 1995-96 program year, of twenty-two Center projects, seventeen were active.

The Information Component

This component conducts research, disseminates information, and provides technical assistance.

The Clearinghouse at Pacific Oaks. The Clearinghouse has a collection of over 3,500 publications and audiovisual items concerning criminal offenders, their children, and their families. The Clearinghouse distributes materials through two catalogs; one catalog lists items available to prisoners free of charge, and one lists items available to all users, including correctional facilities and correctional personnel, for the costs of handling. Items free to prisoners include over 100 documents which concern incarcerated parents and their families and which were originally published elsewhere. Other documents provided without charge include Center project information sheets, seven Center Data Sheets on Children of Incarcerated Parents, a booklist for children of prisoners, two Center research reports written specially for incarcerated parents, information sheets and brochures from model criminal justice programs serving families, five legal information manuals for prisoners with children, Phase ReEntry Program and Prison MATCH materials, a child care contracts package, and two children's books on the issue of parental recidivism. Audiovisuals include "Children of Incarcerated Parents," a videotape of the minor and adult children of current and former prisoners describing their lives in their own words. The videotape focuses on intergenerational crime and incarceration and is available in twelve- and twenty-five-minute versions.

Evaluation and outcomes. Client satisfaction with Clearinghouse services is high for all groups of users, including incarcerated mothers. Since the project does not monitor how ordered materials are used, other types of evaluations are not conducted.

Technical Assistance Projects. These projects have included a range of services, from advising the National Institute of Justice about research on children of offenders, to setting up children's programming in maternal-child residential drug treatment centers, to creating customized parent education curricula for correctional facilities. The Center has provided technical assistance to over 200 correctional and community agencies since 1991. The Center also has provided technical assistance directly to several prisoners' groups in different parts of the United States. Among other projects, Center staff have assisted groups in the design and implementation of waiting and visiting areas for children, development of customized parent education curricula, and the creation of a parents' library.

Evaluation and outcomes. The Center's technical assistance projects typically result in the provision of professional services or the creation of a product for client agencies. Client satisfaction with technical assistance services is high for all groups of users. The Center has conducted only two such projects for groups of incarcerated mothers. Since these projects do not monitor how programs and products resulting from Center assistance are used, other types of evaluations are not conducted.

Research Projects. Research projects at the Center have included the landmark "Children of Offenders" and "Jailed Mothers" studies, as well as smaller investigations. The Center publishes at least one research report per year. These reviews of the literature and reports of our own empirical studies are distributed through the Clearinghouse.

The Education Component

This component includes eight educational projects offered to incarcerated parents, jailed fathers, juvenile male offenders, women probationers, women jail inmates, and substance-dependent parents in residential drug treatment. Since the loss of parental authority both inside and outside the family is a central issue for incarcerated and substance-dependent parents, all Center educational programs use competency-based, empowerment curricula.

The Prison Parents' Education Project (PPEP). PPEP is a parent empowerment course designed and written by formerly incarcerated parents. It addresses topics that over 400 prisoners and former prisoners have identified as being of greatest importance to them as parents.

The project began as a correspondence course in 1990 to allow women prisoners at California correctional institutions with no parent education programming to meet court-ordered family reunification requirements. Subsequently, it was made available through sale of the PPEP curriculum and presentation by Center staff in regional jails and prisons. The sixteen-session PPEP curriculum is the prototype for all of the Center's other parent education projects.

PPEP focuses on the effects of parental incarceration and its causes, including specifically intergenerational childhood trauma. The course format includes readings and/or general classroom discussions, small group exercises, parent peer-support groups, and journal-keeping. Each session involves four hours of student classwork, written homework, and group work.

PPEP was designed to be taught by formerly incarcerated persons. This type of staffing is critical to the project as a parent empowerment activity. Where lack of resources and security restrictions make such staffing impossible, the training and use of current prisoners as teaching assistants should be strongly considered.

The PPEP curriculum manual is written for students who read at an eighth-grade level; however, the PPEP course is also available on audiotape for students with limited reading skills. Curriculum manual sets, which include an instructor's manual and fifteen or twenty student manuals, are sold through the Center's Clearinghouse. The PPEP curriculum can be customized for specific correctional institutions and populations; this service is available through the Center's Technical Assistance Project.

The PPEP correspondence course is conducted once a year, from January through October, free of charge. Enrollment is limited to a first-come, first-served basis to students who write to the Center prior to November 15 of the preceding year. At any time, prisoners may enroll in an eight- to thirty-two-week, independent study PPEP correspondence course for a fee that covers the costs of materials and postage and handling.

Evaluation and outcomes. PPEP students complete written, objective pre- and post-tests that measure their knowledge of the topics covered in the course. These examinations are used to evaluate teaching performance and not student performance. All students who participate consistently in the course, including an 80 percent attendance level and completion of all assignments, receive a certificate. The Center frequently is consulted about the use of PPEP or other parent education curricula to change prisoners' parenting or even criminal behaviors. This is a highly unrealistic and uninformed expectation. Since no evidence exists that purely cognitive interventions can change any type of behavior pattern, let alone compulsive behaviors like substance dependency that impair the ability to parent effectively, attempts to measure behavioral outcomes of PPEP participation are inappropriate.

The Ex-offenders' Parent Education Project (EPEP). EPEP is also a parent empowerment course designed and written by formerly incarcerated parents, based on topics that women—both prisoners and former prisoners—said were vital to them in their parenting role. EPEP is appropriate for community agencies or probation offices.

The project was developed from PPEP in 1991. Its original purpose was to assist recently released, formerly jailed women in meeting court-ordered family reunification requirements in a self-help setting. Naturally, its objectives, format, and contents are similar to those of the predecessor, PPEP program.

Just as PPEP, EPEP examines the effects of parental incarceration and its causes, especially childhood trauma. The content focuses on immediate post-release reunification issues and family reentry. The course format is also similar to PPEP. It includes readings and/or general classroom discussions, small group exercises, parent peer-support groups, and journal-keeping. Each session involves three hours of student classwork, written homework, and group work. EPEP is effective when taught by formerly incarcerated persons. This type of staffing is critical to the project as a parent empowerment activity.

Just like PPEP, the EPEP curriculum manual has an eighth-grade readability level; however, the EPEP course is also available on audiotape for students with limited reading skills. Curriculum manual sets include an instructor's manual and fifteen or twenty student manuals. These are sold through the Center's Clearinghouse. The Center's Technical Assistance Project can customize the curriculum for specific populations.

Evaluation and outcomes. EPEP students complete written, objective pre- and post-tests that measure their knowledge of the topics covered in the course. These examinations are used to evaluate teaching performance and not student performance. All students who participate consistently in the course, including an 80 percent attendance level and completion of all assignments, receive a certificate.

The Reclaiming Parenthood Project (REPP). This project was designed for parents in treatment for substance dependency. Like EPEP, this project was developed from PPEP. In 1993, parents in recovery wrote the original curriculum components. This project has been conducted in residential drug treatment programs, probation offices, and jail drug treatment units by Center staff. It also is sold through the Center's Clearinghouse.

REPP focuses on the effects of parental substance dependency and its causes. Like PPEP and EPEP, the course format includes readings, general classroom discussions, small group exercises and parent peer-support groups. Each session involves three hours of student classwork, written homework, and group work.

The REPP curriculum was designed to be taught by parents in recovery from substance dependence. This type of staffing is critical to the project as a parent empowerment activity and should be possible in all community-based treatment programs. Where lack of resources and/or correctional security restrictions make this type of staffing impossible, the training and use of current prisoners as teaching assistants should be strongly considered.

As in the other two programs, the REPP curriculum manual is written at an eighth-grade reading level; however, the course is available on audiotape for students with limited reading skills. Curriculum manual sets include an instructor's manual and fifteen or twenty student manuals. Customization for specific programs and populations is available through the Center's Technical Assistance Project.

Evaluation and outcomes. Similar to the other programs, REPP students complete written, objective pre- and post-tests to measure their knowledge of the topics covered in the course. These examinations are used to evaluate teaching performance—not student performance. All students who participate consistently in the course (with an 80 percent attendance level and completion of all assignments) receive a certificate.

The Family Life Education Project (FLEP). FLEP is a short curriculum for jailed fathers that focuses on parent-child separation and intergenerational behaviors. FLEP has been offered in Southern California men's jails. This curriculum is sold through the Clearinghouse.

The Young Father's Project. This is a specialized version of FLEP developed for teenage fathers in juvenile detention. The eight-session curriculum has been offered locally in juvenile hall settings and is sold through the Clearinghouse.

The Women's Education and Empowerment Series. This series includes ten to twelve presentations on topics of interest to women offenders. The series has been purchased by or conducted in correctional facilities and community correctional supervision sites in three states. This curriculum is sold through the Clearinghouse.

The Jail Health Education Project. This project is a ten-session curriculum focusing on health issues of criminal offenders and substance-dependent persons. This project has been offered regionally in county correctional facilities.

The Therapeutic Intervention Project (TIP) Training Project. This is a one-day curriculum that trains teachers, correctional employees, social workers, or other professionals to work with traumatized children and their families. This curriculum is offered at the Center by special arrangement and as an annual training event.

The Family Reunification Component

This component consists of two national projects and one local project.

The Child Custody Advocacy Services (CHICAS) Project. Late in 1990, while conducting the Jailed Mothers Study, Center staff repeatedly were approached by the subjects of the study for assistance with child custody problems. This assistance later was formalized as the Child Custody Advocacy Services (CHICAS) Project.

CHICAS provides assistance with child custody and placement issues to substance-dependent parents and parents who are criminal offenders. The project helps parents to locate children from whom they have become estranged, to plan for and make emergency placements, to negotiate child care contracts with the caregivers of their children, to maintain or establish communication with their children, to obtain visitation with their children, to arrange powers of attorney and legal guardianships, to meet court-ordered reunification requirements, to identify resources, and to arrange parent placements in residential drug treatment and other types of service programs.

Potential clients hear about CHICAS by word of mouth; the project neither advertises services nor seeks clients. Persons making inquiries are sent an application packet. When an application is complete, a client is assigned an advocate. Advocates may have minimal involvement with a client (providing a power of attorney form or finding out the name of a prisoner's dependency court attorney, for example) or they may remain involved throughout a client's entire term of incarceration and after their release. There is no charge to clients for project services.

CHICAS served 660 incarcerated parents during its first five years of operation. A description of incarcerated CHICAS clients, their child custody problems and their service needs was published in *The Prison Journal* in June, 1995.

Evaluation and outcomes. CHICAS case files are closed when the client requests termination of the advocacy partnership, when the services requested by the client are complete, and/or when a client's parental rights are terminated. More than 86 percent of clients whose case files have been closed have rated project services as "good" or "excellent."

There has been no way to measure the comparative effectiveness of CHICAS Project services because clients are self-referred, and the Center has been unable to identify and follow matching groups of parents. We have been unable to determine if CHICAS clients reunite with their children at a different rate than other incarcerated parents, because public child welfare agencies do not categorize their data by the parent's criminal justice status.

However, the project report found a dramatic difference in reunification rates between clients who were released from incarceration and entered residential drug treatment (92 percent) and clients who were released and did not enter residential treatment programs (36 percent). Since CHICAS practice guidelines require that advocates recommend long-term, residential drug treatment for all incarcerated parents who are released from jail or prison, this high rate of reunification success may be seen as an indirect outcome of project services.

The MotherRight Project. In 1991 and 1992, newly published studies reported that women serving short terms of incarceration had far worse outcomes of pregnancy than women serving long sentences. The MotherRight Project was designed and implemented to improve the outcomes of pregnancy for jailed women who serve average sentences of less than six months.

The project paired pregnant and screened jailed women with trained, screened, and experienced mothers who served as their advocates and mentors. Jailed women were offered referral and placement services through the Center, while MotherRight mentors provided their partners with individualized advocacy, education, and support. Services focused on placing pregnant prisoners in residential drug treatment, parent support programs, and parent education programs upon release; on arrangements for the protection of the child's custody; and on the placement of newborns in appropriate enrichment or treatment programs with their mothers or caregivers.

MotherRight produced several training documents for advocates and mothers, as well as resource and placement manuals. The staff-intensive project required an experienced volunteer coordinator to recruit, screen, and train advocates and pregnant prisoners, as well as a child development specialist to supervise mother-advocate interaction. In addition, close liaison with and cooperation of jail health services personnel was an essential element of the project that was difficult to achieve. As a result of the high costs of project services and the inability to control the content and format of correctional staff participation in the project, the Center was unable to evaluate project outcomes. The Center placed the project on indefinite hiatus in 1993 but will assist interested agencies in developing their own MotherRight services.

The Parenting Program. This is a new model for services to parents at risk of criminal prosecution for failing to supervise their children. Typically, these parents are neither under correctional supervision nor under supervision of the juvenile dependency court. This project conducts family assessments and provides resources, referrals, and placements to prevent parents from entering the criminal justice system for charges related to ineffective parenting.

The Therapeutic Services Component

This component includes two programs offering similar services to children of different ages in different settings.

The Early Therapeutic Intervention Project (ETIP). This project provides play therapy for young (ages four through seven) children of prisoners in a community setting. The project uses cognitive-behavioral methods and focuses on issues of enduring trauma and parent-child separation.

The Therapeutic Intervention Project (TIP). This project was developed from ETIP in 1991 and conducted at public schools. TIP originally served middle-school children. During its second year, the project was expanded to include family support services; during its third year, teacher training services were added. Currently, TIP offers children individual, group, and/or family counseling, recreational activities, and social skills building. TIP family support services include a parent training institute, parent/caregiver support groups, referrals and placements, and family social activities. TIP teacher services include on-site training and teachers' support groups.

Summary

The Center for Children of Incarcerated Parents offers a comprehensive program of services for criminal offenders and their families, including several specific projects appropriate for incarcerated mothers. All Center staff members are former prisoners. The Center's interventions for jailed and imprisoned mothers are competency-based, empowerment models that meet the women's needs for services addressing loss of parental authority, mother-child contact, and retention of parental rights. The Center offers women offenders information critical to their needs, increases their access to services, advocates for them, trains them to advocate for themselves, and models successful, powerful lifestyles of formerly incarcerated women.

Rhode Island Women's Prison: Mothers in Prison—Children in Crisis

4

Roberta Richman
Warden, Rhode Island Women's Prison

in collaboration with

Alberta Bacarri, MSW
Parenting Program Coordinator
Rhode Island Women's Prison, Cranston, Rhode Island

Rhode Island enjoys the distinction of being the smallest state in the nation. This presents us with interesting possibilities as well as troublesome predicaments. As a result, we have no separate jails. All offenders are housed in the State Prison. Pretrial inmates, and those sentenced to ten days, thirty days, six months, six years, or life without parole, all reside in our facility. We face, therefore, a wide range of daily problems encompassing the crises of newly arrested women concerned about their children's welfare in their absence, those who must explain a three-month separation to their pre-adolescents, and those facing the potential of permanent separation after their parental rights have been terminated because of their conflict with the law. Women who are mothers and find themselves in prison must face dozens of serious concerns and issues during their incarceration.

Rhode Island incarcerates fewer than 200 women on average, about 6 percent of the total adult incarcerated population. Approximately 75 percent of our female population are mothers of dependent children. Some of these children are in family care and others are in the care of the State. While other prison settings this size tend to be more stable, our population is primarily transitory, turning over continually. We do have a small core group serving longer sentences. Our program must be flexible enough to address a whole range of issues—immediate separation crises, long-term reunification issues, maintenance of mother/child bonds during short incarcerations, counseling for termination of parental rights, and counseling mothers serving long terms who have lost control of their children's lives.

Although our primary purpose is to provide incarcerated women with opportunities for treatment and prepare them to lead responsible lives upon release, when those women are mothers of dependent children, philosophically, our first and most important concern regarding their status as mothers is the welfare of the child. With that premise established, our programming is designed to enhance the mother's ability to care for and nurture that child or, if her parental rights are likely to be terminated, to counsel and prepare her to deal with the loss in the child's best interest. We believe in the practice of creating, wherever possible, positive experiences between the mother and child so that the child's memories of Mother are good ones.

Visits

For many of the mothers and children we serve, visits during incarceration are the most positive relationship experiences they have. Mothers are not distracted by the trials and tribulations of daily life. They pay attention to their children, under the supervision of counselors, with dedication seldom found when at home. Our intention is to allow these experiences to build the lasting memories children will take with them to replace the traumatic memories many of them have of violence and substance abuse in the home.

History

The prison reform movement began when Elizabeth Fry, a Quaker living in England in the eighteenth century, discovered the wretched conditions in which incarcerated women and their children were kept. At that time, when women were jailed, their children simply accompanied them and received equal punishment for the mother's crime. Fry's emotional discovery motivated a life-long dedication to prison reform. The concept of motherhood traditionally stirs a strong emotional response in people and provokes action and sympathy even when the mother is in conflict with the law. The desire to assist mothers and children in prison is compelling and often displaces anger and resentment against the offender. Today, of course, we would be appalled at the suggestion that children be incarcerated and punished along with their mothers.

Even when we do have settings in which children spend time inside the prison with their mothers, those instances are unusual and often controversial. Society perceives the babies as imprisoned, even when the infants clearly are not cognizant of their surroundings, only of their loving care. Infants usually are removed when very young and spend only limited periods of time visiting thereafter. Ironically, we are replicating the practices of eighteenth-century British society. When the child is separated from his or her mother, regardless of his or her quality of care, the child suffers the loss of contact with the mother and is, in fact, punished still, in that sense, for the crimes of the mother. How contemporary corrections deals with the incarcerated mother for the most part has not progressed much since the days of Elizabeth Fry. She certainly would be dismayed to see how incarcerated mothers are treated in many prisons still. Although there are some prisons in which the issue is addressed appropriately, for the most part, incarcerated women are treated simply as inmates; their status as mothers with dependent children generally is ignored.

Historically, Rhode Island first addressed the need for programming for incarcerated mothers during the mideighties on a small scale. A weekly parenting education class funded by a grant to a community counseling agency provided services. A modest children's room was created to allow special mother-child visits supervised by state social workers and separate from general visits. When the grant ended in 1988, the program was discontinued. In 1991, the present program was created. This chapter describes the parenting program in the women's prison in Rhode Island, the circumstances surrounding its creation, its philosophical premise, its evolution through several growing stages to its present operation, and the practical learning we have experienced during the four years of its existence.

Rhode Island incarcerates all of its approximately 185 female offenders in two renovated psychiatric hospitals located among five men's facilities. All are in close proximity in Cranston, one of the two largest cities in the state. As a result, unlike states where prisons are far from the urban areas where families of inmates generally live, Rhode Island inmates are easily visited by families via public transportation in usually less than a half hour of travel time. Visits, therefore, are potentially frequent and family members may bring children in three or four times a week. Approximately 55 percent of our mothers have their children in extended family care. The remaining 45 percent are in state care.

The relationship between Rhode Island's Department of Corrections (RIDOC) and its Department of Children, Youth and Families (DCYF), regarding incarcerated mothers with children in state care, has been adversarial. Although gradually changing, remnants of that difficult relationship persist. DCYF social workers viewed mothers in prison as persona non grata, as though they disappeared from the consciousness of their children simply because they were in prison. DOC did its part to create hostility. Correctional staff, in the course of doing their jobs, made it difficult for case workers bringing in children for mandated visits. Children often were traumatized by routine searches for contraband. They, then, often became difficult for both the case worker and the mother to control. It was not unexpected, then, that DCYF case workers believed bringing children to visit their mothers in prison created more bad feelings than good. Mothers, often not wanting their children to know where they were, preferred that children not visit. When visits did occur, inmates with children in state care were supervised by the case worker and visits took place in spaces not usually conducive to putting the child at ease and certainly with no program or plan for the interaction. For those children in family care, visits took place in the visiting room, usually crowded with other inmates and their visitors. The child was required to sit quietly while most of the mother's attention was focused on the adult family member who accompanied the child. In both cases, the child's experience was at best boring, and at worst, traumatic. Any thought of encouraging the mother to communicate and bond with the child was defeated by circumstance.

In 1991, George Vose was appointed as Director of Corrections by Governor Bruce Sundlun, who, partly because of his wife's longstanding interest in female offenders, made the female offender a priority. Director Vose, having had experience with a women's prison while Commissioner of the Massachusetts Department of Correction, was sensitive to the need for changing existing attitudes toward and treatment of this special population. Like most other women's prisons, ours had suffered from neglect which was justified by the administration's argument that women represent under 6 percent of the total prison population, and women present little threat of physical danger or legal challenge. Women in prison, historically, received minimal resources for security and custody, and virtually nothing for treatment or programming in comparison to the male population. In this regard, Rhode Island was no different from the majority of other states.

In June of 1991, Director Vose appointed this author as Warden of the women's facilities. By creating a warden's position to lead the female unit, he reinforced his commitment to addressing the needs of female offenders. When this author was appointed, no programs were operating in the women's prison beyond a meager educational program. No programs addressed the needs of mothers.

Most critical was the need for staff with expertise in programming for parents and children. A well-qualified trained staff member, dedicated solely to the development of competent and meaningful parenting education and mother-child visiting programming, would be essential. Budget constraints hindered the development of new positions. The creative and critical intervention of the Governor's wife allowed us to accomplish this first goal. With her help, we were able to persuade four state departments to contribute to the creation of a social worker position dedicated to creating and coordinating a parenting program for incarcerated mothers. The four departments all had a theoretical interest in the welfare of the mother and child; they were DOC; DCYF; Mental Health, Retardation, and Hospitals; and the Department of Social Services. Although their financial support quickly faded, the position was created and has become institutionally permanent within the women's facility staff.

Simultaneously, we identified a vacant building in good condition which was physically separate from the prison, yet on the grounds belonging to DCYF. The space, ideal for our program, was transferred to us for use as a children's center. Minimum-custody and work-release inmates would spend whole days visiting with their children under staff supervision but separate and away from the prison environment. Children no longer had to submit to the security routine of visiting the prison but were more casually admitted to a neutral space.

At this same time, CODAC, a community substance abuse agency which had experience with mother-child programs, applied for a small grant from the Children's Trust Fund to work with our population in the new Children's Center. Funding was awarded for three years—$6,000 the first, $4,000 for year two, and $2,000 for the third year. When the grant ended, DOC agreed to allocate $30,000 from our Inmate Welfare Fund allowing us to expand the program to a more adequate level. After a competitive process, CODAC, based on its experience and commitment to the program, won a new three-year contract to continue the program. They now provide a director and three program supervisors for our Saturday visiting programs and instructors for the parenting education classes. Working under the supervision of our program coordinator, they meet monthly for clinical supervision and also receive clinical supervision from a CODAC staff psychologist. In 1994, the CODAC contract was expanded to include provision of parenting education classes for fathers in several of our men's units. These have been well received. Plans are in the making to expand further to include supervised visits for fathers and their children.

Community Agencies

Collaborating with community agencies is an integral part of a strategic plan designed to ease each inmate's transition back into the community. Ultimately, it is intended to transfer dependency on the prison, which many of our clients quickly develop, to more socially and fiscally appropriate existing community agencies serving the same population. This strategy has the potential of more effectively assisting women through situational crisis and relapse after they are released. Rather than setting out to be arrested to come back to prison, which many of them tell us they do, we envision them calling community agencies they have become familiar with while incarcerated to provide a safe place.

Program Coordinator Alberta Bacarri was hired to develop and manage the mother/child program. Ms. Bacarri, an MSW with experience working for the State Department of Children, Youth and Families, outlines issues and experiences which gradually have shaped the evolution of the program over the past four years. More than half of the female population is serving six months or less. The majority, technically, have committed nonviolent crimes. It is assumed by the courts and the public, therefore, that their crimes are victimless. Our premise is that for those who are mothers, their crimes are not victimless—their children are their victims. The child suffers separation from mother, movement from home and school, or if they remain in the same school, humiliation and shame because of their mother's incarceration. Our program intends to assist the family in understanding and coping with its new situation. We recognize the need of all children to make peace with, and have a sense of, who they are as individuals and as the children of mothers in prison. While our initial focus was on family reunification, we gradually have adjusted our focus to address the real-life situations our children face day to day. We continue to emphasize maintenance of the parent-child bond, strengthening existing bonds, and in some cases, creating new bonds. To accomplish this goal, our most valuable tool is an assessment procedure developed cooperatively among our staff.

Assessment of Parenting Aspects of a Woman's Life

Unlike the traditional, more comprehensive needs assessment used for women in prison, this assessment addresses only the parenting aspects of the woman's life. An in-depth evaluation is completed of the mother's existing skills, what she needs to learn, and what her plans are for the future care of her children. It is critically important that we also work closely with the State Child Protective Agency to clarify legal status and case plans they have for the children. Rhode Island statute deals harshly with substance-abusing parents and parents whose rights previously have been terminated. Our assessment focuses, therefore, on substance abuse, treatment history and failures, and past and pending legal actions.

Women are assisted in understanding the complex details and proceedings of maintaining legal rights to their children in ongoing education groups which inform them of the changing legislation and legal trends in the courts. Those facing termination are offered counseling. Women are not automatically excluded from the program if their rights are to be terminated. Depending on the case, visits may continue to allow for positive experiences and memories for the child if this is in the child's best interest.

Parenting Education Classes

In addition to assessment of each mother, and individual counseling when appropriate, the program operates regular weekly parenting education classes and extended Saturday visits when the child is out of school. Visits between mother and child occur in supervised structured group settings. Mothers in medium custody and awaiting trial are allowed two and a half hours; mothers in minimum and work release are allowed three and a half hours. Many of our children also visit mothers during regular visiting times in the general population visiting room, which has no special accommodations for children, three times a week, daily for minimum and work release. On these visits, however, they must be accompanied by other family members. Although two or three hours a week may seem meager, the time spent alone with the child takes on great significance. The children are dropped off by family members or foster parents, by DCYF case workers, or by a driver working on contract with our program.

The focus is on mothers; however, participation by women in other caretaking roles, such as stepmothers, grandparents, and any woman playing a significant role in the child's life or to whom the child relates as a parent, may be included with staff approval. The program is voluntary. Demand usually exceeds capacity, although no mother goes without participation for long. Schedules constantly are adjusted and are flexible to suit each individual's needs. Scheduling to accommodate individual women's work schedules, foster family schedules, and children's schedules is difficult and time consuming, but is essential if children are expected to attend. Fortunately, with our relatively small population, this flexibility is possible.

The educational segment cycles in an eight-week curriculum which addresses child development, self-esteem, substance use within the family, discipline, foster parents and their role, and separation issues for mother and child. Two weeks are left unplanned, allowing content to be determined by the participants' needs. We have addressed such diverse issues as coping with the physically challenged child, lying to children and family, and living with disease and the prognosis of AIDS and cancer. When a woman completes the cycle, she may choose to remain for another cycle or spend additional time in longer visits with her child. As women have approached release, they typically shorten their visits and return to the educational group. We understand that, with release imminent, they are eager to relearn skills they know they will need at home. Shortly, we plan to establish a supervised professionally led post-release support group for selected mothers and children where they can seek comfort from a group that shares their particular circumstances.

Preparing for Visits

Over time, it has become clear that long visits require considerable structure and planning to be successful. Recognizing the reality that many of our women have never been mothered themselves was important. In addition to providing time for the women to be with their children, we needed to instruct them on how best to use that time. For many women, these visits may be the first time she spends two or three hours concentrating on relating to her child without interruption or distraction. The program provides midmorning snacks, lunch preparation cooperatively with staff and participants, clean up, seasonal group activities, and quiet time for mothers to read or talk alone with their children. After children leave, staff talk individually with each mother. Problems are discussed and immediate aftercare or counseling is provided, if necessary. This is particularly important if the visit did not go well, if the child was upset either in arriving or leaving, or if the mother has specific concerns about the child's welfare.

We learned early on that this level of individual attention and flexibility is essential. Prison administration is well aware of the sensitive nature of many issues raised during these extended visits. Many women never have experienced the pleasure and stress of coping with their children without the aid of drugs or alcohol. Suddenly, not only is this occurring, but also they are receiving parenting instruction. Applying what they are learning is difficult, particularly in the prison environment where they have so little control over their lives. The support and availability of staff after visits has been extremely important.

Counseling

Individual counseling, which most participants require, is another important aspect of the program. Legal issues and concerns regarding possible termination of parental rights are private and painful topics. Present legislation in Rhode Island is based on the philosophy that permanency planning for children is in the child's best interest. If the mother is incarcerated, permanent planning will not be likely to include her as the primary caretaker. Our staff wrestles with the inherent conflict of who we support—the mother or her children. In our experience with this program, we have learned as much as we have taught. Women share their histories, their present lives, and their hopes for the future with us. We have come to accept the reality that some of our mothers are so damaged by their own victimization that they will never manage their lives independent of a structured setting. Parenting, rather than being a happy and loving experience, is another source of stress and one which can lead to resumption of negative coping mechanisms. For these women, individual counseling assists them in making the best decision possible for themselves and their children. This sometimes leads to acceptance of relinquishing their roles as primary caregiver, while, hopefully, maintaining contact both for the child's sake and their own.

Work with Nonprofit Agencies

Prison-based programs often present conflict with private nonprofit agencies because of the institutional structure and restrictions built into the system. Careful attention must be given to the prison's role and mission which may require more rigidity than most community program providers are used to. Staff working for private agencies interfacing with the prison system require training, support, and supervision regarding correctional issues. Also of concern is the relationship between these community agency prison-based staff with the State Children's Agency, the courts, and other governmental agencies overseeing children and families. They sometimes find the policy of corrections, regarding interagency relationships, in conflict with the policy of their own agency. We have found it most efficient to have one staff person, our program manager, be the designated contact both for information sharing and reporting. Because she is familiar with DOC policy regarding privacy issues, we are able to control confidentiality and information flow.

Contracted community agency staff become aware, through training and experience, that while women are sincerely interested in their children, they also are very concerned with their own survival. Their behavior often reflects a lifestyle based on manipulation and self-serving habits which distract from the care of dependent children. We find that manipulation is decreased if group supervision and collaboration are built into the program. Our program coordinator conducts weekly staff supervision sessions which provide routine oversight, review and evaluation of programs, and debriefing on problems that arise during the week. Consistency with both women and staff form the foundation of a strong and effective program. Unrealistic and broken promises are typical expectations for this population, and they can do irreparable damage to struggling relationships between inmate and staff, and between mothers and children. Staff often have difficulty dealing with the intense level of emotion and pain typical of these women. It is important that we both recognize and address this aspect of work with incarcerated mothers.

Staffing

Our program relies on adequate staffing and constant attentive supervision by the program manager. The Saturday programs can accommodate approximately twelve to fifteen mothers and up to twenty-five children supervised by three staff members. Through various graduate schools with which we are affiliated, we are able to supplement staff with graduate interns. They have enabled us to experiment with various innovative programs such as foster parent follow-up, children's support groups, adolescent sports groups, and a teen discussion group. These each have merit and warrant further development should resources become available. We also have been able to develop modest research projects in conjunction with this and other interventions offered to incarcerated women. Monitoring and supervising students is a mixed blessing; it works well when students are motivated and prepared, but it can present unexpected problems and burdens. We continue to participate because we are committed to developing professional expertise working with this population, and because introducing students to women in prison sensitizes them to the unique needs of this population.

The Future

We consider many possibilities as we envision the future of the mother/child program. We would like to develop more educational and informational groups and a summer camp program staffed by volunteers. Making the program enjoyable and exciting is no less important than the educational component. Children and mothers will retain happy memories and sometimes forget the painful ones. We have proposed a post-release support group which will allow our released women to come together for sharing and assistance once back with their families. Our goal is to create a safe, comfortable environment where people are trained to help each other and themselves without criticism or judgment. Our goal is to build foundations for better lives and create memories that will last a lifetime.

We often must remind ourselves that mothers in prison are often children themselves who never have been mothered. We try to give them back some of their own childhood as we sensitize them to their roles as mothers. We give them opportunities to learn through doing, together with their children, and hope these experiences and memories will replace some of those with which they arrived. Running the program is rewarding and depressing. We see more failure than success and have come to redefine what success means. We celebrate a day without crisis as success, a mother laughing and hugging her child as success, tears and expressions of love and being eager for next Saturday's visit as success. Some of these memories may have to sustain these mothers and their children throughout their lives. We can give the child an opportunity to see his or her mom as the special person they know she can be, at least for a while. It is not unusual for us to hear a child say, "This is the best time I've ever had with my mom."

The "Girl Scouts Beyond Bars" Program: Keeping Incarcerated Mothers and Their Daughters Together

5

Marilyn C. Moses*
Program Manager
National Institute of Justice, U.S. Department of Justice, Washington, D.C.

"Girl Scouts Beyond Bars" may sound like a tabloid headline; however, it does not refer to a group of Girl Scouts who have been paroled after doing time for absconding with the proceeds from their annual cookie sale. It is an inmate mother-child visitation program that began as a National Institute of Justice (NIJ) demonstration project in November 1992.

This first-of-its-kind Girl Scout troop began with more than thirty daughters whose mothers live at the Maryland Correctional Institution for Women[1] (MCIW). The girls meet with their mothers at MCIW two Saturdays a month for a Girl Scout troop meeting; on alternate Saturdays, they meet at a Baltimore church where they work closely with Girl Scout troop leaders on projects just like girls in other troops.

In July 1993, just eight months after the first troop meeting, the National Council of Juvenile and Family Court Judges (NCJFCJ) honored the program with its annual "Unique and Innovative Project" award. In written remarks prepared for those gathered at the ceremony, Attorney General Janet Reno said:

> Creative and innovative solutions come when we work together on all levels [of government] and with the private sector—the "Girl Scouts Behind Bars"[2] project is a classic example. This program has the potential to become a model for the nation.

---

* Findings and conclusions reported here are those of the author and do not necessarily reflect the official position or policies of the U.S. Department of Justice or the American Correctional Association.

Since the Attorney General's remarks in 1993, NIJ has received numerous requests from other jurisdictions interested in forming a Girl Scout council-corrections partnership. With technical assistance from NIJ, similar Girl Scout programs have begun in several other correctional institutions: the Jefferson Correctional Institution near Tallahassee, Florida; Broward Correctional Institution in Pembroke Pines, Florida; Franklin Pre-Release in Columbus, Ohio; the Ohio Reformatory for Women in Marysville; the Estrella Jail in Maricopa County (Phoenix), Arizona; the Kentucky Correctional Institution for Women; the Delores Baylor Women's Correctional Institution in Delaware; New Jersey's Edna Mahan Correctional Institution for Women; the California Rehabilitation Center in Norco; and Dismas House in Owensboro, Kentucky (see Chapter 12). The National Institute of Justice is currently working with officials from ten other states who also are interested in replicating the program.

While the number of sites have grown, so too have those recognizing the novelty and potential of the partnership. In 1994, the Maryland Criminal Justice Association[3] followed NCJFCJ's recognition of the program with their first annual "Outstanding Program" award. Florida's governor recognized the Tallahassee program with his annual "Peace at Home: Preventing Domestic Violence" award in 1995. Later that year, the Maricopa County program was honored by the National Association of Counties with their annual "Achievement" award.

This chapter discusses the social, judicial, operational, and community context for this unique program. Programs in five of the eleven sites will be discussed. This chapter concludes with an examination of the broader issues that these programs should confront to effectively change the lives of high-risk youth.

Children, the Hidden Victims

Parental separation is difficult for children in any circumstance. Many of the adverse effects observed in children of incarcerated persons are also consistent with studies of children placed in foster care, those whose parents have divorced, and those who have experienced the death of a parent.[4]

Maryland correctional officials believe that about 80 percent of the women at MCIW are mothers. "We estimate that for every mother incarcerated at MCIW, three children are affected," reported Deputy Commissioner Melanie C. Pereira. Many experts believe that children deserve an honest explanation when there has been a dramatic change in their home circumstance. "When children don't know, they fantasize," observed Lisa Cid, the Girl Scouts of Central Maryland's (GSCM's) executive director. "They create an image of what happened to Mommy—and some of those imaginary pictures are horrible. They envision their mothers in chains."

Emotional suffering exists on both sides of the prison fence. "You need only impose a sentence of incarceration on a mother whose children are present to know what a terrible impact it has on the children," said Judge Carol E. Smith.[5] Judge Smith also observed that children are the hidden victims of their parents' crime(s) and subsequent incarceration, and their mothers are unable to provide a stable prosocial home environment.[6] Studies have shown that children of incarcerated persons are more likely to experience:

- Anxiety, depression, and aggression [7]
- Decline in school performance, attention disorders, and truancy [8]
- Teen pregnancy and symptoms of post-traumatic stress [9]

Beyond these problems, evidence indicates that many of these children follow their parents into the criminal justice system. A reliable measure to assess the risk that children of incarcerated persons have of becoming involved in the criminal justice system is not available. One study estimated that children with imprisoned parents may be almost six times more likely than their counterparts to become incarcerated.[10] A survey of youth in custody indicated that about a third reported a parent had been incarcerated at some time; a quarter said a brother or sister had been incarcerated.[11]

Since the Maryland program began, one Girl Scout's older sister (who did not participate in the program) already has followed her mother into MCIW. Now, the teenage Girl Scout has a mother and sister in prison at the same time. The Girl Scouts Beyond Bars program may keep her from following the same path. It has the potential of preventing many daughters from following in their mothers' footsteps.

The Partnership

The Girl Scouts Beyond Bars program is based on a unique partnership between corrections agencies and local Girl Scout councils which is designed to respond to needs of children of incarcerated parents and the perceived inadequacies of in-prison visitation programs. Few organized programs encourage children to visit their incarcerated parents. Those which existed usually have depended on one dynamic leader, someone from within the correctional institution or from the community. Thus, many such programs have had a short life expectancy. Existing programs also rarely have offered anything to the child or parent beyond the visit itself.

Considering these observations and the findings of the Carnegie Corporation of New York's Task Force on Youth Development and Community Programs, the Girl Scouts Beyond Bars program seemed a logical response. The Carnegie Foundation study found that youth service organizations "reach many young people, although usually not the ones who need service the most, but their potential remains largely untapped."[12] By creating a partnership between the Girl Scouts and correctional agencies, the potential to reach some of those young people in need is now being realized.

The partnership concept is also supported by the Maryland Governor's Committee to Study Sentencing and Correctional Alternatives for Women Convicted of Crime.[13] Judge Kathleen O'Ferrall Friedman [14] noted, "While the committee did not specifically call for such a partnership, it offers much of what the committee had hoped for. It provides an opportunity for increased as well as supervised visits by children. It also offers the children a chance to be involved with adult Girl Scout volunteers from the community. These women provide an opportunity for the girls to see that different life choices can be made."

It takes a whole village to raise a child. The African proverb indicating the importance of the community in influencing the way a child grows up has new meaning in the United States today. Many major youth service organizations were built on a family model. These organizations historically relied on parents to deliver their program and provide leadership for youths. Most frequently, mothers and fathers served as troop leaders or den mothers. Parents typically purchased the uniforms, books, and supplies. They shared carpooling responsibilities and supervised cookie sales or staffed the hot dog stand at the community fair to raise money for camping trips and other expeditions.

"Family life in America has changed, and so have the nation's communities. Fewer and fewer young adolescents are raised by a caring, supportive family surrounded by a caring, supportive community," reported the Carnegie task force.[15] This situation creates a major challenge for youth organizations. Underfunded youth service organizations, built on a family model, now are faced with the need to provide services to children of "zero parent" families.[16]

Between 1986 and 1991, state prison populations grew 58 percent. During that time period, the number of incarcerated men increased by 53 percent, while the population of incarcerated women increased by 75 percent.[17] Families are more likely to be broken by the woman's confinement within the criminal justice system than by a man's.[18] When a father is incarcerated, the mother commonly continues to care for the child; however, when a mother is incarcerated, frequently the father is altogether absent from the child's life, or is in prison himself. Incarcerated mothers must rely on other family members, many times grandparents, friends, or as a last resort, foster care. Children whose mothers are incarcerated and whose fathers are absent obviously fit the "zero parent" profile.

When a mother is incarcerated, a grandmother most commonly will assume care of the child. Most grandparents have not contemplated full-time care of their grandchildren at this point in their lives. Many are not physically or financially able to provide the ideal level of care their grandchildren need.[19] If a grandparent cannot take responsibility for the child, usually other family members will take the child. Frequently, relatives have their own children whose needs may understandably take priority.

Robin Gamble, GSCM's project coordinator said:

We cannot ask more of the child's caregiver than has already been asked in this circumstance. We must rely on dedicated volunteers from the community. These women have taken a personal interest in these girls and have become the village—they are doing what parents ordinarily would do.

The Maryland Demonstration Project

Except for the atypical location with metal detectors, clanging gates, and razorwire fences, the mother-daughter gatherings at MCIW differ little from Girl Scout meetings held in the community. The daughters, who range in age from five to fifteen, join their mothers two Saturdays each month for a Girl Scout meeting in the prison gymnasium. During these two-hour sessions, the women spend supervised time with their daughters in structured play and working on troop projects.

A strength of the program is that it offers the child more than just a visit. The troop meetings are both fun and educational. Activities have had varied themes such as aerobics, a miniscience fair, and arts and crafts. More serious issues also have been addressed in a creative manner. Mothers and their daughters attended a puppet show on violence prevention. Sessions on various contemporary and family life issues also have been held, addressing such topics as self-esteem, drug abuse, relationships, coping with family crises, anatomy and physiology of the reproductive system, and teenage pregnancy prevention.

On alternate Saturdays, when the girls are not meeting with their mothers at MCIW, they meet at Corpus Christi Church in downtown Baltimore to finish projects and start new ones. They spend time with Girl Scout volunteers, who serve as mentors, and with new friends in the troop.

Occasionally, the girls take field trips with other Girl Scouts in the community. Such activities have included a leadership conference at a beach resort with more than 100 other Girl Scouts from across the state, a day camp experience, a Halloween sleepover, a trip to the Baltimore Museum of Industry, and an evening of roller skating.

Focus on the mothers. Using the prison and community troop meetings as a catalyst, the program is opening avenues of communication between parent and child. One mother remarked, "I've gotten three letters from my daughter this week. That never happened before the Girl Scouts."

As the slogan says, "The Girl is First in Girl Scouts," but in this program, the mother is just as important. In addition to increased visiting time, one aim of the program is to enable the mothers to assume responsibility and develop organizational skills. With Girl Scout staff support, the mothers take responsibility for some of the planning for the mother-daughter meetings. The correctional facility's limit of a one-hour monthly planning session for mothers and Girl Scout staff limits the mothers' ability to take total charge of planning.

Training in parenting. Before incarceration, most of MCIW's inmate mothers were their children's primary caretakers. Although many of these mothers have not been ideal parents, [20] most will resume their parental role when released.

Figure 5.1 Profile of an MCIW Mother

Average age	29.5
Average age of first intercourse	15.5
Average age of first pregnancy	17.9
Average number of children	2.4
Average child's age	7.5
Functioned as children's primary caregiver prior to arrest	68.7
Were single parents	86.1
Received AFDC prior to arrest	45.8
Had not had a visit from children since imprisonment	28.6
Saw their children less than once per month	35.7
Plan to reunite with their children after release	94.0
Women of color	73.9
Had no high school diploma or GED	50.2
Had been incarcerated before	65.1
Were physically or sexually abused (as a child, adult, or both)	51.7
Had a drug/alcohol-related arrest	52.9

Source: Preliminary results of a survey administered by the Maryland Governor's Office of Children, Youth, and Families in 1992.

Given these realities, a link between the Girl Scout program and MCIW's parenting education program and other institutional services would seem sensible. However, the connection has not been made. Maryland correctional administrators cite their need to offer a variety of program opportunities to many women rather than concentrating limited resources on a few.

Mothers receive some training from Girl Scout staff who help them plan and run the mother-daughter meetings, but they need more help with parenting skills. To supplement the Girl Scouts' work, the mothers work in a group setting for one hour each month. While no formal parenting instruction is offered in these monthly Saturday sessions, Deborah Pierson-Agbebakun, a licensed social worker from the community, volunteers her time to provide a forum for the mothers to discuss various family-related concerns and to develop parenting-from-afar coping mechanisms.

While Pierson-Agbebakun believes that both mothers and daughters derive great benefit from the program, she also believes that the program falls short in two areas. First, the girls and their caregivers are not receiving the same mental health support through the program as the mothers.[21] Second, when a mother is transferred to the Baltimore Pre-Release unit, she no longer can attend the regular mother-daughter Girl Scout meetings. The transfer disrupts the mother-daughter communication that is essential to easing the mother's move back home.

Release from prison. Continuity and transitional issues are a concern for both Girl Scout and correctional administrators.[22] Involvement in the program does not end for the children once their mothers are released or transferred to prerelease. However, because the program lacks funds and enough volunteers, when a mother leaves MCIW, her daughter's participation in the Girl Scout program drops from four to two Saturdays a month. She can participate in the community troop meetings but not those at MCIW.

When the mothers return to the community, they are encouraged to continue to participate in the community-based program. In Maryland, most girls continue in the program, but no mother has accompanied her daughter to more than one community meeting. The mothers' lack of continued involvement can be explained by conflicting work schedules, the demands of other family responsibilities, and, in a few cases, a lack of interest. Moreover, research suggests that the desired level of free-world parental participation does not exist in "typical" Girl Scout troop activities. Hence, it seems unfair to hold ex-offenders to a higher standard than nonoffending parents.

Operational issues. Women from all custody levels may participate in the Maryland program if they meet the requirements of the correctional institution's screening process. MCIW Warden James A. Carter explained:

> Among other requirements, the women cannot have a history of child abuse and they must be infraction-free for six months before they can apply. They also must remain infraction-free while in the program. We have a few "charter" members in this group who have managed to abide by these rules for quite some time.

Other requirements are outlined in a memorandum of understanding that each mother must sign.

The mothers are not the only ones who must adhere to tough standards for program participation. Along with taking Girl Scout leadership training, the Girl Scout volunteers must undergo a criminal background check and participate in the department's volunteer orientation and inservice training sessions.

"Contraband is always a concern in correctional institutions," said Assistant Warden Mitchell Franks. Mothers are strip-searched after each mother-daughter troop meeting. Thus far, no serious problems have arisen as a result of these contact visits.

"The most difficult aspect for us has been accommodating media requests," commented Assistant Warden Franks. Over 100 newspaper articles and substantial local and network television time have favorably depicted the program, the department of corrections, and the Girl Scouts.

Program funding. The program offers much in return for a relatively small outlay of funds. The budget for the Maryland troop is approximately $30,000 per year with transportation-related expenses accounting for nearly half. Included in that sum are Girl Scout support staff salaries, accident insurance, supplies, and other miscellaneous expenses.

When GSCM initially took on the project, funds from its operating budget were used to offset initial troop expenses. A one-time-only NIJ demonstration grant of $15,000 partially offset initial costs. The United Way of Central Maryland followed with a $10,000 grant, a continuation award of $8,500, and a $6,500 bridge grant. Later, a one-time-only $20,000 award from the Maryland Department of Public Safety and Correctional Services was made to GSCM. With assistance from a recently formed advisory committee, a strategy for long-term funding to sustain the program is being developed.

Florida's Two-city Program

Tallahassee

Within a few months of hearing about the Girl Scouts Beyond Bars program, the Girl Scouts of the Apalachee Bend (GSAB) and officials from the Florida Department of Corrections had their own program. The Florida groups learned of NIJ's pilot program in October 1993. By late January 1994, they had developed a more intensive program at Jefferson Correctional Institution (JCI).

The Florida Governor's Office is impressed with what the Girl Scouts, the Florida Department of Corrections, and their collaborating partners have accomplished at JCI. In April 1995, the program was recognized by the Governor with his annual "Peace at Home: Preventing Domestic Violence" award.

Focus on training in parenting. Pat Chivers, GSAB's executive director, said:

We were really anxious to implement the visitation program here. I knew that the community would get behind this project. But I also knew we would need to put together a comprehensive program if we hoped to make a difference.

The Tallahassee mother-daughter meeting schedule is similar to the Maryland program. Two Saturdays each month the girls work with their Girl Scout troop leaders in the community. On alternate Saturdays, the mothers and their daughters meet for troop meetings at JCI. Kerry Flack, assistant to Florida's secretary of corrections, pointed out how the program aimed to expand on the Maryland pilot: "We wanted to do all that we could to support this program. Dr. Shayn Lloyd, JCI's staff psychologist, has been assigned to work with the mothers, at no expense to the Girl Scouts, for at least an hour after each mother-daughter meeting."

Not only do the mothers at JCI meet for a longer time than they do in Maryland, they also meet more frequently. Mothers meet four times per month for almost two hours each session. The sessions are a hybrid of formal parenting instruction using a text developed specifically for incarcerated parents and the Girl Scout contemporary issues material. Mothers also have adequate time to plan for upcoming Girl Scout troop meetings.

Partnerships. The program is small, about eight mothers and fifteen girls. Although small, GSAB has made every effort to coordinate with other local agencies. The Tallahassee Girl Scouts work with the local school system to monitor the girls' school performance. In addition, they are collaborating with the Community Intervention Program, Inc. and the Glenn Terrell Foundation, an organization that provides services to inmates and their families, to provide social services for the girls, their guardians, and the mothers after they are released. The services of these organizations are provided at no cost to the program.

Release from prison. While the mother in the Girl Scout program is in JCI, staff from the Glenn Terrell Foundation meet with her to determine her transition needs. A post-release plan that includes job placement counseling and links to other needed social services is tailored to suit her specific needs. Once she is released, the staff continue to meet with her to carry out the plan. The staff also perform a family assessment and collaborate with other agencies and organizations in an effort to meet the entire family's needs. At least once each week, staff members continue meeting with the entire family until the social services are no longer needed.

Program funding. The council initially received a $37,500 Community Juvenile Partnership Grant from the Attorney General's Office of Florida. A continuation grant of $57,848 was later awarded.

Program expansion. The program enjoys strong support from Secretary Harry K. Singletary of the Florida Department of Corrections:

> I am not interested in what people say, I am interested in what they do. I am very impressed with what the Girl Scouts have done here. It is the department's goal to work and make the program available in all four of our women's institutions and in our adult probation and parole populations. It is ambitious, but it is something we need to work toward if we intend to make a difference.

Fort Lauderdale

Secretary Singletary's goal for expansion in Florida is becoming a reality. In February 1994, Girl Scout executive directors from all ten councils in Florida met in Tallahassee to learn about the Girl Scouts Beyond Bars program. Jeannette Archer-Simons, executive director of the Girl Scouts of Broward County (GSBC), attended the meeting. Archer-Simons embraced the program and saw it as an opportunity rather than an obstacle.

Partnerships. Although Archer-Simons had recently moved from Iowa and had been in her new position for only three days when she learned of the program, she immediately went to work building the partnerships necessary to implement a comprehensive program. Archer-Simons said:

> We now have the support of the Broward County Sheriff's Office, a commitment from the Broward County School District, Mount Bethel Baptist Church, the Florida Department of Health and Rehabilitation Services, Women in Distress, Henderson Mental Health Center, Cambell Hall, and Woodson Psychological Services.

After nearly nine months of planning, the program began in November 1994. The Fort Lauderdale program shares common elements with the other Girl Scouts Beyond Bars sites in that it involves alternate Saturdays of in-prison mother-daughter troop meetings and community troop meetings at Mount Bethel Baptist Church. In addition, formal parenting instruction also is offered to the mothers by a certified parenting instructor.

One unique aspect of the program is the emphasis on the mental health of the girl participants. Dr. Pamela Hall of Woodson Psychological Services conducts a forty-five-minute screening session for each girl prior to her entry into the program. Such issues as what to expect when visiting the prison and concerns about seeing mom for the first time in a long time are discussed during this session. In addition, twice each month Dr. Hall conducts a girl-only group session for those participating in the program. A significant turning point for the older girls and their troop leaders from the community was an overnight session facilitated by Woodson Psychological Services. During that time, the girls discussed concerns they had about school, foster parents, and boyfriends with their Girl Scout troop leaders and Dr. Hall.

While all the partners play a critical role in the Fort Lauderdale program, enough cannot be said about one partner—Mount Bethel Baptist Church. The church has embraced the Girl Scout program and provided scores of volunteers to make the in-prison and community programs work for both the girls and their moms. Mount Bethel Church also provides door-to-door transportation.

Neither has Mount Bethel Baptist Church forgotten the sons of the women who participate in the Girl Scouts Beyond Bars program. These boys are picked up each week with their Girl Scout sisters. While they are not included in in-prison mother-daughter Girl Scout troop meetings, volunteer male mentors work with these boys each week on a number of character and skill-building projects.

Release from Prison. As in other sites, the girls continue in the program after a mother's release. Recognizing that the Girl Scout mother faces enormous obstacles upon release, and that achieving rapid family stability is in the best interest of the child, GSBC has formed a partnership with Women in Distress. Women in Distress is an organization serving homeless or otherwise needy women. Thus far, only two mothers participating in the program have been released. One was referred to Women in Distress. They provided housing assistance, a referral to a drug counseling program, and other related assistance. Thus far, this mother continues to succeed on the outside and has made progress toward family reunification.

Program Funding. Over $50,000 has been received from the Henderson Foundation, the Florida Department of Health and Rehabilitation Services, and Mount Bethel Baptist Church.

Program Expansion. At the invitation of the Broward County Sheriff's Department, GSBC is currently planning to expand the program to the Broward County Detention Facility in January 1996. If successful, the Fort Lauderdale site will be the first Girl Scouts Beyond Bars site in the nation to provide a program continuum from point of arrest to long-term incarceration and aftercare.

Ohio's Program

Just one phone call started things in Ohio. Once Dr. Barbara Nichols, warden of the Franklin Pre-Release Center in Columbus, Ohio, learned of the Girl Scouts Beyond Bars program, she called the Seal of Ohio Girl Scout Council (SOGSC).

The Ohio program began in January 1994 and operates much the same as it does in other sites. Twenty-five girls, ages five to eleven, meet with their mothers two times per month but only attend community troop meetings after their mothers have been released. The mothers meet for Girl Scout planning sessions, but the program offers no formal parenting instruction or mental health care. However, SOGSC proudly reports that eighteen of the twenty-five girls participating in the program had the opportunity to attend residential Girl Scout camp last summer.

Program funding. In its first year, the program was funded almost entirely from the SOGSC's operating budget. Later, the Columbus Foundation and Nationwide Insurance provided funding support. In addition to purchasing Girl Scout cookies from their daughters, the mothers raised over $1,700 for the troop from a cosmetic sale they held within the institution.

Program Expansion. In December 1994, SOGSC expanded its program to the Ohio Reformatory for Women. Ohio is the first state to have this program in its prison with transition to a prerelease center. The SOGSC also played a key support role in the Ohio Reformatory for Women's first day camp for children whose mothers are imprisoned there.

Arizona's Jail Program

When speaking of the partnership formed with the Arizona Cactus-Pine Girl Scout Council (ACPGSC), Sheriff Joe Arpaio of Maricopa County said, "The Girl Scouts Beyond Bars program is just going back to basics. Involvement in prevention programs is nothing new for sheriffs." The Maricopa County Sheriff's Office is the first in the nation to implement the program in a jail. In July 1995, the National Association of Counties recognized the Maricopa County Girl Scouts Beyond Bars program with its annual "Achievement" award.

Partnerships. The sheriff's office and ACPGSC also are working diligently to forge links with other service organizations. So far, a partnership with Parents Anonymous was formed to provide formal parenting instruction to the mothers, and ACPGSC has formed a partnership with Valley Big Brothers/Big Sisters.

Partnerships in Action

Maryland

— Maryland Division of Corrections

— United Way of Central Maryland

— Private Donations

Tallahassee, Florida

— Community Juvenile Justice Partnership Program (Administered by the Florida Attorney General's Office)

Fort Lauderdale, Florida

— Henderson Foundation

— Mount Bethel Baptist Church

— Florida Department of Mental Health and Rehabilitation Services

— Broward County Sheriff's Office

Kentucky

— Anonymous gift

— City of Louisville Youth Alliance

— Mercer Transportation Company

— V.V. Cooke Foundation

Ohio

— The Columbus Foundation

— Nationwide Insurance

Arizona

— Arizona Community Foundation

— Arizona's Governor's Office for Children

— Valley of the Sun United Way

— ThunderbirdYouth Fund

Delaware

— DuPontMerck Pharmaceutical Company

New Jersey

— Schumann Fund of New Jersey

— Prudential Foundation

California

— Southern California Edison Corporation

Outlook

The feasibility of a partnership between Girl Scout councils and correctional facilities has been demonstrated. Such a partnership can be formed with any motivated youth service organization, including those serving boys. The partnership can augment an existing parenting or visitation program, or it can be implemented at institutions with no program in place.

Because the programs are based on organizational strength rather than the leadership of individuals, a number of sites have weathered significant turnover in both Girl Scout and correctional personnel. Although organizational reliance provides an "insurance policy," it does not guarantee survival. The jury is out as to whether the Girl Scouts will be able to sustain the program over time.

High-risk children generally, and this group in particular, are an expensive population to serve in terms of human resources and finances. Survival of the Girl Scouts Beyond Bars program will depend, in part, on each participating council's ability to "reinvent" itself to serve high-risk children from "zero parent" families.

Leadership, motivation, management ability, fund development expertise, volunteer recruitment, and coalition building strategies vary from council to council. It is questionable whether councils with insufficient organizational capacity will be able to build the necessary structure to implement or sustain such a program over time.

Survival also will depend, in part, on the correctional institution's willingness to pull its weight in the partnership. Although most correctional facilities cannot contribute direct financial aid, corrections officials can assist Girl Scout partners with coalition building efforts within the criminal justice, business, legal, state, and local government communities. In-kind support, such as providing refreshments for the mothers and their daughters during the in-prison troop meetings would be helpful. In addition, detailing those under community service orders and/or boot camp residents to do maintenance work at Girl Scout camps, also may be appreciated by local councils.[23] Making a match between council needs and those services provided by the institution's state-use industries also could be a valued contribution.

A final challenge to both current and future partners is to reexamine the mission of the program. Will it remain a "visitation plus" program, or will it expand its goals to break intergenerational cycles of criminal justice involvement and other negative social behaviors? If the latter mission is to be assumed, these children and their families will require "high octane" programming. It is not reasonable to expect that a child's negative behaviors will be significantly lessened by a two-hour meeting held once per week.[24] If the program is to effect long-term behavioral changes, partnerships with other organizations offering complementary services and expertise must be made.[25]

Correctional agencies will also have to be willing to coordinate existing institutional resources with their Girl Scout partners to build a comprehensive intergenerational program. Success in family reunification, inmate recidivism, and delinquency prevention for the child participant cannot realistically be expected solely from a visitation program or with a fragmented, less than comprehensive approach.[26]

As for NIJ's continued role, a competitive grant was awarded recently to the University of Baltimore to conduct a research and evaluation effort at the Maryland site. Findings from this study are expected in early 1997. Within budget limits, the Institute plans to continue to provide technical assistance to current and prospective sites. In November 1995, on the third anniversary of the inception of the program, NIJ sponsored the first annual Girl Scouts Beyond Bars conference. The two-and-a-half day conference was attended by more than seventy-five Girl Scout and correctional officials from fifteen states.

Betty Kassulke, warden of the Kentucky Correctional Institution for Women, said:

The Girl Scouts Beyond Bars program is a classic example of synergism at its best. While this program has its limitations and faces many challenges ahead, there can be no question that Girl Scouts Beyond Bars equals a sum greater than its individual parts. As a result of this initiative, visitation programs now exist in a number of correctional institutions across the country that previously had no such program in place. Through extensive national and local media coverage, this program has succeeded, like no other single program to date, to bring children of incarcerated parents out of the shadows and into the public consciousness. Grantmakers, many of whom have never funded a corrections program, have embraced this one. It is clear that none of the parties in the partnership could have achieved this result on their own. Having said this, I believe the Girl Scouts Beyond Bars program has yet to realize its full potential.

Endnotes

1. The Maryland Correctional Institution is a minimum/medium/maximum adult correctional facility.

2. Originally the project was popularly known as the "Girl Scouts Behind Bars" program. However, in 1995 the majority of participating sites felt that "Girl Scouts Beyond Bars" more accurately described the mission of the program.

3. The Maryland Criminal Justice Association is a state affiliate of the American Correctional Association.

4. Hairston, C. F. 1991. Family Ties During Imprisonment: Important to Whom and for What? *Journal of Sociology and Social Welfare.* Vol. 18, No. 1, p. 87-104; and Brown, D. Incarcerating Mothers and Parenting. *Journal of Family Violence.* Vol. 4, No. 2, p. 211-221.

5. Baltimore City Circuit Court Judge Carol E. Smith is a member of the National Association of Women Judges (NAWJ). Judge Smith is a past-president of NAWJ's Maryland Chapter, a member of their national organization's committee on women in prison, and also serves on the Maryland "Girl Scouts Beyond Bars" advisory committee.

6. Gabel, Stewart. 1992. Children of Incarcerated and Criminal Parents: Adjustment, Behavior, and Prognosis. *Bulletin of the American Academy of Psychiatry and the Law.* Vol. 20, 33-45; Hungerford, Gregory A. 1993. The Children of Inmate Mothers: An Exploratory Study of Children, Caretakers and Inmate Mothers in Ohio. Ohio State University (Dissertation), pgs. 85-89, 96, 105-106, 110.

7. Gabel, Stewart and Richard Shindledecker. 1993. Characteristics of Children Whose Parents Have Been Incarcerated. *Hospital and Community Psychiatry.* Vol. 44, No. 7. p. 658 (July); Hungerford, Gregory A. 1993. The Children of Inmate Mothers: An Exploratory Study of Children, Caretakers and Inmate Mothers in Ohio. Ohio State University (Dissertation), pgs. 111-112; Lowenstein, A. 1986. Temporary Single Parenthood: The Case of Prisoners' Families. *Family Relations.* 35:79-85; Koban, L. A. 1983. Parents in Prison: A Comparative Analysis of the Effects of Incarceration on the Families of Men and Women. *Research in Law, Deviance, and Social Control.* 5: 171-83; and Sack, W. H., J. Seidler, and S. Thomas. 1976. The Children of Imprisoned Parents: A Psychosocial Exploration. *American Journal of Orthopsychiatry.* 46: 618-28.

8. Ibid. 658; Hungerford, Gregory A. 1993. The Children of Inmate Mothers: An Exploratory Study of Children, Caretakers and Inmate Mothers in Ohio. Ohio State University (Dissertation), pgs. 107-108, 112-113, 116; and Stanton, S. 1980. *When Mothers Go to Jail.* Lexington, Massachusetts: D. C. Heath.

9. Hungerford, Gregory A. 1993. The Children of Inmate Mothers: An Exploratory Study of Children, Caretakers and Inmate Mothers in Ohio. Ohio State University (Dissertation), pgs. 104-105; Bloom, Barbara. 1992. Why Punish the Children? A Reassessment of the Impact of Incarceration on the Children of Women Prisoners. Paper presented at the American Correctional

Association, 122nd Congress, 1992; and Jose-Kampfner, Christina. 1991. Michigan Program Makes Children's Visits Meaningful. *Corrections Today*. August. 132-134.

10. Barnhill S. and P. Dressel. 1991. *Three Generations at Risk*. Atlanta, Georgia: Aid to Imprisoned Mothers.

11. Bureau of Justice Statistics. 1987. *Survey of Youth in Custody*. See also American Correctional Association. 1990. *The Female Offender*. Laurel, Maryland: American Correctional Association. 1991. *Statistical Summary*. Laurel, Maryland: American Correctional Association (over 50 percent of all juvenile delinquents imprisoned in 1990 have a parent who has been incarcerated).

12. Carnegie Council on Adolescent Development, Task Force on Youth Development and Community Programs. 1992. *A Matter of Time: Risk and Opportunity in the Nonschool Hours*. New York: Carnegie Corporation of New York.

13. State of Maryland. 1988. Governor's Committee to Study Sentencing and Correctional Alternatives for Women Convicted of Crime (Final Report).

14. Baltimore City Circuit Court Judge Kathleen O'Ferrall Friedman chaired the Maryland Governor's Committee to Study Sentencing and Correctional Alternatives for Women Convicted of Crime. Judge Friedman is also a member of the National Association of Women Judges (NAWJ) and is a member of their national steering committee on women in prison. In August 1993, Judge Friedman convened a subcommittee of the NAWJ-Maryland Chapter to revisit the 1988 Governor's Committee report. Judge Friedman also serves on the Maryland Girl Scouts Beyond Bars advisory committee.

15. Carnegie Council on Adolescent Development, Task Force on Youth Development and Community Programs. 1992. *A Matter of Time: Risk and Opportunity in the Nonschool Hours*. New York: Carnegie Corporation of New York. p. 26.

16. Carnegie Council on Adolescent Development. Ibid. 12, 88.

17. Bureau of Justice Statistics. 1994. *Women in Prison*. March.

18. Datesman, Susan K. and Gloria L. Cales. I'm Still the Same Mommy: Maintaining the Mother/Child Relationship in Prison. *The Prison Journal*. Vol. LXIII, No. 2, Autumn-Winter 1983, 142.

19. Hungerford, Gregory A. 1993. The Children of Inmate Mothers: An Exploratory Study of Children, Caretakers and Inmate Mothers in Ohio. Ohio State University (Dissertation), pgs. 90-100.

20. See Gabel, Stewart, and Richard Shindledecker. 1993. Characteristics of Children Whose Parents Have Been Incarcerated. *Hospital and Community Psychiatry*. Vol. 44, No. 7, p. 660; Hungerford, Gregory A. 1993. The Children of Inmate Mothers: An Exploratory Study of Children, Caretakers and Inmate Mothers in Ohio. Ohio State University (Dissertation), pgs. 88-90, 117, 124-125; Neto, Virginia V. and LaNelle Marie Bainer. 1983. Mother and Wife Locked Up: A Day With the Family. *The Prison Journal*. Vol. LXIII, No. 2, Autumn-Winter, p. 124.

21. See Hungerford, Gregory A. 1993. The Children of Inmate Mothers: An Exploratory Study of Children, Caretakers and Inmate Mothers in Ohio. Ohio State University (Dissertation), pgs. 142-145 (discussion of the need to link children of incarcerated persons with local child welfare and mental health services).

22. While the need for transition from prison to prerelease is acknowledged, it also should be recognized that the first break in an inmate parent-child relationship takes place at arrest and jail detention.

23. See Pitts, Chrystal. 1994. Federal Partnerships at Work. *Federal Prison Journal*. Winter, p. 15 (a discussion of use of federal inmate work crews to maintain and construct facilities on U.S. Forest Service properties).

24. See Gabel, Stewart, and Richard Shindledecker. 1993. Characteristics of Children Whose Parents Have Been Incarcerated. *Hospital and Community Psychiatry*. Vol. 44, No. 7, p. 660; See Carnegie Council on Adolescent Development, Task Force on Youth Development and Community Programs. 1992. *A Matter of Time: Risk and Opportunity in the Non-School Hours*. New York: Carnegie Corporation of New York. p. 12.

25. Arella, Lorinda R. 1993. Multiservice Adolescent Programs: Seeking Institutional Partnership Alternatives. *Journal of Youth and Adolescence*. Vol. 22, No. 3, p. 283-284.

26. See Carnegie Council on Adolescent Development, Task Force on Youth Development and Community Programs. 1992. *A Matter of Time: Risk and Opportunity in the Non-School Hours*. New York: Carnegie Corporation of New York. p. 12.

The PROGRAM for Female Offenders, Inc.

6

Tracie M. Haigh

Associate Director

The PROGRAM for Female Offenders, Inc., Harrisburg, Pennsylvania

The PROGRAM for Female Offenders, Inc. was established in Harrisburg, Pennsylvania in 1979 to serve any woman who had had a "brush" with the law. The focus of the agency at that time was employment readiness and employment placement. The PROGRAM's services have expanded as the population of women in the criminal justice system has exploded. Our menu of services now includes substance abuse case management, HIV/AIDS education, supportive counseling, and alternatives to incarceration.

Because the prisons have two and sometimes three generations of women offenders incarcerated at the same time, The PROGRAM's focus in the past three years has been concentrated on the children of offenders. The goal of our children's programming is to stop the intergenerational cycle of crime.

The PROGRAM for Female Offenders, Inc., along with Penn State Cooperative Extension and Dauphin County Prison, collaborate to provide incarcerated mothers with an intense parenting program called P.A.T.C.H.—Parents And Their Children at Home— designed specifically to meet the needs of women parenting from prison.

P.A.T.C.H. offers mothers at Dauphin County Prison a full-scale two-month curriculum of parent education. The training officer from the prison teaches cardiopulmonary resuscitation, first aid, vital signs, kids in safety seats, and fire safety. The education director teaches children's literature and the importance of play. The treatment counselor conducts individual and group counseling and parental support sessions. The Penn State extension agent teaches parenting courses designed by extension agents throughout Pennsylvania on topics such as discipline and self-esteem, positive image for parents and children, leisure time, and age-appropriate expectations of kids. The PROGRAM for

Female Offenders, Inc. is the liaison between the prison and community-based agencies which teach such courses as toys and gender expectations and health issues. The PROGRAM also facilitates projects where the mothers create gifts for their children such as "love boxes" (boxes which the mothers decorate and fill with affirmations), tape recordings, handmade cards, and books.

Simultaneously, the collaborating agencies conduct two evening visits with the P.A.T.C.H. children at the local YMCA. There, we help them make gifts and crafts to give to their mothers at the special visits. We also get to know the children so they feel comfortable with us during the visit.

After completing the eight-week course, the women have two special contact visits with their children. These visits are conducted in the multipurpose room of the prison without glass windows between them and without correctional officers. The room has been decorated, and there are snacks and games on the tables. The children are required to remove their shoes so the staff can search them, but it is done playfully. The children enter the visiting room through a front door, so they do not go through gates or through the corridors of the prison. Only P.A.T.C.H. staff are with the children and their mothers, and the women use this time to implement their newly acquired parenting skills. The visits last three hours, from 6:00 PM until 9:00 PM.

The first visit is planned by P.A.T.C.H. staff. Afterwards, an evaluation meeting is convened with the mothers and the staff to review the visit's events and plan the second meeting. After the second visit, a task force consisting of the deputy treatment warden at Dauphin County Prison, prison counselors from the female wing of the prison, and a volunteer from the community, convenes to evaluate the overall effectiveness of the program with the P.A.T.C.H. staff. A qualitative evaluation is conducted after each class focusing on the relevance of the material and the effectiveness of the trainer. This allows us to continually improve the program.

Goals

One goal of P.A.T.C.H. is to foster communication between incarcerated mothers and their children, and to increase the mother's knowledge of age-appropriate developmental capabilities and needs of their children. We teach fundamental safety and health courses. Some of what we teach is extremely basic, but necessary, as illustrated by the comment of one woman in her evaluation, "This is the first time I ever knew how to take my child's temperature."

Another goal of P.A.T.C.H. is to help children of incarcerated mothers learn to socialize effectively with other children and adults. We try to emphasize positive self-esteem and encourage them to feel special and unique. We also provide a place where these children can talk openly about their mothers' incarceration because all the children present have mothers in prison. We provide an atmosphere of acceptance and inclusion for these children.

At our last evaluation of the P.A.T.C.H. program, the collaborating agencies realized a vital component was missing to address the special needs of the P.A.T.C.H. children. The agencies recognized that we needed a program parallel to P.A.T.C.H. which specifically addressed the children of offenders and provided them with a continuum of care. We decided that teaching parenting skills to incarcerated mothers without serving their children was short sighted. We needed to intervene early with children of offenders in order to stop the intergenerational cycle of crime. To that end, Penn State Extension Agents, Dauphin County Prison staff, and The PROGRAM for Female Offenders, Inc. designed the L.I.N.K.—Life Is Nurturing Kids—program.

L.I.N.K.

L.I.N.K. was designed to address the needs of offenders' children. These needs include: skills training in self-esteem, conflict resolution, decision making, coping, and healthy modes of recreation. Our goal is to foster values, teach the tools of self-help, stress the importance of education, and teach street survival skills which include drug, alcohol, and HIV/AIDS education.

The cornerstone of the L.I.N.K. project is thirty volunteers. Each child is matched with a volunteer from the community. Volunteers act as mentors and friends to the children. The mentors spend two hours with the children each week at the YMCA surrounded by other L.I.N.K. children and their mentors. In most cases, these meetings provide the only time the child is able to behave as a child—to relax, play, read, be read to or talked to, and be able to experience unconditional positive regard from an adult.

From the outset, we attempted to recruit volunteers whose ethnicity closely matches the L.I.N.K. children. We contacted area churches and schools, set up information booths at local shopping malls, and were interviewed by the local newspaper. Upon application, all volunteers are screened by the local prison for a criminal background; once cleared, they spend eight hours in training provided by The PROGRAM for Female Offenders, Inc. and Penn State Cooperative Extension. The training includes information on age-appropriate expectations, discipline, and the importance of the volunteer's commitment to the program.

Weekly group meetings at the YMCA enable the volunteers to meet with their L.I.N.K. child once a week for a period of nine months. During this meeting, special projects are planned for each age group. While the mentors and children work together on projects, the mentors attempt to foster a sense of accomplishment in each child. Bonds between mentors and their children form very quickly.

Mentors also work with the children to expand their range of responses to conflict. Many of the L.I.N.K. children show signs of anger and respond to conflict in destructive ways. They are accustomed to dealing with chaos by fighting, uttering harsh words, or violence. By offering alternatives to violence, we teach and reinforce conflict resolution and decision-making skills. L.I.N.K. uses an empowerment model of skill building to develop competencies to enable children to achieve independence.

Kids In Control, a course developed by Penn State Extension Services, is the basic educational component of the L.I.N.K. project. The curriculum includes lessons on learning to deal with loneliness and boredom, being alone at home, getting it together and keeping it together, self-esteem (I'm glad I'm me), taking care of yourself, handling emergencies, what to do if you're afraid, you and friends, you and your younger brothers or sisters, saying no and talking about it, and making decisions on your own. The curriculum combines education with role-play, projects, worksheets, and group support. This curriculum is designed to build independent living skills and self-esteem for children.

Another course and book, also developed by Penn State Extension, is *The Stress Connection, A Kid's Guide*. This book also uses exercises, worksheets, journals, puzzles, and group activities to allow open discussions about stress, its causes, symptoms, and worries; healthy ways to respond to stress; personal privacy; assertiveness; feelings; self-esteem; relaxation techniques and exercises; imagery and fantasy; and getting in touch with feelings.

Evaluation

Evaluation of the L.I.N.K. project is completed by the L.I.N.K. project director. At the beginning of the program, each child receives a questionnaire. The questionnaire asks the children to explain their relationship to their family, school grades, activities, and interests. The Piers-Harris Self-Concept Scale also is administered. This instrument measures the child's level of self-esteem at the beginning of the program. The self-esteem concept scale and the questionnaire document the needs of the children entering the program. The self-concept scale is administered again at the end of the nine-month period of L.I.N.K. to measure changes in self-esteem and behavior after completing L.I.N.K.

At project end, the L.I.N.K. project director conducts an in-depth individual interview with each of the caregivers, the children, and the mentors who were matched with each child. Each L.I.N.K. child "draws a person" as their evaluation. The children draw their caregiver, volunteer mentor, themselves, mother, and father. They, then, discuss the drawings and what each means. The personal interviews with the caretaker and mentor focus on how effectively the program met the needs of each child. The interviewer asks for specific examples of any changes observed in the child while a L.I.N.K. participant. The interviewers ask for specific skills that were learned. Questions also focus on behavior changes and performance and attendance in school.

Upon completion of the evaluations, all L.I.N.K. children are invited to return for a second year, and mentors also are invited to return. To date, no mentor has opted to leave the L.I.N.K. program. Additionally, mentors and their children are encouraged to continue their relationship through the Big Brothers and Big Sisters organization.

Funding for the L.I.N.K. project comes through the Children's Trust Fund of Pennsylvania. The grant requires a 25 percent match from the local community which increases to 50 percent after two years. At the end of three years, The PROGRAM for Female Offenders, Inc. will seek funding from local foundations to continue this program, since we have been able to document its effectiveness.

Incarcerating an adult in Dauphin county costs taxpayers almost $26,000 per year. For a juvenile offender who must be placed in secure detention, that figure escalates to over $60,000 per year. It is imperative that we address the needs of incarcerated mothers and their children. Otherwise, the results will be more prisons, more sanctions, more money spent, and more lives lost to the "system."

Long after we leave, the mothers and children who participate in our programs will possess the skills that we impart. What better legacy can we leave than healthy and resilient children, children who break the cycle of crime?

The Children's Center Programs of Bedford Hills Correctional Facility

7

Kathy Boudin
Inmate 84G0171
Bedford Hills Correctional Facility, Bedford Hills, New York

Dear Mom,

I hope you're feeling better. You're the only mother that I ever had. I hope you get out of jail soon. I love you.

Denise (nine years old)

Right now it's like I'm helpless. I can't reach out to my daughter the way I'd want to. Time is so limited. I feel angry at myself for doing the things I've done, things that could have been avoided, leaving her out there all alone, with no one to reach to as much as she could have with me. I had an addiction and I wasn't thinking of nothing else but the drugs. I didn't actually have the full control that I thought I had over myself, trying to fight my addiction and take care of my daughter at the same time. It was a struggle, I was trying to keep both going and I couldn't.

Lonnie, Denise's mother [1]

Lonnie and her daughter are two of the many thousands of mothers and children who have been separated by the mother's incarceration. Children of incarcerated mothers are the unseen victims of the criminal justice system.

Lonnie is at Bedford Hills Correctional Facility, New York State's maximum-security prison for women, located one hour from New York City where the vast majority of the inmates' family and children live. Throughout the country, mothers such as Lonnie are coming to prison in increasing numbers. In the past decade in New York State alone, the number of incarcerated women tripled from 1982 to the end of 1990, increasing from approximately 800 to 2,700. The rate of increase in state prisons nationally from 1980 to 1989 for men was 112 percent and 202 percent for women (Bureau of Justice Statistics [BJS] 1991).

For some children, the loss of their mother to prison may be like a death. When a mother is incarcerated, children generally lose their primary caregiver. Many children come from families already in crisis from drug abuse, family or neighborhood violence, and poverty. They face enormous psychological damage from the accumulation of losses—separations following separations—due to the instability of their home life. Now, they face the likelihood of increased material hardship as the new caregivers take on an additional economic burden. These are children at risk, our next generation (Bloom and Steinhart 1993). The overwhelming majority of women in prison will get out and return to their children as mothers (Bureau of Justice Statistics 1994). They and their children need the opportunity to relate to one another during their separation and to lay a strong foundation for their reunion. Even mothers who stay in prison for much of their children's childhood usually will remain importantly connected to their children—as the mother who gave birth to them, who may have raised them or their siblings, and as a person whose love for them is certain. In either situation, the mother-child relationship will continue to have an impact on both. Across the separation, now so total, mother and children continue to reach towards one another.

Fifteen years ago, the New York State Department of Correctional Services recognized the special needs of incarcerated women and their children and acknowledged the responsibility of corrections to strengthen that relationship. The 1981 Statement of Need for the Children's Center of Bedford Hills Correctional Facility puts forth the rationale for this commitment (Bedford Hills/Bayview Children's Center Program, p.1):

> The inmate-mother represents a special prison population: she cannot be viewed in isolation but must be seen in the context of her life and role with her dependent children. When a mother is put into prison, her children are very likely to suffer with her. . . . These children of inmate-mothers are subjected to serious mental health and development problems, as are their inmate-mothers who suffer with them. . . . It is clear that these families need extensive supportive services to maintain and strengthen their relationships, so that when the mother leaves prison, children and mother will be an intact family able to cope with whatever problems await them.

The Children's Center Program has expanded steadily over the fifteen years since its formal inception. Its vast array of activities meet four critical needs of the population of Bedford Hills Correctional Facility, 75 percent of whom are mothers:

1. To maintain and strengthen the relationship between mother and child

2. To provide support for the children in their day-to-day lives around problems they face and to involve their mothers from prison in developing this support

3. To educate the mothers in three areas: their children and parenting, themselves as people, and the foster care and family court institutions

4. To meet the special needs of pregnant women and mothers and their newborn babies

The Children's Center Program is vitally important for inmate mothers and their children. I know this from personal experience as an inmate, a mother, and one of the inmate staff of the Children's Center. I was arrested when my son was fourteen months old. Today, he is fifteen years old. The Children's Center has encouraged me to be a mother, not to give up the effort in spite of my life sentence. My son and I have a wonderful relationship which has been sustaining to both of us during the past fifteen years. And I, like many other prisoners, want to do something meaningful with my time—to help others, to contribute, to give back to the community. As a member of the Children's Center Program staff, I am able to do that.

Crucial Program Elements

What are the critical qualities of the programs that can be reproduced elsewhere? The most crucial element is that the Children's Center Program is inmate-centered. This begins with the recognition that when a woman goes to prison, her relationship to her children is a central emotional focus: she is torn by guilt, anxiety, and a sense of failure, yet, her child continues to be a source of hope, a motivation for change, and an inspiration. This crisis is potentially an opportunity for enormous growth, growth in a woman's ability to mother and also growth in herself as a woman, as a person, and as a citizen. The Children's Center responds to this crisis by creating a range of programs. As women participate throughout the facility, seeing the differences in their relationships with their children and within themselves, some want to help other women and their children here. They become part of the Children's Center inmate staff, leading and creating new programs, further expanding the potential of the programs to meet even more needs of the children and their mothers. This is a cyclical process—of meeting personal needs, growing, then contributing to the community.

Inmate-centered means that inmates are responsible for teaching the classes, developing new curricula, working as advocates and peer counselors for other inmate mothers, and administering the many programs of the Center. They identify programmatic needs out of their own experience; their personal stake provides committed inmate staff; and their involvement generates self-reliance, responsibility, and positive peer role models.

The philosophical underpinnings of many prisons echo the importance of independent thinking and responsibility among inmates, qualities necessary for both mothering and inmate initiative. Yet, prisons by their very nature foster dependence and passivity. Generally, the primacy of security works against inmate initiative. These contradictions within the prison environment must be faced when developing and implementing effective programs for women and children.

This chapter describes how the Center programmatically addresses each of these four critical needs, viewing them through the two lenses of the children's emotional well-being and the prison environment. It then revisits the issue of "inmate-centered" while examining the main factors which allow the Children's Center Program to flourish. The conclusion considers how the successes of the Program raise issues for our broader society.

The Beginnings

The roots of the current program stretch back to the early 1970s, when Sister Elaine Roulet, then a liaison family worker funded by Catholic Charities, set up a special area with toys in one corner of the visiting room for children visiting their mothers. She also held support groups for mothers. In this small beginning were the seeds of commitment and content for the program that ultimately bloomed. In 1979, Superintendent Elaine Lord, then a program developer with the New York Department of Correctional Services, began investigating programming for mothers and children in prisons throughout the United States. Ultimately, a proposal was developed and a contract was signed launching the Children's Center Program with Sister Elaine as Director (Correctional Service News 1981).

Inmates were active from the start. Ms. Lord and Sister Elaine asked for an inmate advisory committee, and as Sister Elaine said, "They [the inmates] have input on the actual, final design of all programmatic components." The inmates' first job was to construct the Children's Center playroom and to involve the inmate population in defining program needs.

Inmate Population

Bedford Hills Correctional Facility has grown from a women's prison of 400 and a receiving center for an additional 250, to a prison of 750 and a reception center for more than 3,000 women who are distributed to several other state prisons (New York State Department of Correctional Services [NYSDOCS] June 1995). The average sentence of the women at Bedford is eight and one-third years. Almost 200 women are serving sentences in excess of ten years while the majority of the women who come through Bedford have shorter sentences (Lord 1995). The Children's Center has accumulated experience in mother-child relationships with both "short-termers" and "long-termers." Its programs are carried out bilingually, and the inmate staff is ethnically balanced to meet the needs of the population which statewide is 50.6 percent black, 34.4 percent Latina, and 14.3 percent white (Division of Program Planning, NYSDOCS 1995).

Program Components

The Children's Center Program has expanded into three distinct physical spaces harboring a multitude of programs and services. What started out as a sole corner in a visiting room has expanded to today's Children's Center play area, an inside children's playroom with an additional patio. Our Parenting Center is comprised of the lower floor of the school building, which includes a large room for inmate and civilian advocates; several classrooms for parenting and prenatal classes; a prenatal center; and an infant day-care center. The Nursery, created in 1901, also has expanded and now occupies two floors of the hospital building. The Children's Center, the Parenting Center, and the Nursery, are the three components of The Children's Center Program. Although the present programs are vast and may appear impossible to duplicate, they have developed gradually over a fifteen-year period.

The Women

Today, many of the mothers at Bedford come from families that were torn by poverty, drugs, violence, homelessness, and AIDS. The statistics of women in prison reveal common experiences: 75 percent are mothers, 65 percent are victims of both physical and sexual abuse, 75 percent have a history of drug or alcohol abuse (Bureau of Justice Statistics 1994), 20 percent enter prison HIV positive in New York State (NYSDOH AIDS Institute 1994). Most know that even before their arrest, they were living on the edge and their role as a mother was troubled. Now in prison, torn away from their children's lives, they have both the time and the need to reflect on who they are as people, as women, and, most painfully, as mothers. They need to work on their own issues in order to be the mothers that their children need.

> I grew up in the country. I had to cut wood, get the stove going and take care of my five younger brothers and sisters while my mother was off doing her thing. I wanted to have some fun, get away from it. I got married at sixteen, dropped out of school in the tenth grade, and got pregnant. My first baby was planned and wanted. [By] my second, we were having problems, my husband beat me, I tried to hide my black eyes, my cut lips. I began drinking. I drank all through my pregnancy. Two months after my second was born, my marriage went down the drain. I came to prison. After four years away, my boys have turned into young men. I want help preparing to reconnect to them. Who will I be to them now?

*   *   *

> I never chose to be a mother. I became one. I was using drugs on and off. I never looked at it as a problem because you feel as long as you give them food and a roof over their head, you're taking care of your children. Also, my family was real supportive. Whenever I went on a binge, my family took over. I never felt that my life was out of control. We went on trips around the city to the museum, the planetarium. I was the youngest of eight, smart . . . I wanted to do what boys could do and I couldn't. I wanted to be an engineer, but my father told me black women can't be engineers. I couldn't find my place, so I kept having kids. Now I'm here for ten years, and I need help connecting to my children the best I can. My oldest is thirty, my youngest is ten.

Each woman's voice and self-examination resounds with a common echo: the request for help in her relationship with her children. The thread that weaves through the entire history of the Children's Center is Sister Elaine's desire to honor that request; she believes in the capacities of the women. Sister Elaine works with their strengths and her words convey the fervent belief that it is never too late to do better (Willens 1995, p.7):

The women's best friend before they come to prison has always been failure. They basically feel they were failures as mothers. We say to them, "Now here is an opportunity for you to learn."

Maintaining and Strengthening the Mother-child Bond

Coming to the Children's Center meant breaking the barrier of the real prison and the horrors that my children thought it was. I think it was a miracle done in the prison and without that environment, I don't know if I would have been able to present my children to the world I live in.

Children often have a relationship with a parent who resides elsewhere. Whether it is because of divorce, immigration, foster care, or incarceration, geographic or physical absence does not eliminate the parent/child relationship or bond. The core of the Children's Center Programs is to provide opportunities for children and their mothers to develop a positive relationship in spite of the separation of prison.

Contact Visiting in a Child-centered Space

Contact visiting in a child-centered special place is necessary for a meaningful visit between an incarcerated mother and her children. At Bedford Hills, one third of the visiting room is a separate Children's Center playroom. As the children skip or gallop past the visitors' tables, eagerly waiting for their mothers, they enter what is clearly their own magic space. For many years, over the entrance of the Children's Center was a rainbow stretching from one wall to the other with the words "Joy Is Unbreakable. So it is perfectly safe in the Hands of Children." The walls below were covered with handprints of children. Now the entrance is decorated with brightly colored children's paintings. The children know immediately that they are welcome.

On any Saturday or Sunday, toddlers can be seen sliding down the wooden slide, or playing house in the play corner with their cups and plates. A mother is curled up in the reading area with her eight-year-old son; lying on large stuffed animals, they are reading a story picked from the Center's children's library. A group of six-year-olds is playing in the block corner, building a castle, and a teenage daughter is sprawled out on the rug talking to her mother about the latest neighborhood gossip. In the paint corner, the littlest Van Gogh in her paint smock is painting for her mother. A mother is changing her baby's diaper on the changing table in a corner. At the end of each visit, mothers and children go their separate ways out of the visiting room. Children leave hugging their paper bird or popsicle stick house, the mother holds a painting from the child. Each carries something tangible to sustain the connection over time and space.

The Children's Center includes a small outdoor patio directly adjacent to the visiting room. The patio is big enough for a volleyball game. And in the space provided, children can play handball against the small brick wall or jump rope, play in a sandbox, or splash and leap in and out of a large plastic pool in the summer. Here, mother and children can enjoy the changing seasons and even build snowpeople.

Children communicate through play. Much can be said when they have a place to be active, to be normal, with their mothers.

I think the Children's Center formed a much stronger bond than I would have without it. The activities help, because if I just sit with my son in a chair, he'll just sit there, he won't speak, but if we're doing something, when we're working on a project, that's when he opens up. I don't know why, but it's the distraction, and he'll confide.

Trained inmate caregivers plan arts and crafts projects as well as games, coordinate all the activities in the Center, and help the children and their mothers during the visits. They work with the civilian coordinator of the Children's Center who is usually an early childhood specialist. Although the space is not physically large, its design is that of a modern multi-age playroom.

Diversity of Visiting Programs

Visiting at Bedford Hills takes place every day from 9:00 AM to 3:30 PM. An important feature is that children of mothers in Bedford can come into the prison unescorted by their caretaker families. They are safe in the hands of the civilian caregivers. This gives mothers and children a chance to be alone without the distraction of adult visitors while also reducing the burden on the caretaker families. Bedford also has several special visiting programs.

The Summer Program is when children can visit for five days in a row during one of ten weeks between June and August. Children either live with host families in the neighborhood or they are picked up as far as an hour and a half away in New York City, and driven back and forth each day by volunteer drivers. Usually eight or nine children come from out of state or even from Puerto Rico. The intensity of being together for five straight days allows for an expression of feelings and an exchange that is difficult to obtain in a one-day visit. This also permits children to build friendships with other children similarly situated, and to not feel secretive, alone, or abnormal. The inmate caregivers organize activities such as a carnival, T-shirt design, a talent show, or play in the gym. A plastic pool is on the patio for water play. Each day, a small table is set for lunch with placecards bearing the names of the mothers and children. Lunch is an important family event each day. The Summer Program is a vast mobilization of energy and resources; this past year more than 230 children participated.

The enormous success of the summer program laid the basis for the *Weekend Visiting Program*, in which the children can come one weekend each month for two days in a row. They stay overnight with host families, often the same ones that took them over the summer. Children also come to know one another from the weekend programs, extending the experience from the summer and having a peer group with whom they have a shared experience.

Finally, the *Family Reunion Program*, run by the Department of Correctional Services, allows mothers to visit with their children for forty-eight hours in mobile homes situated in a fenced-off area on the prison grounds. Eligibility is determined after thorough investigations. This program allows for an even greater exchange between mothers and children. They can cook, read bedtime stories, and have the time and privacy to share an even more real-life experience. The Children's Center supplies toys and games and frequently helps with the coordination of these visits.

The Meaning of the Visits for Children and Their Mothers

The visits have special meaning for mothers and children. When a mother goes to prison, children miss their mother, blame themselves, and are angry, hurt, or filled with grief. They may be anxious and fearful that other significant adults will leave them. Most of all, they wonder whether their mother continues to remember and to care about them. Visits allow children to see their mother and be reassured that their mother has not forgotten them. The child remains loved and central to that parent's life (McGowan and Blumenthal 1978). One woman describes her seven-year-old son after a visit:

> I realized how much my just being with him, for me to say "Keith, I love you" meant to him. Like I would go to the bathroom and when I came out he would be waiting for me and he would say, "You didn't tell me where you were going." They called him my "shadow." He was everywhere. He asks me now if when I go home if I could be good because he doesn't want me to come back here.

Another woman speaks:

> When he wasn't seeing me he was having problems in school. Every time he sees me he makes a promise that he's going to be good. He messes up a little bit but not as bad as it was before.

Even before their mothers' incarceration, many children were part of extended families, often cared for cooperatively by aunts, sisters, and, most often, by grandmothers. The children may have a number of significant relationships in their lives and their mother may not be a stable figure for them. Yet, usually the mother remains a central person emotionally. The visits give the children a chance to connect to that part of themselves, to root themselves in their family. One woman says about her children:

> They were telling me about their school and their grades; they've improved but all of them do horrible with math. They asked me about math and I said, "I did bad, too." They said, "Ohh, it's hereditary!" and we all laughed.

Another mother talks about her twelve-year-old son from whom she has been separated for eight years:

> I have been visiting with my son for eight years, now he's twelve. My mother is raising him. It turns out he is so much like me—he is very orderly, very organized and amazingly, he is an artist like me. He is so good. When he visits, we do a lot of art projects together. I'm looking for an art school for him.

Also, children worry about the mother who is not present. For those children who know that their mother is in prison, their fears and fantasies about prison, fed by the images from comics, movies, TV, and popular culture, will further their anxiety that their parents are hurt, cold, or sick. Coming to prison, seeing and talking with their mothers and others, and learning firsthand that she is all right can allay their fears (Baunach 1985). One woman says her children always ask if they feed her bread and water. Another woman says:

> My kids are more calmed down now that they get to see me. They see horror stories about beatings. It was okay that they pulled my blouse down a little to see that I didn't have marks. I reassured them that what they see on TV isn't what happens here.

Finally, visits may be difficult, but those difficulties are often a necessary part of a path towards recovering or repairing damage (Johnston 1995). Children have strong feelings about their mothers not being with them, and mothers feel shame and guilt or humiliation about having left the child. Sometimes, these feelings come out in ordinary moments together. One woman remembers:

> When my son was seven, there were two small trees on the patio and he climbed up into one and started telling me, "You're stupid, you're stupid, why did you leave me, you were stupid." I told him he was right, I was stupid, I was wrong, and he had a right to be angry. As sad and painful as it was, I knew it was important that he felt safe enough to express his anger, that there was the space for him to say it. It gave me a chance to say that what I did was wrong, "you're right," and then for us to have three more days to recover and heal and play. The summer program gave us that gift.

Visits are a chance for children to begin to come to terms with their mother's behavior which led her to prison. Most children at some point will ask the mother what they did or why they did it.

> "Mom, why did you give me away to Grandma?"
> "Because I was using drugs and I couldn't take care of you like Grandma."

> "Ma, I know why you're here. You hurt someone."
> "You're right. I did hurt someone."
> "Well, I still love you anyway. I wish you hadn't done it."

These short conversations constitute initial steps of children trying to come to terms with their mother as someone who has committed an offense. Children must learn to distinguish good behavior from bad in a context of loving and being loved. That can be done best by "knowing" the incarcerated parent herself, not simply from the crude stereotypes they may hear such as "drug addict," "prostitute," or "convict." Both mother and child grapple with positive and negative qualities which make up every person and define much of family relationships (Gamer and Gamer 1983).

I told him "we need to talk." At first I didn't know how he would respond and it was kind of scary, but then when I was able to be open with him, then he began to be more open with me. He asked me why I was here, he wanted to know what happened. Being able to talk made us closer than we were because I don't get to see him often, like we formed a bond.

Visits Help Mothers Take Responsibility

Visits give mothers a chance to actually work on their parenting. Even though women cannot spend time with their children outside prison, the same types of issues arise in the visiting room as at home. Sometimes women do not feel confident resolving basic problems that might occur in an average day on the outside. One mother speaks about a visit with her eight-year-old son:

The visit was hard. First, he was playing with that small tennis set outside, and the other boy won. He felt really bad that he lost. I explained to him that the other boy had practiced more and that he could be good if he practiced, but he still felt bad. Then he came out crying because someone took his toy. I tried to comfort him, but he said he didn't want to stay. Now, I'm afraid that he won't want to come back, and I'm afraid his father will use this as a reason not to bring him back. When he left, he finally came to me. I held him and said "I love you very, very much." And he hugged me back and said, "Mommy, I love you, too." But I'll be woman enough to admit, I don't know how to be his mother. I didn't know what to do in that situation. I need help.

The Children's Center provides concrete ways for mothers to express their love and caring for children, even though they are in prison. For Christmas, the Center receives community donations of new toys and clothes. In a room transformed into a "children's toy store," women may pick and wrap two gifts for each of their children and one for each of their grandchildren. They can give them during a visit. On the child's birthday, the Center provides a birthday cake enabling the mother to host her child's birthday party.

The Center has a long history of encouraging women to help their children learn to read. Past activities included scheduling a special quiet time for reading during each day, offering a certificate to each mother and child who completed reading ten books together, and group storytelling. Presently, through our Family Literacy Program, interested mothers are learning how to work with their children on reading. The following flier was put on each living unit to involve mothers:

Dear Inmate Mothers,

It is a well known fact that mothers' encouragement is a very important part of a child's ability to acquire good reading skills. The Children's Center will be offering a program for mothers on how to help your child with their reading skills. The program will consist of a weekly class running for 10 weeks on Saturday mornings, as well as tutoring time in the Children's Center.

Family Literacy Program

The Need for a Support System

Tears, frustrations, and jealousy all emerge in prison visits, creating conflict and crises. These mutual experiences are good because they reflect real life, which mother and child need to share. Simultaneously, they are hard because visits are not real life and there is additional pressure for everything to work out well. This pressure to make each visit be a "perfect experience" adds to the difficulty of being honest, tackling painful matters, and working on things that are troubling. This is why experience, guidance, debriefing, and structure all matter.

For women at Bedford, this supportive system takes place in different ways. A volunteer psychologist is present to speak with mothers and children during the summer program. In addition, we have foster care and children's advocate programs (see next sections), parenting classes, a mother's support group facilitated by a volunteer social worker, and one-on-one support by inmate staff. Also, a subculture of support exists among women throughout the prison; women return from visits to their living units where they give each other advice based on years of experience.

Children benefit from support as do the families who are raising them. Visits can stir up feelings of enormous sadness or anger which emerge when the child returns home. They may act out at home or in school, or have nightmares. The good-byes at the end of visits are repeated separations which can be painful.

> When my daughter first came, after she hadn't seen me for a while, she wouldn't hug me when she left and she threw the painting she had made on the ground. When I talked to her on the phone, I told her we would be seeing each other again, it wouldn't be so long. The past two times that she came she left smiling. She knew that it wouldn't be such a long time again and she felt calmer about saying good-bye.

The stronger the system of support for the children and their families outside, the more the children will be able to work through the issues that are raised on visits with an incarcerated parent (Brooks 1993, Gaynes 1993).

Connecting from a Distance

We have found that the children yearn for contact with their mothers between visits. Also, many children are never able to visit. They may live too far away, in another state or country, or their caregivers may not allow them to visit. The Center has programs which allow the child to feel her mother's caring and love from a distance.

Story Corner, carried out in English and in Spanish, gives women the opportunity to select books and read them on tape once a week. The Children's Center sends both book and tape to the child. On tape, the mother can sing to the child, read a poem, describe the child's birth for her birthday, and tell her or him how much she loves them. The children can listen to their mother's voice whenever they want. Once a week, our *Card Shop* provides a group of mothers the opportunity to make a greeting, a birthday, or other holiday card for their child.

Summary of Visiting Programs

The Children's Center is eagerly used by both mothers and children. In one month during the winter of 1995, 338 children visited 174 mothers. In the course of 1995, there were 2,837 visits by children.

The meaning of the visits varies for each child and mother, depending on the prior relationship between the two, the frequency of visits, who the child's caretaker is, the child's age, the length of sentence, and the personalities of mother and child. Not every child wants to visit or connect, and each situation must be assessed on a case-by-case basis. Yet, the enormous use of the visiting and other programs for mothers and children suggest that they meet very deep needs for both mother and child to connect.

For children, the visits remove the mystery from the child's life. Children need help with the visits, but they also benefit from them. For the mothers, the reassurance, the ability to rebuild or to learn, and the time to lay a foundation for her future with the child, all become factors which help inspire her as she tries to survive and grow during incarceration.

Visits do not equal a normal interaction. The separation by incarceration, under even the best of circumstances, cannot allow for the kind of contact needed to nurture a mother-child relationship. Yet, the visits, although limited in time and frequency, allow the mothers and children to develop a relationship. The hugging, the emotions, the game playing, the hair braiding, the story reading, and the conversations are the seeds of the relationship which grow in both mother and child—even when apart.

Supporting the Children and Enhancing Parental Responsibility

Angelo is thirteen now. He was eleven when his mother was arrested and his father had just died. In the courtroom at his mother's sentencing, he learned that she would be away for eight years. He wanted to hug her but the judge wouldn't let him. Together with his younger brother and sister, he went to live with his paternal grandmother who was seventy-four. The grandmother was angry at his mother and believed it would be bad for the children to visit a prison. "They're all criminals there," she said. She didn't want the kids to visit. Angelo missed his mother, so did the two younger kids. Now, Angelo is in special education classes because his mother used drugs when she was pregnant, but he takes care of his younger brothers.

The children of incarcerated parents have many needs. Where will they live? Are they living in a house that is safe or is it racked by drugs or violence? Is there anyone with whom they can share their feelings about their mother being in prison or are they acting out in school, taking medicine for being hyperactive, or in a special education class? How are they going to see their mothers, and will their caregivers allow visits?

The *Foster Care* and *Children's Advocacy* programs have two interrelated goals: to support the children and to involve their mothers in carrying out parental responsibilities from prison. Support for the children must come from the combined efforts of the incarcerated mother, the families raising the children, and community resources. These programs work to achieve this cooperation.

Support for the Children in Maintaining Contact with Their Mothers

Increasingly, it is understood by professionals and the caregiver families themselves (Bloom and Steinhart 1993) that children need to have the opportunity to relate to their incarcerated mothers, and they need support around this relationship. Yet, in our experience, families also have many valid questions with which advocates can help them. Repeatedly, inmate mothers raise these issues to the inmate advocate:

"I can't get a visit. They feel I haven't been a mother to my kids, so why would I want to start now, while I'm in jail."

"My mother-in-law says this is a place for criminals, and they don't want to bring my children here."

"My mother doesn't have a way to get here. She's got my sister's kids too, and she has a block on the phone, so I can't even have a talk with her about the Children's Center."

"Their father has them. He lives with his mother. He's angry at me, and his mother thinks they're her kids."

When children get support after a visit, they may work through emotions stirred up by the visit. Yet, sometimes families reluctantly allow visits or refuse them until compelled by court order to do so, thus placing the child in a destructive conflictual situation:

Juan is nine. Recently, he saw his mother for the first time in five years. He lives with his father and his father's parents. Really his nana takes care of him. He always hears them talk bad about his mother. He wants to see her because she's fun and he calls her "Mom." He knows she can't come home. Maybe not until he is grown up. He can't understand twenty-five years. When he sees her in the prison, he has fun because they make drawings and play games. He doesn't want to go too often. But he doesn't like it when his grandma and father call her a jerk, a murderer, a bad person. But he can't say anything.

Civilian advocates work with the families to try and separate what is in the best interest of the children and what are adult concerns. One civilian speaks about this:

The family is usually very angry at the mother in prison. I can listen to them and validate their anger and frustration. Just that alone helps. I talk about the mother and her participation in programs, her struggle to change, that maybe this is a possibility for growth. I can talk about the child's needs to have some contact with the mother, why this can help the child. They are able to hear me in a way that they couldn't hear the mother who is in prison. Or, even if it's just my describing the visiting conditions and how positive it can be. They will trust me more.

Social attitudes about children visiting their mothers in prison had an impact on the laws governing children in foster care. Until 1983 in New York State, children in the foster care system did not have a legal right to visit their parents in prison. The assumption was that visiting was not good for children with incarcerated parents. Thus, in the early 1980s, children in foster care often did not get to visit their mothers in prison. This created a need for intervention on behalf of these children, who were almost always living with unrelated families, in unfamiliar neighborhoods. At the time, Sister Elaine suggested that women at Bedford form a committee to work on this issue and the Foster Care Committee was born among women who were unable to get visits with their children.

The combined efforts of the Foster Care Committee and outside advocates to educate lawmakers led to new legislation in 1983 that gave incarcerated parents with children in foster care the same rights and responsibilities under the social services law as those parents who were not incarcerated. One of these rights was monthly visitation with children, if the prison was not too far away. [2] This approach of involving women in problem-solving has been a pillar of the Children's Center programs. Women felt a sense of their own efficacy by being a key part of initiating and aiding the passage of legislation to enable their children to visit them.

Parental Responsibility: Enhancing the Mother's Capacity To Negotiate the Foster Care and Family Court Systems

The new social service law of 1983 imposed legally required responsibilities on incarcerated parents. These include maintaining contact with their children, communicating with the social service agency, and participating in rehabilitative programs. Women became empowered to meet these parental responsibilities through contact with the inmate Foster Care Committee and its civilian advisor. The inmate coordinator helps women learn to read their court papers, to write letters to the agencies and family court, and to make decisions about and prepare for court appearances. She encourages mothers to build working relationships with their social workers.

The civilian advisor works as a liaison with the social work agencies, encouraging them to understand the issues of incarcerated mothers and facilitating visits, court appearances, and custody decisions. The Foster Care Committee holds a Social Worker of the Year Ceremony—now in its tenth year—to recognize those workers who have done a special job. This ceremony is a way to build a bridge between workers and incarcerated mothers around a concern for the children.

Women develop the skills and confidence to work with the foster care system and family courts. With this foundation, mothers are better equipped to negotiate with other government agencies—education, health, and welfare—on behalf of their children after release from prison.

Supporting the Children in Their Daily Problems: Mothers Take an Active Role in Their Child's Life

Mothers in prison have great difficulty helping their children with daily problems. Prison means separation. Their absence often means they learn of a problem long after the fact. A frequent comment is, "My daughter's grandmother didn't tell me she got suspended. They said they didn't want to worry me, and what could I do anyway?" The mother must struggle with feelings of passivity, and a lack of initiative which is the inevitable outcome of being absent. This feeling is multiplied by the prison context which encourages dependency and lack of initiative; every decision is regulated, from the smallest details of what color clothing a woman may wear, to what time she goes to bed. When crises occur with their children, women experience enormous anxiety, frustration, and resignation. "What can I do? I'm in here. I have to learn to let go," is a common reaction. Mothers must fight this constant inner battle. The Foster Care and Children's Advocacy programs help mothers overcome their frustration by connecting them with the outside world.

Sometimes the best way to help a child is to connect the mother to community resources. The Children's Advocacy program has helped a mother talk to the doctor of her child who was in a hospital, put a mother in touch with a child's therapist or teacher, and helped a woman develop a custody plan with her lawyer. One inmate describes her experience:

> I learned that my daughter was acting out in school. I spoke with the inmate advocate and together we met with the civilian advocate who called the teacher in the school. It turned out that the teacher knew that I was in prison and she also knew that four or five other children had parents in prison. They all agreed about the idea of creating a support group for the children to talk about their feelings and experiences. The teacher with the support of the civilian staff member created the group. The group helped the children release their feelings and the behavior of my daughter improved.

Other times, children receive support from the families charged with raising them. Families of incarcerated mothers carry enormous burdens (Bloom and Steinhart 1993). Often, caretakers are grandmothers who are stressed by the economic and physical burdens of raising their grandchildren. Advocates find that the family member sometimes will talk about their burdens and then become open to suggestions, overcoming their initial suspicions of outside interference by "strangers" and "professionals." One advocate describes the situation:

> A grandmother was raising the children of the mother in Bedford plus other grandchildren. She used a lot of corporal punishment as a way of controlling the situation that was overwhelming her. The mother in Bedford, although raised with corporal punishment herself, had changed her views as a result of her own education and was concerned for the children. The civilian was able to build a relationship of trust with the grandmother through arranging visits. The mother was taking a lot of initiative in her own life, and the grandmother was open to talking. The grandmother agreed to go for supportive counseling

and through that process, she developed means of control and discipline and decreased the amount of corporal punishment.

A crisis in a child's living situation is often serious because this stability is the foundation for his or her well being. Although most children are situated by the time their mother arrives at Bedford, crises do arise. The programs help the mothers develop new possibilities such as moving a child out of a friend's house into foster care, or moving from one relative to another.

In order for children to have more options, Sister Elaine created My Mother's House, a foster home run under the auspices of St. Joseph's Family Services. The home is staffed by nuns. Sister Elaine chose the name so that no child would feel any stigma when asked where he or she lives. They can say to their friends in school with pride, "I live at my mother's house." One woman whose daughter lives in My Mother's House, describes how she used the Foster Care/Child Advocacy programs:

> My mother has been raising my twelve-year-old daughter during the eight years that I have been in prison. But my mother has a drug problem, and that's what I'm here for, too. I could feel things were getting out of control, but one day I found out that she had been arrested. I had to get help immediately. I was very frightened and in a state of panic. Where was my daughter going to live? Who would take care of her? I was devastated that my own mother was in jail. I went to Sister Elaine, and she sent me to the Children's Advocates. We talked about the idea of My Mother's House and then I began working with the inmate in charge of foster care. The civilian advocates made the phone calls. My daughter moved into My Mother's House. My Mother's House has given her so much—a place where she can be a child, know that she is being loved, taken care of, and allowed to blossom. And we get to see each other once a week.

Advocacy for the Children: Helping the Mothers Place Their Children's Needs First

> And it's not just about getting the mothers' visits. Women are learning how to write a decent letter to a guardian, learning the communication rapport with people in charge of their children. Even avenues they never even thought about for their children. "Therapist? No way. My child's not crazy." And then, things they never dreamed of they would find themselves suggesting. When people come in, I lay out the possibilities. "Do you think they're taking good care of your child? Do you think you're doing the right thing by your child? What's best for your child?" That's the focus I push for.
>
> Inmate Staff Advocate

Our experience teaches the necessity of helping mothers focus on the needs of their children. Many mothers in prison focus on their own pain of separation and punishment and have difficulty thinking of their children's needs. Moreover, before they came to prison, many women were so driven by their own needs, reflected in drug abuse or the struggle to survive abusive relationships, or too young to handle responsibility, that they could not focus adequately on their children (Baunach 1985). One woman speaks about a new awareness of herself from her parenting class:

> It made me realize that I wasn't ready to be a mother when I became a mother. When I got pregnant, I thought, "Hey, isn't this cool, this is great." It made me finally somebody. I had such low self-esteem that I didn't think I was anybody before, and then I thought I would become somebody, but it was somebody I couldn't be when it happened. I was on drugs, I gave him to his father, and I went on to be the teenager that I was.

Inmate staff struggle with their peers to focus on the needs of their children as separate from adult arguments, or the mother's own personal needs, and encourage them to act on behalf of the interests of their children. Sometimes, these discussions happen in very hard situations, and the mother is faced with painful decisions.

> Anna is eleven. Her mother has AIDS and will be in prison for eighteen months. Before her mother went to prison, Anna was in foster care, and she saw her mother sometimes regularly and sometimes not. Now, the foster family wants to adopt her. She likes them because they are always there. The court is having a hearing to take away her mother's parental rights; then she'll never see her mother again. She doesn't want that either.

Through hours of discussion with the inmate foster care worker, Anna's mother came to terms with the need to create a permanent living situation for her daughter. She currently is working with a lawyer to determine how to achieve this while still legally permitting visits between mother and daughter.

Often, these hard discussions happen concerning visitation. A child may be too angry to visit except occasionally; perhaps the child is becoming a teenager and is setting other priorities. One woman speaks about her own development:

> I wanted the kids to visit here so bad. The Agency said they didn't have to bring them since they were way up state, and they just didn't think it was right, yet, for the girls. I wanted to blow them away. Then, I got to talk to the therapist. She told me the girls had other more important needs. They were acting out, fighting, and they were going to be put in therapeutic homes, separate from each other. The therapist asked for my help. They said I could write them background information. So I've been writing them, with help from the women in the Children's Center. Telling them about me and the girls' past. Now I feel like I can see, I wasn't thinking about their mental status, their emotional needs. The therapist tells me the letters are really important, and I feel good about that. I feel now if they come, they come, but if they can't come, I can accept that.

Education for the Mothers

> Giving birth to my son did not make me a parent;
> Giving birth to my son did not make me a mother.

> —Woman at Bedford, 1995

The *Parenting Center* offers education programs, aided by inmate-instructors, based on the premise that knowledge can help mothers and that the time during incarceration can be an opportunity to learn and grow. The education programs focus on three areas: child development and topics of parenting, the foster care and family court systems, and learning about ourselves.

Learning about Children and Issues of Parenting

Parenting Through Films is a twelve-session workshop series, offered in English and Spanish, that gives women opportunities to examine difficult parenting issues and chances to reflect on their own experiences as children, and provides new options for their own children. Women discuss topics such as discipline, abuse, play, step-parenting, sibling rivalry, discrimination, teenage pregnancy, sex, and gender stereotypes. Past workshops have focussed on child development, future possibilities include a series on adolescence.

For women who have little or no contact with their children while in prison, the classes offer a way to connect with them. While parenting classes appear to be more immediately useful for mothers with child contact, even inmates applying what they are learning still have to work within the limits of parenting from prison. One inmate-teacher cites an example:

> One woman became aware through the films that the way her child was being treated and talked to really was a form of emotional abuse. But, she was reluctant to tell the caregiver of her child, for fear it would insult her and then she wouldn't get her visits. It's tough.

The prison context also impacts on motivation. One inmate-teacher says:

> Some women take the program just because the court ordered it so that they can get their children back, or to get a certificate for the parole board. But others take it because they are really working on being mothers.

Ann is one of those mothers. She is deeply interested and urgently trying to use her time in prison to prepare for going home:

> I'm going to be here for a year. My daughters live too far away for me to have visits. I talk to them once every other week. I send them things. I got pregnant in high school, didn't finish; that's all I ever wanted, to be a mother. I want to learn all I can about parenting, and about myself while I'm here. I've been drinking since I was nine, and I don't want to go back to it. My daughters are everything to me.

Foster Care and Child-custody Workshops

These two workshops, each a series of eight one-and-a-half-hour sessions, offered in English and Spanish, assist women working with the foster care system and the family courts. Inmates developed these workshops over a period of years, first learning from lawyers who taught the material, then writing a handbook of rights and responsibilities about the foster care system for incarcerated parents, and finally creating the curriculum by drawing on their day-to-day experiences as advocates.

The foster care committee offers additional education by providing question-and-answer sessions with family court judges, workers from social service agencies, foster care mothers, and legal guardians.

Many workshop participants use the Foster Care and/or Children's Advocacy programs when they face immediate situations which require them to apply the information they have learned. One woman describes how the workshops helped her:

> I think society stigmatizes the child because "his mother's a convict, his mother's in prison." So my own mother didn't think it was good for my son's school to know I was in prison. But I think my being here is where his frustrations came from, and if they had addressed his problem, I don't think he would have been put in a special school. But I was new to it, new to having a caseworker. I didn't know there were certain rights I had. But by being in the foster care workshops I learned, things opened up. So I spoke with my social worker and I found out about my rights, that I can let the school know about my son. Now he is in counseling. His therapist tells him to ventilate with me and he's doing better. There's always somebody out here to help. I didn't know that, but I know that now.

Learning about Ourselves

The Children's Center provides a network of programs that provides women opportunities to look at their own lives—their childhoods, their adulthoods, their experiences as mothers, the relationships between their own histories and the impact on their children. These ninety-day intensive programs meet five days a week for three hours each day. Brief descriptions follow:

Choices and Changes: Women examine their own repetitive activities such as risk taking, enabling, drug use, and abuse in their own lives, to help them develop insight and inner strength to do a better job with their own children.

Fountain of Youth: Adolescent inmates, living in a world of adults, have the space to focus on their own particular needs. This group follows a similar process as Choices and Changes.

Parenting from a Distance: Women explore their experiences as mothers before incarceration; they work on taking responsibility as mothers from prison, and plan for the future when they will return home.

Breaking the Cycle: Women explore family behavior patterns that influenced them in negative ways; they define their strengths which helped them in the past and which they can rely on to help them redirect their lives.

We ask women how these programs affect them. One woman reflects on how she is changing her patterns of interaction with her children:

I was feeling a lot of guilt, shame, and fear. I didn't see how my drinking was affecting the children until the group. And I can see how with my oldest, I'm not so hard on her now. I can see, I expected her to be an adult. Now I'm telling her it's okay to be the little girl. You don't have to worry about big people things. I don't tell her things that her little mind can't handle—before I never hid anything from her.

Another woman says the class affected her plans for returning home:

For the first two years at least when I go home, I see him still living with her. I have certain goals, but I need stability in his life until I can get stability in my life. What I did last time, was I just snatched him, even though my mother ended up with him. That was one of my mistakes last time. I should have just visited him, now I know I have to work on me and get myself more stable.

For some, the self-examination has given them a place to say that they are not ready to be mothers—that their children may be better off with someone else:

I felt it was good for me because I was able to speak about things in front of other people and not feel like I was being judged, like not knowing whether I was ready to be a mother. Even now, maybe subconsciously, I was thinking about it, but until I said it out loud it wasn't really an option. But I'm not sure I am ready to take on the responsibility now. I want to see her, but maybe I can't be a mother to her.

Support for Pregnant Women and Mothers with Their Newborn Babies

Nursery moms sometimes say, "Look, look what he's doing." Before, they didn't have the time to do that, to just look at their child, life was so crazy. It's like this is their first child, the first child that they are actually being a part of. It's sad to say that it happens in here, but at least it happens. And all that comes from the programs that the Children's Center has with the prenatal, the

Parenting Through Films, the course with the Public Health Nurse. And the mother is happy to be with the child. Finally they are drug free, and all want to be able to be the best mother they can be while they're in here.

—Inmate Nursery Aid

Sometimes I can't believe I'm in prison with my newborn. She is so special to me. I feel a closeness to her that is unlike that of my other two children. I couldn't have taken the time to breastfeed at home. I also wouldn't have had the slightest idea how to. But the prenatal classes with advice from other breastfeeding mothers here on the Nursery helped me 100 percent. Being an alcoholic, raising my teenage daughter and becoming incarcerated just three weeks after my two-year-old son was born, I barely had the opportunity to be a completely sober mom. Little things I notice that my daughter does now I might not have noticed with my thirteen-year-old when she was this age. Nothing can compare to having your freedom and being home with all your family and friends. However, I feel the quality time I have now with my daughter I would not have at home. Looking at my daughter at this very moment with her charcoal gray eyes, I thank God for both her and this Nursery Program.

—Nursery Mother

The Nursery at Bedford, established in 1901, was the first in the nation to consistently remain open from the time of its inception.[3] At a time when ever-increasing numbers of pregnant young women are coming to prison (estimates range from 6 to 10 percent) (Bloom and Steinhart 1993), and more lives are torn by involvement with drugs, the Nursery program has taken on even greater meaning. The program begins with prenatal classes in which the women participate in a twenty-eight-day program where they learn about important prenatal and postbirth information; share experiences on being mothers; and make quilts, first year books, and other crafts as they prepare for their babies. The special space, with its cushioned rocking chairs, makes the setting comfortable for pregnant women. Inmates on the staff of the Parenting Center teach the prenatal class using a curriculum which was also inmate-designed. A civilian volunteer leads the weekly craft workshop.[4] Prenatal medical care is provided by the Bedford Hills medical department in cooperation with local hospitals.

Although every pregnant woman is part of the prenatal class, not every woman is accepted into the Nursery. Factors considered include the nature of the instant offense, prior parenting of children, and prison disciplinary record. Most importantly, decisions are made on a case-by-case basis.[5]

Those women not accepted into the Nursery may feel heartbroken. Yet, just being pregnant in prison and being part of prenatal education is often an appreciated gift:

Well, I might have enjoyed my pregnancy more on the streets. My son's father never saw my belly because I was in jail for both pregnancies. I would have more things to eat, I would have more things to buy, it's nice to go on your own. But if I'd been on the street, I would have been using drugs, because for both pregnancies I didn't know I was using. I was small, because of the drugs, so I didn't know I was pregnant. And, I would have lost both my kids. What messed me up was the drugs.

Once a woman is accepted into the Nursery, she enters a structured program designed to enable her to bond with her baby, to develop confidence in herself as a mother, and to grow personally. The mothers spend a part of each morning in sessions taught by civilians and inmate staff about child development, parenting, and women's health. Afternoons are spent in educational or work programs.

Ongoing parenting education is needed after the women give birth. Many of the mothers are young—in their teens or early twenties. They do not know how to burp a baby, warm a bottle, or cope with many developments that occur with babies. They need options. For example:

> A civilian giving a child development course was teaching about language development, like how important it is for the mothers to talk to the children even before they can talk. That was new to the women. She also gave one on discipline. One of the kids was starting to bite. The mother said, "Bite him back." But the caregiver led a discussion on discipline, and explained a better way to work with a baby who is biting, by distracting him, giving him something to bite. That gave the woman a different outlook.

The Nursery consists of two separate living areas, one for babies zero to six months and another for those who are six to twelve months. Each unit has a civilian manager, an inmate aide, and an assigned officer. Women live two to a room, with their two babies, until the babies become older and the mothers are given single rooms. In addition to the inmate aides, other inmates care for the babies when a woman has to go to the hospital or court or be away for any other reason. An average of seventeen mothers reside on the two nursery units with their babies.

When mothers go to their morning and afternoon assignments, they bring their babies to *The Infant Center*. This area is filled with sun, a soft rug, toys, color, quiet music, cribs, and a changing table. The Infant Center is staffed by inmates and civilian volunteers, and has a civilian coordinator.

Prison conditions impact on the experience of mothering an infant. Living together in a small area, two women and two babies in a room, would be difficult under any circumstances; the rules of security and control can increase stress on mother and baby. For example, if the baby has to go to the outside hospital for care or surgery, the mother may not go with her; when mother and baby go to the visiting room, both are searched. Conflict resolution meetings occur for the nursery mothers once a week with the goal of helping reduce these stressors. One inmate aide says:

> People are able to speak out, face each other, they get to cry, they get to laugh, they get to release all these feelings that they have. I think in a group that comes out better instead of letting things build up. I notice that the women are getting along better with these groups.

Prison conditions also can mean an accompanying loss of maternal control in decision making, and therefore impact on the goals of autonomy and self-reliance for the mothers. One inmate who teaches the Nursery mothers says:

Mothering involves taking initiative, making decisions, and being mature enough to take responsibility for another human being. Yet, sometimes, encouraging the development of these qualities in the mothers must be balanced against enforcing certain basic decisions about the babies that are determined by the Children's Center based on its experience and common sense about what things are safe for the babies. For example, in the Nursery, you can't leave the baby propped up with a bottle; you cannot curl your hair with a curling iron in the same room as a baby because the baby could get burned; you cannot feed a baby solid food until four months because the baby could choke; you cannot lie in bed with a baby. These rules may be objected to by some mothers, but if they want to keep their babies with them in the Nursery, they must abide by them. It is part of educating the mothers. Those of us who work with the Nursery mothers have to work with this tension between encouraging confidence and decision making by the mothers and enforcing rules deemed important by the Children's Center. It means sorting out which are the critical rules which must be enforced and which ones can be recommendations, but the final decision must be up to the mother.

The benefits of a mother being able to spend the first year with her child are enormous. The mother spends this year deeply involved with her child. An inmate aide observed:

This may not be her first child, but it is may be the only time that they learn to deeply love and bond with that child. There's no drugs, there's no men, there's nothing else. Here you really understand that you brought a human being into this world. They are very protective, they learn that.

The first-year bonding between mother and child sets the stage for subsequent involvement. Pediatric studies all emphasize the importance of the baby's first year in establishing the intellectual, emotional, and social qualities of a lifetime. The Nursery program provides concentrated time for mother and child, as well as opportunities for growth by the mother in other programs: parenting, academic education, substance abuse treatment, family violence, and AIDS education.

The babies are in excellent condition. Each baby receives good medical care and periodic developmental assessments. Observations of Nursery babies over many years reveal a remarkable fact: these babies of high-risk mothers, many of whom have drug histories, are thriving. They are physically healthy, precocious in certain areas of development, socially active, and happy babies.

Policy states that babies must leave at one year of age; however, if a woman definitely will be released within the next six months, the baby may remain the extra six months. The overwhelming percentage of mothers—close to 90 percent—go home with their babies. Even when the mother must serve more time, she has the initial year in which to establish a secure placement for her baby.

The Nursery program works with the mothers in planning their future. Sister Elaine created a halfway house for mothers and babies so that women who are not going home to families may have housing with their babies on release. In addition, the *Sponsor-a-Baby* program provides for the immediate material needs of the baby since many of the families are indigent. Sponsor-a-Baby reaches out to churches and communities, asking groups and individuals to donate items such as cribs, formula, car seats, high chairs, and diapers to send home with the baby.

When asked whether the Nursery program is a good idea, one inmate aide summarized the benefits by saying:

> You can only imagine what would happen if we didn't have a Nursery. The child would be placed for a year, the mother would then go home, look at a child she doesn't know and who doesn't know her, and start from the beginning when the beginning already happened.

Factors Underlying the Success of the Children's Center Programs

Inmate Centered: The Women at Bedford

When visitors from correctional facilities throughout the country sit at the long table in the Children's Center to learn about its programs, they often are shocked to realize the inmates' level of initiative and responsibility:

> "I teach the prenatal class with another woman. We are finishing the curriculum for it that we have written."

> "I am responsible for setting up the summer program; this year we had 400 host families and 236 children. I coordinate all the housing, transportation, and work preparing inmates for the week."

> "I coordinate the Sponsor-a-Baby Program."

> "I am the inmate coordinator for the Children's Advocacy Program and I work with four civilian advocates."

> "I coordinate the foster care program, teaching workshops, helping women prepare for court hearings, teaching them their rights and responsibilities as incarcerated mothers with children in foster care."

> "I work in the Infant Center; I am a caregiver in the Children's Center."

I sense that visitors listen with some combination of awe and uneasiness. Perhaps the level of inmate responsibility breaks with their conceptions or stereotypes of "convicts" as being "limited." They may wonder how inmates have developed such abilities. One answer is the cyclical process of growth the programs generate. When a mother reads a book on a tape for Story Corner, participates in the family literacy program, or writes a letter to a judge, she is developing her literacy ability. When a woman goes to an advocate in preparation for a court hearing, she is learning to use resources and to nego-tiate social institutions. This process, which repeats itself in women throughout the facility, develops the women's potential until they are able to help others through work on the Children's Center staff. Sister Elaine's deep belief in women's capacity for growth de-fines her leadership and fuels the process. [6]

Two women speak about their personal development:

The first thing that drew me to work with [the] Children's Center was that I could be in the visiting room with the children, a way to be with my own chil-dren since I can't be with them. After working with Sister Elaine for almost three years, I feel very confident that I will be able to offer more to my chil-dren. And now I am a teacher in the parenting class, giving information.

*   *   *

I wasn't sure I even wanted it when they asked me to work here. I was being lazy, just being a porter and clerk on my unit. But how long would I just be here sitting up here and doing time, that would really be time doing me. I knew my daughter needed the service, it would be a challenge to take on a program. And I knew I had to grow. I've learned a lot about so many things, how the shelters work, how the foster care system is, how to find missing kids in the schools, how to help women help themselves and focus on their chil-dren's needs.

The uneasiness of the visitors also stems from anxiety around issues of security and control within the prison setting. How are inmates allowed so much responsibility with-out undermining security? The next three factors—firm leadership, civilian staff, and community participation—encompass and support the inmate role.

Firm Leadership

Security and control are the foundation of this maximum-security prison for women. The Children's Center programs sit squarely in this reality, beginning with the leadership from the highest administrator, the Superintendent herself. The impact of her commitment to the Program sets the direction for security personnel throughout the facility. Security issues inevitably arise: what kinds of craft projects may a mother bring out of the visiting room as a memento from her child? A painting is allowed, a paper silhouette of her child is not! Although children are not permitted within the prison interior, is it possible to allow them into the gym during the summer program because teenagers need space for exercise? These and hundreds of other issues arise, and under the direction of a Superintendent who recognizes the priority of helping women support their children, these issues are ad-dressed.

This commitment also sets the direction for civilian personnel and programming. Currently, twenty-seven paid prison jobs exist for the Children's Center inmate staff. An additional forty-five female inmates participate in Children's Center education programs as their paid institutional assignment.

Sister Elaine, as the Director of the Children's Center, provides day-to-day leadership, vision, and commitment. She carefully screens and supervises all staff. Staff meetings are held once a week for the entire staff and mini-meetings for each area of work occur as needed, along with constant informal communication. Strong leadership and structure are key factors that allow the high level of inmate initiative.

Civilian Staff

The civilian staff work hand-in-hand with the inmate staff, as a team. Without them, the programs could not function. Twenty-five civilians work on the Children's Center staff, four are paid, and the rest volunteer. Additional community volunteers donate time to provide civilian coverage for such areas as the visiting spaces or the Infant Center.

The unique pairing of civilians and inmates in most programs both meets security needs and enhances work environments. Staff includes an inside and outside Sponsor-a-Baby coordinator, civilian nursery managers and inmate nursery aides, a civilian foster care committee advisor and an inmate foster care coordinator, and one inmate children's advocate with four civilian advocates. Each civilian provides a link to the outside community; she is able to place phone calls to courts, hospitals, or social service agencies, calls which inmates are not permitted to make. Inmates are on duty twenty-four hours a day; living in the prison enables them to be in touch with the crises—a child taken to the hospital, a child moved with no forwarding address. In these teams, civilians have final responsibility and authority, creating conditions in which inmates can discharge their responsibilities.

Civilians bring their unique skills from jobs or work in the outside community: nurse, social worker, writer, financial manager, lawyer, psychologist. One civilian speaks about why she volunteers:

> It's the fulfillment that I feel. I gain more than I could ever give. It's hard to put into words. Most important, it is about the bond between the mother and the child. It needs to be strengthened—in some cases it shouldn't, but in most it should. The children deserve to know their mothers. They need the mothers to be honest with them and they need to feel loved. Hopefully from the honesty, caring, and loving—which is hard to do from behind bars—the children can avoid the same pitfalls as their mothers. We hope that by keeping the connection going, we're achieving communication and, in some cases, the children will blossom. And, hopefully, in the long run it will work out for them. That's really my strongest emotion for being here.

Outside Community

The outside community support is rooted in a common concern for mothers and their children. The Children's Center Program develops this support in the adjacent suburbs through announcements and discussions in churches, speeches at clubs and libraries, newspaper articles, and word of mouth. Of the 400 host families on the list, usually 90 of them make possible the summer program and weekend overnight visits in any given year. Host families provide lunches on the weekends for the children in the overnight programs. The Center now also receives donations from the community. This community support includes Pampers, T-shirts, and baby carriages for the nursery babies; Christmas gifts for the children; items for Sponsor-a-Baby, and children's books for the Story Corner program and the Children's Center library. Community volunteers often extend their commitment as civilian staff.

Transportation

Transportation for children is a necessity. Although some women's families can bring their children, others need help. Perhaps a grandmother is caring for many children and has to be with them on a Saturday, or a family may not be able to afford the trip or may live too far away. The Children's Center provides chaperoned buses which come once a month from each borough of New York City, and the Department of Corrections Ministerial Services provides a monthly bus which stops in major upstate cities. These buses are provided at no cost to the families or children. Children's Center buses also bring children for weekend programs.

Funding

Funding for the entire Children's Center Program comes from the Department of Correctional Services of New York State and is administered by Catholic Charities. However, without the role of inmate staff, civilian staff, and community support, neither money nor human power alone could make the Program possible.

Conclusion

We are trying to make changes, and the changes may be wonderful and marvelous, but the bottom line is that this is still prison and an abnormal place. It's hard to make it normal, but the tragedy would be not to try.

—Sister Elaine Roulet (Rule 1981)

If we are ever going to effectively intervene in the intergenerational connections of crime, abuse, drugs, and incarceration, we must recognize that these are families at risk. To effect change and enhance the healthy nurturing potential of these mother/child relationships, we must face that this can occur only in the context of consistent relationships and cannot occur in isolation. These relationships cannot thrive on two hours a week or month, and they cannot thrive on one week a year—they cannot thrive in prison. Everything that we are doing in prison to address family issues we can do better in free society and at considerably less cost.

—Superintendent Elaine Lord (Lord 1995)

The Children's Center programs offer hope for the children of incarcerated mothers. Children have an opportunity to sustain a relationship with their mothers while they are separated, and mothers and their newborn babies can bond and spend a healthy critical first year together. Programs develop support for the children while enhancing the mother's capacity to take responsibility as a parent from prison. Also, peer teachers, counselors, and administrators become positive role models for their children, a factor that is well-documented as positively influencing a child's future.

The Children's Center programs also meet other rehabilitation goals of the institution. Women grow stronger and more capable through their participation in the programs; some become teachers, counselors, advocates, or administrators. Finally, the vast participation of women in the programs contributes to the goal of maintaining order in the prison, a key prison goal.

When prisons make a commitment to working with and supporting families, they must grapple with basic prison contradictions. But, in so doing, they offer a future not only to the children and mothers, but also to the broader community. Working with and strengthening families is one of the most important ways to prevent crime (Gaynes 1993). In this way, prison programs such as the Children's Center offer hope to society at large.

Even while advocating for the creation of successful prison programs for mothers and children, we must wonder, "Is there a better way?" Sister Elaine asks (DeFilippis 1982, p.4):

> But is this where we should be putting our energy, into prettying up the prisons? Or should we be trying to find an alternative to incarceration, an answer to what we can do to prevent people from doing things that put them here?

The majority of women in prison are being arrested for crimes which, while unacceptable, pose little threat to the physical safety of the community. The enormous increase in women in prison has developed primarily because of the nation's war on drugs and the related mandatory sentencing laws and policies. Violent crimes committed by women actually have decreased (Bureau of Justice Statistics 1994). Research stresses the prominent roles of substance abuse, physical and sexual abuse, poverty, inadequate education, or poor work experience in the lives of female offenders (Owen and Bloom 1995). Women have particular needs for help in these areas which, if addressed, impact on the roots of their crimes. If we increase community-based programs where women and their children can live together, or which seriously consider the mother-child relationship, then we can address the issues of mothers and children in both more effective and less expensive ways.

The very elements that make the Children's Center programs a success can be applied outside prison. The visiting programs are a strong model for other contexts in which children are trying to form a relationship with their mothers who live elsewhere; other child welfare programs—such as those involved with foster care, residential drug programs, hospitals, mental institutions, or divorce settings—could benefit from our model. Training women, both in society and institutions, will enable them to cope with foster care agencies. Models such as ours can be applied within hospitals, schools, welfare systems, and community groups. The development of community-minded teachers, counselors, and advocates, who work with their peers, will positively effect communities which desperately need such resources.

The PROGRAM for Female Offenders, Inc.

Harrisburg, Pennsylvania

(Chapter 6)

LEFT, BELOW AND BOTTOM

The L.I.N.K. (Life is Nurturing Kids) program, a part of the PROGRAM for Female Offenders, Inc., delivers smiles to children.

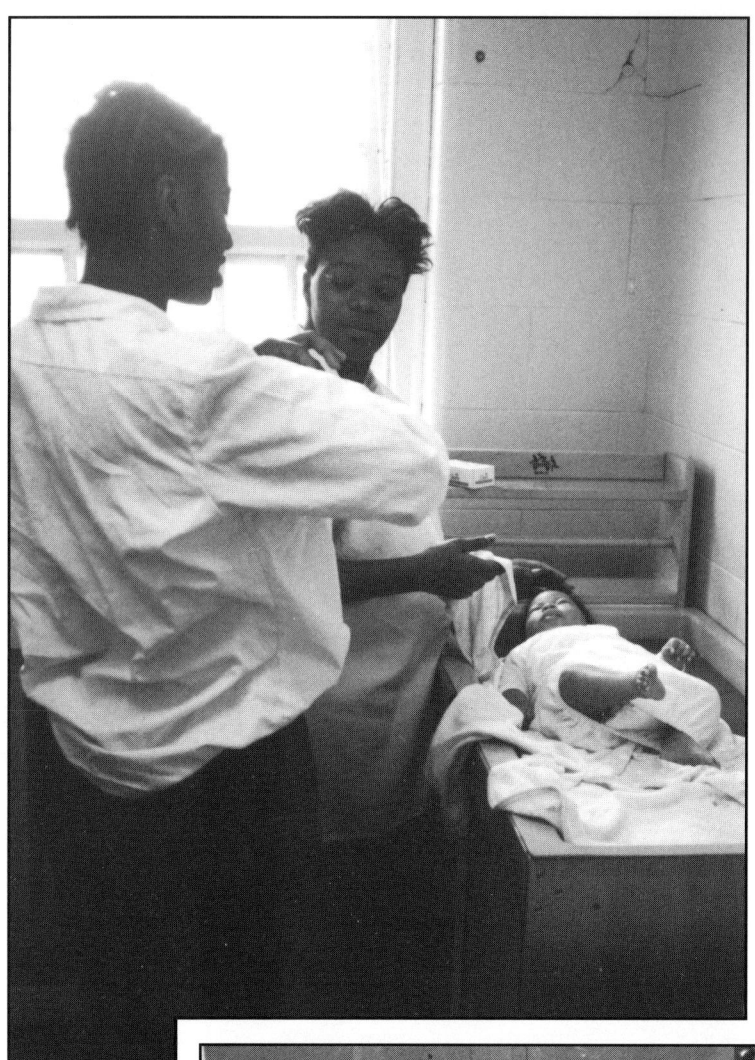

Bedford Hills Correctional Facility

Bedford Hills,
New York

(Chapter 7)

LEFT

An inmate mother teaches another inmate —soon to become a mother—about changing diapers.

BELOW

Story corner: a mother records a story on tape. The Children's Center will send the tape and book to her child.

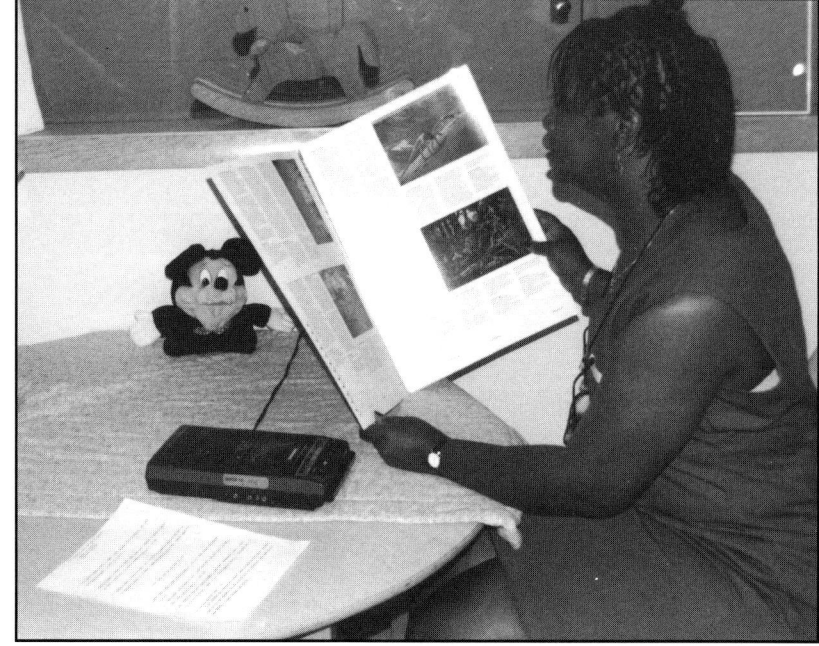

Bedford Hills

(Chapter 7)

RIGHT AND BELOW

Inmate mothers with their babies in the common area of the nursery.

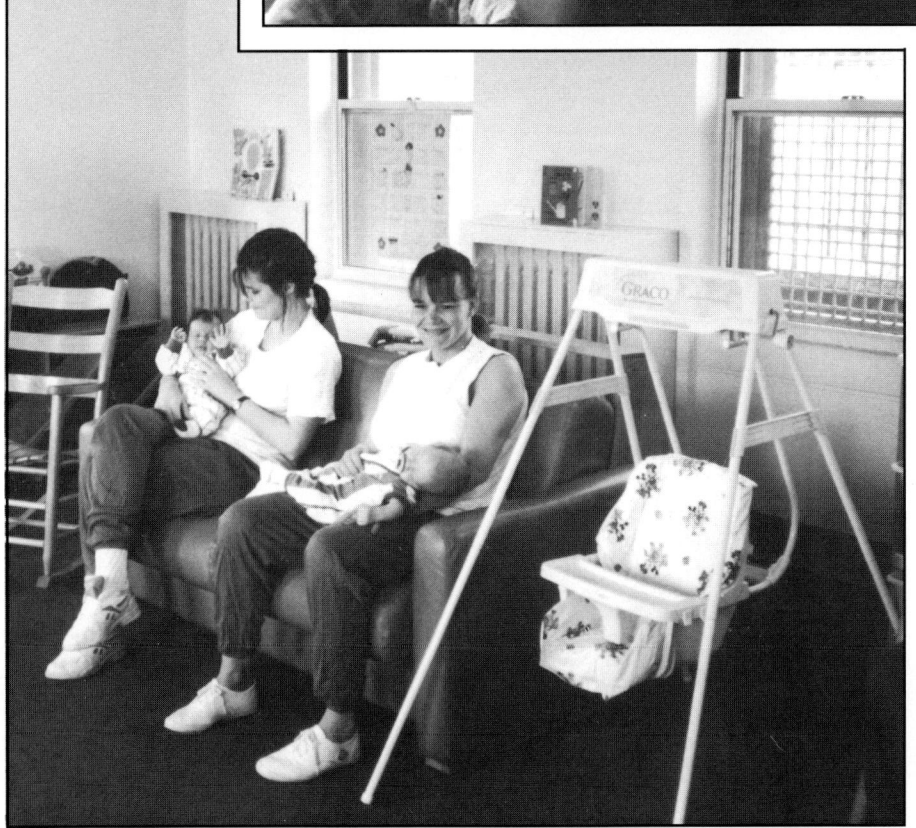

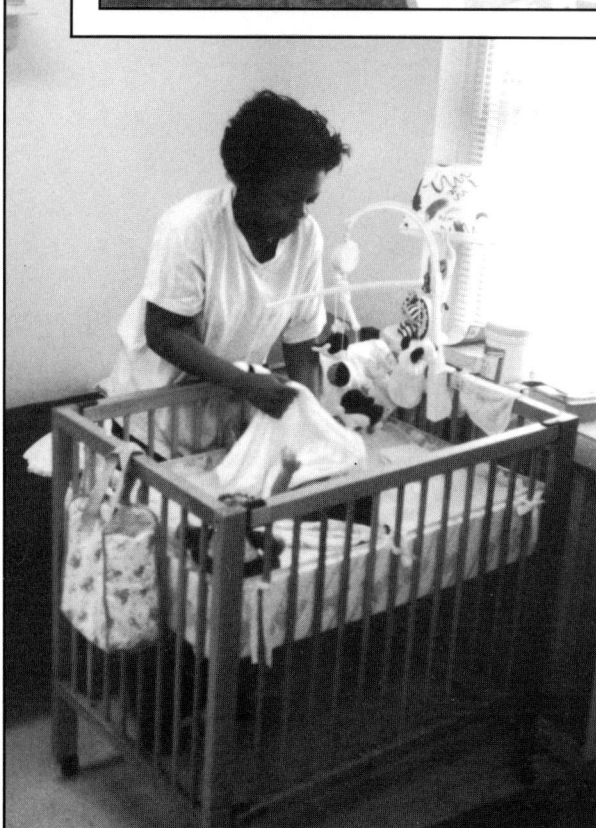

The infant daycare center: inmate caregivers watch the nursery mothers' babies while the mothers go to school or work.

LEFT

An inmate mother puts her baby to bed in her room in the nursery.

Bedford Hills

(Chapter 7)

Women's and Children's Halfway House

Norwalk, Connecticut

(Chapter 8)

LEFT

During the summer program, mothers and children play outside in a plastic pool. Inmate Children's Center caregivers help out.

RIGHT

Mothers and their children make an arts and crafts project in the Children's Center playroom.

Summit House, Inc.

Greensboro, North Carolina

(Chapter 9)

LEFT

A mother takes a late afternoon walk with her children near Summit House.

Neil J. Houston House

Roxbury, Massachusetts

(Chapter 10)

BELOW

The Neil J. Houston House is located in a Boston suburb.

ABOVE AND LEFT

Mother Offspring Life
Development (MOLD)
program activities
keep mothers and
children happily
involved with each
other.

The MOLD
program at the
Nebraska Center
for Women

York,
Nebraska

(Chapter 13)

Preungesheim Prison

Frankfurt, Germany

(Chapter 14)

Mothers and children enjoy the fresh air outside the "open" Mutter-Kind-Heim (or Mother-Child House).

Perhaps the important lessons from the Bedford Hills Children's Center stretch beyond a model for other correctional facilities, beyond any one specific program, reaching to the underlying philosophy of our programs and offering some hope for society. If women can be treated with respect, as agents of their own recovery, if they can get help, gain skills and confidence, and grow through contributing to others, then perhaps the very problems that bring them to prison can be addressed, preventing future crimes and separations between mothers and their children.

Update

As of December 1, 1996, the Children's Center at Bedford Hills implemented "Even Start" with a two-year grant from the federal government. This family literacy program involves three prongs of instruction. Inmates are instructed in (1) adult literacy, (2) parenting classes, and (3) reading readiness for their children. This is the first time Even Start has been piloted in a prison context.

Development of Children's Center Programs, 1970-1990

1970-1980 Period Before Formal Contract

Sister Elaine Roulet begins work at Bedford Hills Correctional Facility as "Family Liaison." She brings children to their mothers in prison twice weekly; once weekly she works in the thrift shop to raise transportation funds. She helps staff the "Sesame Street Play Area" in one corner of the visiting room. She works with mothers in the Nursery, which has been in existence since 1901 when it was part of a reform school.

1980 Formal Contract for Children's Center at Bedford Hills C. F. between NYSDOCS and Catholic Charities

Sister Elaine Roulet; Napoleon Mitchell, Senior Counselor; and Cori Maas, Community Volunteer, work with Superintendent Elaine Lord, then a program developer for NYSDOCS, to create the proposal and contract for the Children's Center Program.

1980-1985 Children's Center constructed, using one-third of the visiting room area.

- Daily visiting and most activities occur in Children's Center Playroom.
- Staff consists of three paid civilians, five civilian volunteers, fifteen inmates, and five community support families.
- Summer program begins; two children stay with two families.
- Weekend overnight program begins with two children.
- Busses bring children twice monthly.
- Christmas toy program is initiated.

- Foster Care Committee educates women; Civilian Advocate works with foster care agencies.

- Prison Nursery formally joins Children's Center program.

- Prenatal education and parenting class are initiated for Nursery mothers.

- Mothers' Support Group formed.

- Transportation Committee formed and phone calls made to families about children.

- Twelve mothers in Nursery.

1985-1990

- Expansion into school building, Infant Center, Parenting Classroom, and office for Sister Elaine.

- Staff consists of four paid civilians, twenty civilian volunteers, twenty-eight inmate staff, and 150 community support families.

- Parenting Through Films program.

- Children's Advocacy Program; one Child's Advocate.

- Foster Care Workshop Series.

- Choices and Changes program.

- Infant Day Care Center opens, with Child Development Associate credential program.

- Weekend Overnight program continues.

- Summer Program has 100 children.

- Thirty-one mothers in Nursery.

- Taconic Correctional Facility Nursery opens with twenty-three mothers.

1990-1996

- Expansion into basement of school building, Infant Center, Prenatal Center, two Parenting Classrooms, Advocate Office, Story Corner taping room, Card Shop, and Inmate Staff area.

- Staff consists of five paid civilians, forty civilian volunteers, thirty inmate staff, and 400 community support families.

- Expansion of Children's Advocacy Program to six civilian advocates.

- Summer Program serves 216 children.

- Children's visits: 2,900 in one year.

- Transportation Clinic: five inmate staff coordinate eight buses.

- Bilingual Parenting Program.

- Foster Care workshops, Parenting classes, and Mothers' Corner all provided in Spanish.

- Child Custody Workshop series.

- Parenting from a Distance Program.

- Fountain of Youth Program.

- Nursery expanded to two floors.

- Nursery mothers are provided morning parenting classes.

- Breaking the Cycle Program.

- Mothers of Adolescents Program.

References

Baunach, P. J. 1985. *Mothers in Prison*. New Brunswick, New Jersey: Transaction.

Bedford Hills/Bayview Children's Center Program (A cooperative effort between New York State Department of Correctional Services, New York State Division of Parole and the Port Washington EAC. Inc. Education Assistance Center).

Bloom, B. and D. Steinhart. 1993. *Why Punish the Children? A Reappraisal of the Children of Incarcerated Mothers in America*. San Francisco: National Council on Crime and Delinquency.

Brooks, M. K. 1993. How Can I Help? Working with Children of Incarcerated Parents. *Serving Special Children, Volume I*. New York: The Osborne Association.

Bureau of Justice Statistics. 1991. *Special Report: Women in Prison*. Washington, D.C.: U.S. Department of Justice.

―――. 1994. *Special Report: Women in Prison*. Washington, D.C.: U.S. Department of Justice.

DeFilippis, B. 1982, May 9. Sister: "Bonding is so important." *The News-Times*, p. 4.

Gamer, E. and C. Gamer. 1983. There is No Solitary Confinement—A Look at the Impact of Incarceration upon the Family. Paper presented at a meeting of the Association for the Professional Treatment of Offenders. April. Pine Manor College, Chestnut Hill, Massachusetts.

Gaynes, E. 1993. How Can I Help? Sustaining and Enhancing Family Ties for Children of Incarcerated Parents. *Serving Special Children, Vol. II*. New York: The Osborne Association.

Gaynes, E. and J. Schreiber. 1993. How Can I Help? Resources for Supporting the Children of Incarcerated Parents. *Serving Special Children, Vol. III*. New York: The Osborne Association.

Johnston, D. 1995. Parent-child Visitation in the Jail or Prison. In K. Gabel and D. Johnston, eds. *Children of Incarcerated Parents*. New York: Lexington Books.

Lord, E. 1995. A Prison Superintendent's Perspective on Women in Prison. *The Prison Journal.* 75 (2), 57-269.

McGowan, B. G. and K. L. Blumenthal. 1978. *Why Punish the Children?* San Francisco: National Council on Crime and Delinquency.

New York State Department of Correctional Services. April, 1981. At Bedford Hills: Parent-child Program is Thriving. *Correctional Services News.* 6(4).

New York State Department Of Health AIDS Institute, Focus on AIDS in New York State, AIDS in Prison Project Fact Sheet. April, 1994. Miki Conn, ed. Albany, New York: New York State Department of Health AIDS Institute.

Owen, B. and B. Bloom. 1995. Profile of Women Prisoners: Findings from National Surveys and a California Sample. *The Prison Journal.* 75(2), 165-185.

Rule, S. 1981, July 31. A Prison Is a "Home" to Babies. *The New York Times.* B1.

Willens, K. 1995, September 4. New York Prison Nursery Gives Rare, Gentle Break to Inmates. *Daily Freeman*, 7.

Endnotes

1. The quotes throughout the chapter are taken directly from women inmates with whom I work and live, from their writings, or from civilians who work in the Children's Center.

2. New York Social Service Law 384-b (7)(f)(2). 18. N.Y.C.R. 430.12(d)(1)(I).

3. The Bedford Hills Correctional Facility Nursery works in coordination with the Taconic Correctional Facility Nursery; in addition to these two nurseries, nursery programs exist both at Rikers Island and at the Nebraska State Prison for women. (Editor's Note: See also the Introduction by Mary Q. Hawkes for further information on the history of prison nurseries in the United States.)

4. A public health nurse also taught in the prenatal program until recent budget cuts at the county level.

5. Editor's Note: According to Sister Elaine, the safety of the children is of primary importance. Before admission to the Nursery, the nature of the crime is considered. Arsonists are not permitted on the unit. Also excluded are inmates showing any signs of overt psychotic behavior.

6. The Children's Center also has drawn on contributions from other facility programs, especially the four-year college program that helped women develop confidence and skills. However, the Mercy College four-year college program was disbanded in June, 1995, along with all other publicly funded correctional facility college programs throughout New York State, when the funds were eliminated.

Women's and Children's Halfway House Program Model: NEON, Inc.

8

Lysa K. Judson
Program Director

Lee Pratt-Beardsley
Director of Women's Residential Programs

Dona Ditrio
Deputy Director
Women's and Children's Halfway House, Norwalk, Connecticut

NEON's Women's and Children's Halfway House (WCHH) model is a unique program, serving women incarcerated for state and local crimes who are completing their sentences for the State of Connecticut's Department of Correction (DOC). This unusual halfway house program has filled a painful void in many lives, including those of the incarcerated women and their temporarily motherless children.

Parent Agency History

Norwalk Economic Opportunity Now, Inc. (NEON) is the operating agency of the Women's and Children's Halfway House model. NEON is a community action agency serving the Greater Norwalk area. This area is comprised of three suburban communities and one urban community. Established in the 1960s, NEON provides a wide range of human services such as day care, Head Start, job training, adult education classes, fuel assistance, weatherization of low-income homes, a retired senior volunteers program, and housing assistance. Through its four community centers, NEON is able to provide adults and youths with educational, recreational, and social programs in their immediate neighborhoods.

In 1975 NEON began its first effort with Connecticut's Community Justice System by placing staff in the Norwalk court office of the Bail Commission. Since then, our community corrections program has increased to include community reentry services, an Alternative Incarceration Center, and a twenty-four-bed halfway house for men.

Women's and Children's Halfway House Model History

In 1984, the Connecticut Department of Correction settled the *West v. Mason* lawsuit, which was initiated by female inmates and litigated by the American Civil Liberties Union. The settlement established a task force on inmate mothers with children under thirty months of age. This task force was comprised of four individuals: Walter Baker, MSW, Department of Children and Youth Services Program Manager; Charlene Perkins, Deputy Superintendent of the Connecticut Correctional Institution at Niantic; Sally Provence, MD, Yale Child Center Studies, representing the child plaintiffs; and Albert J. Solnit, MD, Yale Child Studies Center, designated to represent the inmate plaintiffs. The task force accomplished several activities over the next year.

The first phase included data gathering from the available literature concerning women offenders with young children, visits to correctional facilities providing services for mothers and children, and interviews with identified experts in the area of services to female inmates and their young children. The data collected included information regarding efforts both in the United States and abroad.

The second phase undertaken by the task force was the identification of existing infant/toddler programs, which became the basis for a model in Connecticut. The task force identified three viable infant/toddler program models appropriate for inmate mothers at different stages and with a continuum of services. The three models identified included a community residential program using community services, a minimum-security program in a community which would be largely self-contained and rely on a significant amount of in-house services, and a program available on-site at the correctional institution.

The third activity of the task force was to develop guiding principles through which the inmate mothers could reach their fullest potential. The elements they deemed ideal for a successful program included: consideration of the developmental needs of the children; support of mother/child relationships; placement in the least-restrictive environments available; and services to provide optimal personal growth and development for the mother, especially through parenting programs.

The final activity undertaken by the task force was to develop an evaluation process to measure the success of each model identified as viable for incarcerated women. After studying each model and considering the state's needs, the task force reached the conclusion that a community-based model would best serve the needs of Connecticut. A deciding factor for the task force was that the children not feel locked up. As such, the community-based model was selected.

In June 1985, the task force for inmate mothers with children under thirty months made a report to the commissioner with four recommendations. First, for purposes of participation in a mother/child residential community program for released inmates, the Department of Correction (DOC) only should consider releasing inmates serving four years or less. Second, the DOC, in conjunction with the Department of Children and Youth Services (DCYS), should establish one or more community-based residential programs in areas interested in and willing to provide quality services to this population. Third, the DOC should contract for services and/or facilities with agencies trained in the provision of child care. Lastly, the initiation and operation of a community-based infant/toddler program should be monitored by an advisory board of interested professionals to assure that the needs of both children and mothers would be maintained.

In 1987, the Connecticut State Department of Correction awarded a planning grant to NEON to develop a twenty-bed halfway house for incarcerated women with children between the ages of birth and five years. NEON met with an advisory committee throughout that year, to review various program models and NEON's ability to meet the specific population's needs. The advisory committee membership was composed of representatives with decision-making authority from community agencies that would be called upon to assist in designing the program model as well as to provide needed services. The membership included: Norwalk Hospital, Mid-Fairfield Child Guidance Center, Catholic Families and Community Service, Norwalk Health Department, Norwalk Public Schools, Connecticut DCYS, Connecticut Department of Human Resources, the Connecticut Department of Income Maintenance, the Coalition for Children and Youth, First Congregational Church (owner of the building we were renting for the program), and the Correctional Center at Niantic. Also, Eleanor Craig-Green, a well-known author and correctional consultant participated. The program model included some aspects of the effective programs studied as well as elements experts consider important when assisting incarcerated women who are also mothers of young children.

After receipt of a planning grant in 1990, NEON solicited architectural input for the development of an appropriate physical plant. The completed facility would address both custodial issues relative to inmates living in a residential facility as well as the sensitivity necessary to having young children in an environment which would delegate implementation of custodial issues.

Paul Benowitz, an architect from Rye, New York, designed a halfway house which created living situations similar to those residents experience when living in the community. Many potential applicants would have experiences in extended family situations or shared living arrangements with others. Further, the high cost of living in Fairfield County frequently would preclude the women from living alone. For this reason, emphasis was placed on the women developing positive relationships and sharing responsibilities such as caring for their child, cooking, and cleaning. Often, a woman's reintegration into the community would be especially painful due to her high expectations, which were not based in reality. Group responsibility for cooking, rotating child care responsibilities, and sharing suites, rather than single apartments, addressed these problems. Common rooms were designed as a separate space for children's play areas and visiting areas whereas living rooms were for families and adult visitation. Meeting rooms, counseling space, and offices were designed to be separate.

In accordance with the planning and zoning regulations for the City of Norwalk, NEON had to apply for a special permit to run a halfway house. As part of this public hearing process, NEON had to notify all landowners adjacent to the proposed property at 8 Lewis Street, Norwalk, that a halfway house was being considered for this site. Prior to that formal notification, NEON had not encountered any opposition to the halfway house. However, at the public hearing, several residents spoke out against having a halfway house in their neighborhood, stating they felt the halfway house could be construed as a prison and questioning whether it was appropriate for young children to be housed in a prison-like setting. Subsequently, the Planning and Zoning Commission ruled that the use of this land as a halfway house was inappropriate for the zone and denied the permit. NEON, together with the First Congregational Church—the owner of the proposed site— joined to sue the City of Norwalk Planning and Zoning Commission for arbitrarily misusing the criteria available for denial of permit.

While the litigation was undertaken, the DOC provided NEON an opportunity to find another Connecticut location for operation of a women's and children's halfway house based on the model designed in Norwalk. To that end, NEON approached New Opportunities for Waterbury, the Community Action Agency serving the Greater Waterbury area, for assistance in developing relationships with their sister agencies in Norwalk and in the opening of the halfway house in their locale. NEON was fortunate that it was able to open a halfway house in Waterbury within four months.

While the physical plant at the Waterbury location provides a setting more apartmentlike than homelike, NEON appreciates the efforts of the Waterbury community and their commitment to provide a location to run a women's and children's halfway house. The women's and children's halfway house in Waterbury opened and operated with significant success. This supported our belief that the thoughtful planning and consideration undertaken by the Norwalk Site Advisory Committee was crucial to the success of the mothers and their young children. Women having graduated from the program were remaining arrest free with few substance abuse relapses.

Approximately two years after NEON was denied a special permit for the halfway house site in Norwalk, the court ruled that the City of Norwalk Planning and Zoning Commission had ruled arbitrarily and inappropriately in denying the special permit and ordered it to grant a special permit. At that point, NEON began development of the physical plant in Norwalk and reconvened the advisory committee to finalize the development of the halfway house model for the Greater Norwalk area. After the program model was established, a monitoring panel was convened to oversee operations. This panel remains in place today.

The two program sites are operated with the same standards, policies, procedures, rules, and regulations. Efforts are made to maintain consistency between the programs.

Philosophy and Goals

While many complex, sophisticated goals and philosophies are involved in the operation of a correctional program for women, NEON focuses around two primary goals involving human behavior and relationships. The behaviors of both the women and children are usually multifaceted. Their relationships are strained and sometimes weak. These facts form the foundation for the program's philosophy and goals.

The most basic philosophy underlying this endeavor recognizes that during the early, formative years of a child's life, the performance of his or her primary caretaker (here the biological mother) must be as consistent and free of interruptions as possible, to provide the child with a constant sense of being loved, cared for, and nourished, as a basis for the child's future ability to form meaningful life relationships and patterns of behavior.

The primary goals of the program are twofold. The first of these is to ensure the mother's continuity of care of her child to the best extent possible given the reality of mother's legal incarceration. The second primary goal is to help the mother to become a more skilled parent, and then to use the growth in her caring ability and her relationship with her child as motivating factors in her rehabilitation.

The program offers services through a case-management model. All individual services to residents and children are provided through local community service agencies. The goal of maximizing a woman's independence through accessing community support is vital to her sense of connection to the community following her discharge from a structured correctional setting.

The residential model provides twenty-four-hour alert staff for supervision. The physical site is equipped with an alarm system to inform staff of movement in and out of the building; the system also provides fire/smoke detection and an emergency panic system to summon the police. Urinalysis testing is used as a preventive measure as well as for detection of individuals who may relapse.

To defray some of the children's expenses and to promote the women's responsibility for their own incarceration, residents are required to pay room and board monthly. Some women are eligible for Aid to Families with Dependent Children (AFDC) benefits while residing in the program. Forty percent of their monthly income is designated for paying room and board. Thirty percent is allocated to savings, which often is used at discharge for a security deposit on housing or other expenses. The remaining 30 percent of their monthly income is used for the personal needs of the mother and her child/ren.

Upon admission to the program, the family is provided with bed linens, towels, personal hygiene products, and other necessary items. If a woman is admitted without sufficient clothing, the program financially assists with her initial clothing purchase. The program usually is reimbursed for this financial assistance by the woman before discharge.

Referrals

Referrals to the Women's and Children's Halfway House come either from the two correctional institutions for women, Connecticut Correctional Institution Niantic (CCIN) and York Correctional Institution (YCI), or are made for women under parole or transitional supervision status who are at risk for reincarceration. Connecticut Correctional Institution Niantic is the minimum-security prison for women. York Correctional Institution is the maximum-security prison, which also houses all pregnant women due to its twenty-four-hour medical care unit. These two institutions provide most of NEON's applicant referrals.

The applicant criteria states that on admission to the program, women must be at least eighteen years of age and pregnant or mothers of children between birth and ten years of age. Pregnant women who are methadone-dependent are accepted for admission and continue the methadone until delivering the baby. Upon discharge from the correctional system, the mother must be the primary caretaker of her child/ren. The mother may not necessarily have been the primary caretaker before incarceration, but this has since become the goal upon her discharge.

Each applicant must be serving the last eighteen months of her sentence before applying to the program. The applicant's ability to make a commitment to the length of the program and the program concept is determined as part of the formal screening process. The formal screening is done by one of the program directors in a face-to-face interview at the institution.

Interview and Assessment

Typically, the formal interview comes after several informal interviews have occurred to discuss the program. Informal interviews may be conducted by the applicant seeking to determine which program would be most conducive to her rehabilitation while incarcerated. Formal interviews are conducted when the woman has completed the necessary paperwork, allowing the institution to formalize her application. The papers include the woman's authorization for release of information and basic demographic information about her and her child/ren.

The Department of Correction supplies the program with a formal packet of information including classification levels for behavior, mental health, substance abuse, education, and medical condition. An applicant must be at a minimum-security classification level, and free of any current disciplinary charges from the institution. Assessment of mental health and substance abuse levels is imperative to determine if obstacles are present that may prevent her from caring for her child/ren; however, the program does not exclude women who are in recovery from drug and/or alcohol addictions. The packet also includes the woman's transfers in and out of the institution, discipline reports, medical information, arrest record, and a Pre-sentence Interview report (PSI).

Applicants are considered for admission based on information gained from the interviews, both informal and formal, and the DOC packet. If the woman appears sincere, motivated, and genuinely interested in her child/ren, the process of assessing her appropriateness for the program continues. Mothers whose child/ren are under the temporary custody of the Department of Children and Families (DCF) and/or the Probate Court must receive a recommendation for the restoration of the mothers' custodial rights prior to acceptance into the program. All applicants are screened through the Department of Children and Families for security purposes.

All children entering the program undergo a child assessment; the child's current caretaker also is interviewed. For children who are under the care of the Department of Children and Families, or another caretaker who has been through Probate Court, an agreement must be made that upon discharge from the halfway house if accepted, the mother will be the primary caretaker of the child/ren. We believe it would be detrimental to the mother/child relationship established for the child/ren to return to a different caretaker.

Children not involved with the Department of Children and Families who are informally with another caretaker are interviewed, and their caretaker is assured that the environment the children are entering is conducive to enhancing their growth and highly supervised. Most caretakers voice reservations about the children being bounced around from person to person and place to place. Often, in the early years of a child's life, he or she may have been cared for by several different persons because no one individual was able to assume full responsibility for the child. We have found this in cases where the mother has an extensive history of substance abuse and/or criminal behavior. By conducting the interview with the caretaker, the program begins to form an alliance with the previous caretaker who usually provides a support system for the mother and children.

At the interviews with both the applicant and the caretaker or Department of Children and Families, the length of stay in the program is discussed. The applicant must agree to the program length of stay, which is designed to meet the needs of the family. Although individual needs of the woman and child/ren are addressed, one of the most important focuses is how the family functions as a whole unit. The length of stay may vary from twelve to twenty-one months, depending on the needs of the family and the mother's length of sentence. The program will allow for short extensions of stay for those families where the woman is having difficulty finding independent housing or supervised living within the community upon her release date.

Following the interviews, the number of children to be involved in the program with the mother is determined, based on information gathered. Typically, the program can accommodate mothers with one or two children. However, exceptions allowing more than two children may be made on an individual basis with the permission of the parent agency and funding source. With women who have more than two children under ten years of age, we have found it to be destructive for the mother to have to single out one or two children from the others. In other situations, the living arrangements of the other children may be less favorable than our structured program. All applicants and their children are assessed on an individual basis.

The criminal history of a woman is considered during the application process. The program needs to assess continuously how each woman will impact on the program and the other families in the program. Women with nonviolent criminal offenses are primarily accepted.

Exceptions are made, based on review of the Pre-Sentence Interview report and a personal interview with the applicant. Some of the most common offenses in program participants' histories include charges and convictions of welfare fraud, prostitution, violence against property, larceny, and breach of peace. The issue of child abuse is handled individually based on the circumstances. Women who have left children unsupervised while abusing substances during active addiction may be accepted for admission, because we closely monitor substance abuse of program residents. Risk of injury charges against a woman also are reviewed on an individual basis. When a woman has directly physically, verbally, or emotionally abused a child, the assessment is conducted with extreme caution. The risk of putting all the children served by the program at risk is weighed against the benefits of serving the applicant in question.

Based on all the information compiled from the DOC packet, Department of Children and Families screening, caretaker interview, Applicant Assessment Form, and interviews, a final decision is made to either accept or deny a woman for admission. An objective position must be held by the professional deciding if the woman applying to the program will benefit and, most importantly, if it is in the child/ren's best interest to be reunified with their mother. Each case is unique.

Admission

Applicants accepted into the program are admitted to one of two program sites. These sites are identical except for the physical plant of the buildings and the location within the state. Placement in one site over the other frequently is determined by bed availability. If a woman is more familiar with one town due to her criminal history, she is apt to be admitted into the other town's program. Or if a woman's children and her family support network are in one of the towns, if possible, she may be admitted to that program site.

Upon admission to the program, the women are referred to as residents. Newly admitted residents are in a probationary status for their first thirty days. During this time, residents get to know the program, its rules, and the community, and the program assesses the resident's motivation to participate. The probationary period is crucial, for this is the time when family reunification begins and the program determines what services each resident needs.

Case Management

Six primary case managers (PCM's) work with up to ten families at once. Usually, a primary case manager carries a caseload of one or two families, which allows for individualized assistance. Upon admission, each resident is assigned a primary case manager who works closely with her throughout her stay.

Primary case managers and residents work together to plan for reunification visits with the children and to develop individual service plan goals. During reunification, it is imperative that staff observe the interactions between the mother and her child/ren. Visits always incorporate activities preplanned by the mother for her child/ren, ranging from board games, to story time, to time on the program's playground.

All staff observe and supervise the visits to determine each mother's interest in and motivation for reunification and for remaining in the program. Should program staff believe the mother does not have a genuine interest in reunification with her child/ren, she is returned to the correctional institution or referred to a halfway house whose primary focus is not the children.

For continuing residents, the primary case manager quickly becomes the valuable liaison between the resident and staff at formal staff meetings. Requests for expenses, passes, furloughs, child/ren's visits, among other things, are conveyed to the primary case manager during weekly one-to-one sessions.

Weekly meetings for the residents and primary case manager initially focus on the development of an individual service plan (ISP). Although the primary goal of the program is parenting, we believe many other areas of a woman's life must be addressed so she may be the best and most productive parent she can be. If a resident is only working on her parenting and, for example, not her substance abuse or medical issues, then she eventually may fail to be an effective parent.

Multitudes of concerns or needs surround incarcerated female offenders. In the Women's and Children's Halfway House experience, many women in our program have been sexually abused and/or assaulted, are substance abusers and addicted, have been in relationships of domestic abuse, have lived in poverty, and are children of incarcerated parents. Some women are in denial, but the issues will surface and women begin to identify each need as it arises. For the individual and family needs eventually identified, goals and objectives are developed. Most of the services for residents and families are received within the local community. The resident and primary case manager are responsible for arranging for these services. In-house support through staff provides hands-on direction and redirection around these issues.

Because the services are provided by resources in the community, mothers must learn how to use the services within their communities. The feeling of self-dependence and accomplishment contributes towards building a woman's self-esteem. The ability to access community services is one of many tools every woman carries with her when she leaves the program.

All residents must address their parenting skills. They often learn skills they have never known before, and refine parenting skills they already possess. Some women find it insulting to be taught "how to parent," but their needs are the reality. Sometimes, the children entering the program can be "parentified" because they have acted as a parent to siblings at a very young age. When children's lives are unstructured due to living with substance abusing parent(s), frequent changes in caretakers, and/or a lack of parental emotional support, poor parent-child relationships often result. The children's strongest family bond is frequently with their siblings. Sibling relationships develop over a period of time when siblings take care of each other's needs, which forces them to grow up more quickly than do children raised in stable homes. As a result, children tend to have emotional, behavioral, and medical needs themselves, upon admission.

Significant changes must be made in the previously developed parent-child relationship. To this end, parenting training classes are offered in-house as a service. Many families need to augment the basic in-house training by accessing family counseling from community service providers. Parenting and family communication is practiced daily. All staff supervise interactions and provide feedback to the residents. This feedback based upon staffs' observations is one of the most valuable aspects of our program. Mindful of each resident's need for dignity and respect, staff are careful to address those actions of mothers or children which need correction when the children are not present. To do otherwise could hinder the process of building the mother's self esteem and respect.

Most mothers in the program need substance abuse services. If substance abuse is not addressed, this, in itself, may lead to relapse and possibly put the woman's placement at the Women's and Children's Halfway House in jeopardy. To assist with detecting any relapses, all residents must take drug and alcohol tests. The testing is done after all passes and furloughs, randomly, and upon suspicion of substance use. Within the community, the women attend two to three 12-step self-help meetings weekly. Many women also access individual substance abuse counseling from a local service provider in the community. In the Women's and Children's Halfway House, residents frequently discuss substance abuse in weekly house meetings.

Many women entering the program also must seek out individual mental health counseling. Although most of us experience trauma to some degree, many incarcerated women have not had the support to grapple with past experiences. We believe that our staff and the program's structure encourage many women to address these issues while enrolled in the program. The halfway house becomes a safe haven, where other residents and staff help the woman through treatment accessed from community providers.

As the residents begin to view the halfway house as a safe nurturing environment, the lack of guidance and support they have had in the past becomes evident. Many women appear to have previously yearned for this type of environment. Once settled, residents frequently challenge themselves to confront fears they long have retained. Medical and health conditions are important for many of the women and some children. Sometimes the women and children need to just have a physical examination to reassure them of their physical health. However, the results of medical testing are not always as positive. Some women find they need surgery, and/or have life-threatening diseases, and must begin planning for changes in their lifestyles. Others can put closure on worries they have carried for quite some time.

Education and Vocational Training

After our intense program, one significant issue remains in need of attention: educational and vocational training. To prepare for the future is important. A woman may be a wonderful parent, but she must also be able to financially support her family. The educational goal of obtaining her General Equivalency Diploma (GED) is significant for many residents. The woman often expresses feelings of having let someone down by never completing high school. For women who already have their high school diploma or equivalency, their ambitions may include college courses or a specialized training program. Vocational training addresses a variety of the women's interests, including cosmetology, computer programming, nursing assistant training, office technical skills, and carpentry skills. Educational and vocational training resources are provided through community services while women reside in the halfway house.

After gathering information from the resident, the primary case manager can formulate her Individual Service Plan (ISP). The Individual Service Plan then is discussed in weekly meetings with the resident and is subjected to a formal staff review each quarter. Feedback is provided to the resident in two forums: individually in meetings with staff and formally in group meetings where residents join staff for an overall presentation of feedback.

Verification

Staff closely verify services provided from community resources. Verifications may be done visually, by telephone, or by written correspondence—depending on the immediacy and location of the resident. Residents know these verifications are required because of their incarcerated status. Verifications of whereabouts and appointment attendance are conducted randomly by staff.

Residents in the program are adults who have committed crimes and, we believe, are in the process of taking some responsibility for their actions. Just as the residents are responsible for their whereabouts and actions of remaining substance free, they also are responsible for the care, supervision and well being of their child/ren. At all times, the mothers are responsible for assuring that children are free from harm and are being treated in accordance with the program model. The program does not allow corporal punishment. Physical force or punishment is forbidden, as are verbal abuse and/or the denial of basic physical, medical, or emotional needs of one's own child/ren or any child/ren under one's care.

Cooperation Among Residents

Frequently, residents assist one another with babysitting or day care. By working cooperatively, all residents are able to fulfill both daily program responsibilities and individual responsibilities.

Daily responsibilities help instill the values of task completion and personal accountability for the residents. Each resident is responsible for the care of her personal living area, laundry, and the common living areas; she also is responsible for meal preparation, light cleaning chores, and a variety of other daily tasks. These responsibilities are stepping stones to the women's futures, and to their being able to provide nurturing homes for their families.

Performance Measurement

A resident's performance within the program may be measured by a number of indicators. Upon completion of the initial probationary period and reunification with her child/ren, and when responsibilities at both the personal and program levels are being met, a resident earns the privilege to attend community service programs. The resident is allowed three adult visitors on the visitors' list, who may visit biweekly. She may apply for passes into the community for activities, beginning with four-hour passes, and building to eight-hour, then twelve-hour passes, upon successful completion of each previous pass.

After the passes are all completed successfully, the resident may apply for furloughs. Furlough sponsors must be interviewed by the program director then submitted for approval to the DOC. The furloughs again successfully build upon completion of the previous one, and are in increments of twelve hours, twenty-four hours, thirty-six hours, then forty-eight hours. The biweekly passes and furloughs are another method by which the resident may express her responsibility and motivation for change.

Given the number of goals and objectives each resident must achieve, and the individual attention each resident receives, the program completion takes a minimum of twelve months. When a resident is within ninety days of her discharge date, she may become anxious. Worries about where she will live and how and what she will do when on her own often surface. During the ninety days preceding her discharge, the resident and primary case manager formulate discharge plans.

Discharge Planning

Discharge plans are more involved than even the Individual Service Plan that was completed at admission. Housing is always difficult to secure. Women must assess the desirability of either remaining in the community where they have spent the last twelve to twenty-one months or relocating their families elsewhere. The Women's and Children's Halfway House staff provide suggestions about what they feel may be in the family's best interest; however, the ultimate decision of the resident is always supported.

Predischarge planning involves two steps. First, the Exit Service Plan reviews all services the resident has received while residing in the program, and attempts to match all services the resident and child/ren were using within the local community to those the family will need in its new community. If the family remains in the same community, the services already established are maintained. Second, the Ninety-day Reentry Plan, an agreement between the resident, primary case manager, and the program, outlines a formal plan for monitoring progress upon discharge. Once a resident has completed her program time, she is considered to have successfully completed the residential phase of the program. For a resident to be considered a graduate of the program model, she successfully must have completed the Ninety-day Reentry phase.

Conclusion

Women who participate in our residential program are afforded the tremendous opportunity of living with their children in a safe, secure, and nurturing environment. The program's parenting focus encourages women to consider their substance abuse, criminal activity, domestic violence, and lack of education or employment as these impact on their ability to provide a stable, secure home environment for their children.

In our six years of operation, we have seen women establish strong maternal bonds with their children. This factor seems to be the strongest motivational tool for women to remain in treatment and to master alternative coping skills.

Summit House: A Program to Keep Families Together While Changing Women's and Children's Lives

9

Karen V. Chapple, M.A.
Chief Executive Officer

E. Paula Cox, Ph.D.
Director of Evaluation and Training

Jamie Macdonald-Furches
Public Relations Consultant
Summit House, Inc., Greensboro, North Carolina

Introduction

A mother imprisoned is a family fractured. The punishment of incarcerating mothers and pregnant women goes far beyond the direct impact on the mother as the children become the unwitting victims of their mother's debt to society (Bloom and Steinhart 1993). In North Carolina, 78 percent of all incarcerated women are mothers, and 83 percent are single parents. These mothers must relinquish physical custody of their children. Perhaps more unfortunate are the cases of pregnant women who are forced to give up their newborns within twenty-four to forty-eight hours after birth, thereby eliminating the opportunity for that initial and valuable bond with their children. During 1993, over 150 pregnant women were admitted to the North Carolina Correctional Institution for Women. On any given day, over 1,400 women are incarcerated in the State of North Carolina, leaving over 3,000 children without their mothers. Consequently, these children are cared for by extended-family members or foster parents. The issue of justice becomes a double-edged sword as the children bear both edges, a mother removed and a family dispersed.

When a mother is sentenced to prison, she faces the reality of losing direct involvement in her child's life during her incarceration. This separation can severely affect the mother-child bond for infants and younger children, and can result in behavior problems for older children (Fritsch and Burkhead 1981). The likelihood of problems increases when the source and quality of custodial care for the child are inadequate or inconsistent.

Sadly, the children of incarcerated parents face an increased likelihood of being involved in deviant activity as juveniles or adults (Gabel and Johnston 1995, Spindler and Key 1993). Summit House seeks to avoid this family disintegration and cycle of criminal activity by keeping mothers and children together, and strengthening family ties through treatment and rehabilitation.

Summit House is a nonprofit, community corrections program where mothers and pregnant women who have been convicted of nonviolent felonies receive residential and/or day-reporting services. These mothers, who otherwise would be sentenced to prison, come to Summit House as a condition of their probation. Mothers admitted to the Summit House residential program live here with their children.

The purpose of Summit House is to strengthen the mother-child bond and to change behaviors and attitudes that relate to committing crimes by providing a closely supervised and highly structured program of therapeutic intervention and rehabilitation. At Summit House, clients must address major life issues such as parenting, substance abuse, life trauma, relationship skills, child and maternal health, education, employment, financial management, and other crucial life skills.

History

The concept of the Summit House program was conceived by a group of community leaders concerned about the implications to the family when a mother goes to prison. Of equal concern was the status of the children, who usually are placed in foster care or with extended-family members. The latter source of care can be of lower quality than foster care (Gaudin and Stuphen 1993) and fraught with the same risk factors which affected the mothers.

In the 1970s, the Greensboro Commission on the Status of Women discussed the need for alternatives to prison for mothers and pregnant women. As a result of these discussions, the Commission created Another Way, Inc., a program designed to document the need for this vision of an alternative to prison. In the 1980s, a steering committee was established to address the needs verified by Another Way, Inc. This group evolved into a board of directors, which created a program that included residential and day-reporting elements. In 1987, the program was incorporated as the Guilford County Women's Residential/Day Center.

The residential program was designed to enroll women for at least eleven months and provide a structured context in which counseling services, life skills training, and parenting classes were offered. Both the residential and day-reporting programs opened in January 1988. True to its mission, the residential and day-reporting programs allowed the female residents to retain primary care of their children. Thus, the vision was born and the philosophy was becoming a reality. In January of 1989, the Guilford County Women's Residential and Day Center changed its name to Summit House. More importantly, three residents became the first graduates of the residential program, and state government provided funds for the program's operation.

The program experienced growing pains. In 1988, the day center closed due to transportation difficulties. In 1990, the residential program closed for five months because of a financial shortfall. However, a strong commitment to the vision remained. Clients were referred to other programs, or released and continued on probation. When Summit House reopened, a behavior modification program, based on the Teaching Family Model of the Bring It All Back Home agency in Morganton, North Carolina, was implemented to address the women's behavior while they lived in the residential setting.

In the Nineties

While the program stabilized in 1991, the Z. Smith Reynolds Foundation funded an evaluation of Summit House—one of two evaluations to occur that year. The evaluation results were extremely positive. During that same year, new management was hired and Summit House received substantial funding from the state government. In 1992, the local Junior League funded the Women's Learning and Resource Center, the program's day-reporting component, to be located beside the residential facility in Greensboro.

In 1993, expansion plans were approved for developing the residential programs in Charlotte and Raleigh, and reopening a full day-reporting and resource center in Greensboro. A committee of volunteers reorganized Summit House into a true statewide agency. A board of governors was formed as the overall policymaking board, and each site continued to be governed by a local board of trustees. Two representatives of each local board were chosen to serve on the board of governors. The Greensboro Women's Learning and Resource Center (WLRC) opened in early 1994. This innovative program was the first day-reporting center in North Carolina. In April 1995, the residential programs in Charlotte and Raleigh accepted their first families.

Due to the expansion of programs in North Carolina, Summit House is striving to provide services to approximately twenty-one women and thirty-five children in the residential programs across the state, and sixty-five active day-reporting clients annually in Greensboro. Summit House recognizes the strong need for day-reporting services since at least 725 women are on probation in the local county service area. North Carolina's structured sentencing laws, enacted in October 1994, were intended to place increasing numbers of nonviolent offenders into local community treatment programs, thereby reserving prison space for violent and repeat offenders.

However, since the enactment of structured sentencing, North Carolina has witnessed an alarming increase in convictions mandating prison sentences for women who are repeat offenders. (Formerly, these women would have spent a few days in jail and been released.) This rise in the need to serve prison-bound women offenders is a definite call to action for developing more community programs like Summit House.

Funding for Summit House

Initial Justification for Funding

For the first year and a half of its inception, funding for Summit House was derived primarily from foundations and private contributions. During that time, the groundwork was laid with the Guilford County Commission and the legislature for future funding. The justification to these potential funders came from cost analyses of prison incarceration. The total costs include not only the direct costs of imprisonment, but also additional expenses such as foster care for children, medical costs, varying costs for remedial services, and more. To this day, based on expenditures alone, a Summit House placement is far more cost effective than incarceration. Beyond cost, our funders are motivated by the disturbing fact that children of incarcerated parents are more likely to be involved in future crime themselves. Our funders recognize that, as a preventive measure, the preservation of family is paramount.

Continued Strategy for Funding

The original Summit House board members were leaders within the community who brought with them a high level of respect for the programs they represented. Due to that respect, the community advocated for Summit House by targeting donors and elected officials. The long-term strategy for funding Summit House was more complex. After the first two to three years, the foundations who normally fund pilot projects or flagship programs were no longer funding the organization. That the Summit House staff leadership was restructuring during this same period caused concern with funders. This shift in agency leadership also delayed the search for additional funding from governmental bodies and the community, despite the initial $75,000 appropriation of state funding received in the fall of 1989. Further, up to this point, the board had not taken an active role in fundraising, a move crucial for financial solidity. The sum of these elements caused the Summit House residential program to close in May 1990.

This interruption in the history of Summit House, although disheartening for all involved, gave the board and staff an opportunity to reassess their level of commitment to the program and to reorganize their efforts. The board became recommitted to their role as a leadership body to advocate and raise funds for the organization. The staff reevaluated the program model, which had been fairly punitive, and changed to a model emphasizing positive behavior modification and empowerment.

The North Carolina General Assembly reestablished their commitment to Summit House by increasing their appropriation to $165,000, which allowed the program to reopen on October 31, 1990. At the same time, a large foundation in the state, the Z. Smith Reynolds Foundation, decided that prior to continuing their involvement, they would fund an evaluation of the program to determine whether the new model was appropriate and successful with similar populations. An evaluation by Dr. Paul Gendreau, a noted researcher and program evaluator from the University of New Brunswick in Canada, was funded by the Foundation to determine the potential effectiveness of the program. Dr. Gendreau's evaluation of the program model was positive and he recommended continued funding.

In 1991, the second executive director in the four-year history of Summit House tendered her resignation. The board began a national search for an executive director with a strong fund-raising background, and experience managing nonprofit organizations. The new executive director was hired in April 1991 at a point when most board members did not expect the organization to survive beyond the three or more months remaining in the legislative funding cycle.

Continuation of the funding from the General Assembly was the first order of business for the new executive director. A bill was introduced for $250,000 when a state budget deficit existed. The philosophy behind this decision was to alert the legislature to an increased need when the funds became available; eventually $165,000 was appropriated. The executive director and the board worked as partners to rebuild the pool of volunteers. Volunteers were given the option to resign; vacant positions were filled with members who had clout in fund-raising. This included members from the corporate community, civic leaders, and elected officials. The program participants, staff, and board then became involved in a long-range planning process to provide a collaborative vision to the organization. This plan included a five-year projected blueprint for fund-raising, and training on the board's role in fund-raising. The plan was adopted in the spring of 1992 and became the road map for the organization's future.

The fund-raising portion of the plan addressed the need to diversify the organization's funding base. The board agreed the organization needed to include funding from all levels of government, foundations in a decreasing amount, local United Way affiliates, contributions, and special events. The board and the executive director began to approach all areas identified. Grant proposals were written to the city and county; advocacy began with members of the General Assembly for increased funding; membership applications were filed with local United Way chapters; innovative special events were developed and produced; and, with funding by a local foundation, the organization hired a part-time public relations consultant who assisted with heightening the community's knowledge of the program and, therefore, increasing donations.

Evaluation and Funding

Simultaneously, the ongoing evaluation of the program, which was always willing to adapt or change to assure success, remained extremely important. Funders and those involved in the criminal justice system were impressed by the leadership role the organization was providing in community corrections. Staff members began serving on state boards and committees to review changes in sentencing guidelines.

The success of this recipe for long-term funding has been impressive. The state funding has increased from $165,000 to $900,000 annually during the three and a half years following the acceptance of the long-range plan. The funding from the state General Assembly has allowed the expansion of the programs as outlined by the original plan. The City of Greensboro and Guilford County both fund the Greensboro program. Two United Way affiliates have granted membership and a yearly allocation. Annual special events have taken place which heightened community awareness while raising funds.

A contract with the Federal Bureau of Prisons was investigated, but the board and staff chose not to contract due to the punitive changes which would have been required for the program to meet the federal guidelines. Most recently, fund-raising counsel has been hired, and the board of governors will be devising a strategic plan for the next five years since all of the goals of the 1992-1995 plan have been achieved.

The Summit House Setting

Each of the Summit House residential programs operates in a homelike setting. Dwellings with multiple bedrooms in residential communities provide women and children with housing that not only feels safe and comfortable, but also models a neighborhood setting toward which the women may aspire. If space in a given residence allows, each Summit House client and her children share a bedroom with another resident and her children. A sense of community and cooperation is fostered as the women and their children share meal preparation and dinner times, and take turns with chore responsibilities. The clients make arrangements with each other for occasional, brief childcare needs, and for bartering chores. As long as no unfair advantage is taken, staff encourage these kinds of prosocial encounters between clients.

Program Description

Summit House provides a structured approach and blends a comprehensive selection of services. Each woman's progress is guided by a behavior modification and empowerment model where behaviors are rewarded or discouraged relative to goals set by the woman and Summit House staff. The treatment program accesses many local agencies, professionals, and schools to provide services. Elements of service include therapeutic intervention, classes, and workshops on major life issues such as positive parenting skills, good health practices for mother and child, addiction education and addiction-free living through 12-step programs such as Narcotics Anonymous, formal academic education, family relationship enhancement, self-management skills, job-seeking and employment skills, and social skills training and practice.

The rehabilitation program of Summit House borrows from the most successful applications of learning and human behavior theories that include incremental learning and immediate reinforcement, while emphasizing positive reinforcement. Staff members serve as positive role models for appropriate behaviors, thereby giving clients the opportunity to observe and practice positive behaviors. Staff members establish a therapeutic relationship with clients—unconditional positive regard is balanced with a supportive environment, which encourages clients to take responsibility for the consequences of their behavior. The staff-client relationship is built on the principles of empowerment; staff members support and facilitate self-sufficiency and success in clients at whatever level is needed for any given situation.

Goals

The goals of the Summit House program are as follows:

a) To provide a structured and supportive environment for mothers, pregnant women, and their children which will offer comprehensive substance abuse treatment, counseling, medical care, and family services

b) To strengthen the relationship and functioning of the family system

c) To decrease the number of mothers and pregnant women incarcerated in the North Carolina prison system, and, after birth, to prevent the separation of infants from their mothers

d) To assist the courts and state human service agencies in fulfilling their responsibilities to mothers and pregnant women in the criminal justice system

The program and management staff at Summit House are dedicated to individualized treatment where services and rehabilitation are tailored to the specific needs of each mother and her children. This provides a woman entering Summit House the empowerment to participate in setting goals relevant to her needs and the needs of her family. Progress toward achieving these goals follows a unique pathway for each client and her children. Therefore, no absolute length of stay is set for women residing at Summit House. Depending on each woman's rate of progress, it takes between one and two years to achieve the requisite skills for graduation. Alongside her own goals for achievement, each client must attain a standard set of expectations held by Summit House. During their involvement in the Summit House program clients must:

1) Obtain a General Equivalency Degree (if they do not already have a high school diploma)

2) Attend college or vocational training

3) Participate in substance abuse counseling/treatment (if substance abuse by one's self or a family member is an issue) and counseling on victimization

4) Learn parenting, financial management, relationship, mediation, and coping skills

5) Live cooperatively with other residents and their children

6) Play an active part in the daily operations of the home and eventually share in the management of the day-to-day operations of the home including Family Conference (the Summit House self-government system)

7) Obtain employment at a full-time position with earnings above the present minimum wage in order to be self-supporting

8) Obtain appropriate housing for themselves and their children preferably outside of public housing and not with family members whenever the relationships tend to be dysfunctional, and

9) Begin paying restitution

Women also must perform community service.

Summit House Staff

Summit House maintains a team of professionals to work with the women. The residence is supervised at all times by at least one staff member, and during normal weekdays, at least two staff persons are scheduled. Direct-line staff working with the residents have earned college baccalaureate or master's degrees and/or have extensive experience in settings with populations having some degree of similarity to Summit House clients. Most often, these professionals come to Summit House with counseling or social work backgrounds via education or experience.

Description of Services

Summit House has a cohesive network of community resources to provide services for women and children living under its care. Many services offered to day-reporting clients are identical to those provided to the residents. Benefits accessed by the women and children residing at Summit House include various forms of public assistance such as WIC, AFDC, and Medicaid. The public health department provides family planning assistance, well-child clinics, immunizations, and medical assistance. A diagnostic agency performs an assessment on each child and assists in procuring various therapeutic services, as needed. A family assistance agency provides individual counseling services for women; family counseling for women and children, when needed; and child play therapy as deemed appropriate. Substance abuse treatment is provided by local alcohol and drug service agencies, and on completion of detoxification, women begin attending Narcotics Anonymous or Alcoholics Anonymous meetings to continue their recovery.

Summit House Life Skills Classes for Women

— Assertiveness/Self-esteem

— Birth Control

— Budgeting/Credit

— Career Wardrobe

— Child Development: Ages and Stages

— Child Health

— Child Management and Discipline

— Communication Style

— Conflict Management

— Dressing for Success

— Etiquette

— Exercise for Healthful Living

— Food Preparation

— Handmade Toys and Games (children's)

— Hobbies and Crafts

— Hygiene

— Insurance

— Job Hunting

— Making Decisions

— MOTHEREAD

— Nutrition

— Parenting: SOS, Active Parenting

— Prenatal Care

— Self-esteem/Relationships

— Sexually Transmitted Diseases

— Substance Use and Abuse

— Therapy: Group/Individual/Family/Child

Life skills classes on a variety of topics, such as budgeting and finances, HIV/STD prevention, relationship skills, nutrition and food preparation, parenting, and dressing for the job are provided by the Agricultural Extension Service. The Women's Education and Resource Department of a local hospital offers information on ages and stages of child development, and prenatal classes. Training on conflict management and mediation skills is provided to clients by the staff of a local alternative sentencing center. Various Summit House staff members provide training programs such as parenting, MOTHEREAD,[1] study sessions for General Education Development classes, and other fundamentals for competent living.

Local colleges and universities assign interns to Summit House and students volunteer for experiences to fulfill class requirements. A local consulting psychologist provides staff with insights on the women living at Summit House and interprets psychological assessments completed by the women prior to coming to the program. Many local churches and civic groups donate time, volunteer services, financial resources, and material goods to Summit House. Community support is significant and serves as reaffirmation of the Summit House mission. Assistance ranges from local drug stores donating overrun or discontinued cosmetics and toiletries, to large corporations renovating an entire facility. A number of other nonprofit agencies provide assistance; one is low-cost food made available by local food banks. We believe that connecting Summit House clients with these community resources enlarges their formal support networks when they ultimately leave the program.

The behavioral rehabilitation portion of the program at Summit House is an adaptation of the Teaching Family Model promoted by Bring It All Back Home (BIABH) in Morgantown, North Carolina. The Teaching Family Model is based on a national prototype that has proven successful in adolescent group homes. This model combines a behavior-modification approach with a cognitive component and individual empowerment. While in the Summit House program, a woman's behavior is overseen by direct-line staff who address appropriate and inappropriate behaviors relative to her goals. The intent is to provide a sound, reliable, consistent method of identifying women's behaviors that relate to their goals while providing rationales for changes which will be useful to the women after leaving Summit House. The process involves a multilevel approach whereby new skills are acquired, new insights are gained, and privileges are earned at each level.

To maximize the benefit of information gleaned in classes, the Summit House staff members encourage the women to demonstrate learned skills and concepts in the residential program. For example, positive child-management skills learned in parenting classes are acknowledged by staff when they witness the skill's implementation. Budgeting behaviors are generalized outside the classroom as women develop a budget which includes planning for payment of rent and fees from their monthly income. In this way, productive skills that enhance each woman's life, her children's lives, and the parent-child relationship are practiced and reinforced to become an integral part of the woman's natural repertoire of responses. The intent is that, given enough time and practice, these skills will replace former behaviors that were less successful for the women.

Parenting is an essential focus of the Summit House program. Each mother coming to Summit House sets goals for herself regarding parenting and the mother-child relationship. Many of the services and programs implemented to facilitate the attainment of these goals have been mentioned previously. They include MOTHEREAD, family counseling, and various parenting classes. Parenting classes include a wide range of topics such as ages and stages of development, child management and discipline, positive communication with children, child safety, and development of handmade toys and games for children.

Mothers have many opportunities to ask questions and share insights since classes provide an open, nonjudgmental forum. This open forum allows for any disagreements between mothers, concerning child management techniques, to be aired and addressed.

Because Summit House uses an empowerment model, the intent is to blend current conventions of good parenting and child management skills with each mother's particular style, culture, and value structure so that new behaviors can be integrated more acceptably into the mother's responses toward her child.

Scheduling in the residence is geared toward promoting the mother-child relationship. Whenever possible, meetings are scheduled in the evening after children are in bed or during the day while they are in school or day care. Play time is scheduled several evenings per week where mother and child are encouraged to spend quality time engaged in nurturing and developmentally appropriate play. Special arts and crafts activities where mothers and children collaborate on a finished product also are planned. Mothers are encouraged to read to their children at bedtime and are positively reinforced for doing so. Mothers also are reinforced according to the appropriateness and quality of their engagement with their children. Staff are available and ready to bolster the mother-child relationship with guidance and suggestions.

Classes are taught and managed by various Summit House staff and professionals from agencies in the community. Individuals teaching the parenting classes share class goals with Summit House staff so that concepts and behaviors learned in classes can be encouraged and positively reinforced. Summit House staff members receive training in many of the same areas of child development and child management as clients. This educates staff in positive parenting skills which they, in turn, may promote to the mothers. While positive parenting practices generally are reinforced, skills that relate to a mother's specific parenting goals are emphasized individually.

In parenting classes, women often ask, "What should I do when my child . . .?" The question is asked partly to seek information and partly to test the staff. It is information seeking because mothers at Summit House truly are interested in what is best for their children. The question is a test to see if the class leader is sensitive to the woman's particular point of view, culture, and value system. Parenting classes for these women include a delicate combination of gentle guidance, compassion, affirmation, and, of course, humor. Women who come to Summit House have encountered the repeated criticisms and advice of friends, relatives, and "the system." Summit House staff harbor a genuine belief in the capacity and desire of these women to become better parents, and a sincere willingness to listen to each of their individual needs. Such a stance is paramount for the positive impact of training to take hold.

The Client Population

Referrals to Summit House come from the court system, probation officers, alternative sentencing programs, and attorneys for mothers and pregnant women throughout North Carolina. These agencies and individuals refer women who need a structured program but are not candidates for other less restrictive options, such as home confinement or intensive probation.

To make the best use of resources, Summit House accepts women who are deemed high-risk offenders (for recidivism), and for whom there is reasonable expectation of adapting to the Summit House environment and benefitting from the program. Criteria for admission of women into the residential program as approved by the Summit House board of governors include all of the following:

1) She must be eighteen years of age or older.

2) She must have children for whom she has been the primary caretaker or must be pregnant and planning to keep the child with her at the residence.

3) She must be convicted of a crime and have a sentence disposition of an intermediate sanction (as defined by the state's structured-sentencing guidelines).

4) She must follow any treatment ordered by her physician for regulation of physical or psychiatric conditions.

5) She must be able to participate in all facets of the program including provision of adequate supervision and care for her children, academic and vocational training, food preparation, household cleaning, laundry and clothing care, the point system, lifestyle regulations, and volunteer community service.

6) She must be willing to refrain from use of illegal substances, nonprescribed prescription drugs, alcohol, and intoxicating substances, and be willing to submit to frequent substance abuse testing. Prior to entrance, she must be detoxified if she is chemically dependent.

7) She must desire to be self-supporting and willing to work toward obtaining marketable job skills.

8) She must be able to live cooperatively with other women and children in the home.

9) She must not pose a threat to the safety or health of herself or others.

Children who reside at Summit House must be able to benefit from a close relationship with their mothers and be able to live in a congregate living setting with other mothers and children. Child residents must meet the following criteria as established by the Summit House board of governors:

1) Children must be no older than seven years of age at the time of admission.

2) Children must be able to participate in normal activities of childhood.

3) Children must not pose a safety or health risk to themselves or others.

4) Children must follow any treatment ordered by his/her physician for regulation of physical or psychiatric conditions.

Upon meeting these criteria, a potential client is interviewed by the program staff and a resident. Every candidate's admission screening also includes one or more standardized diagnostic tests (such MMPI-2), a review of criminal and social history, and an evaluation of the needs of the woman and her children. The women's level of motivation to change is a critical factor in her being admitted into the Summit House program. Ultimately, the court, the woman, and Summit House must agree to the admission. Summit House strives to maintain an equal balance of Caucasian women and women of color in the program.

Admission criteria for the day-reporting center are identical to those of the residence with regards to age, motherhood or pregnancy, following medical treatment as dictated, detoxification if chemically dependent, and showing a strong desire to work toward rehabilitation. What differs with this clientele is that they may be living within the community either on probation or parole and their children may be older than seven years.

Most of the mothers who have attended Summit House have been between the ages of eighteen and thirty-five; have not completed high school; have two children; are long-term substance abusers; and have been convicted of felonious forgery, counterfeiting, credit card fraud, or drug possession, sales, or trafficking. Studies show that the rate of incarceration for this population in the United States has doubled during the past ten years, and in North Carolina has almost doubled in the past year.

A history of substance abuse is a key characteristic of this population. Nearly 80 percent of the women attending the Summit House program have substance abuse problems, and almost without exception, the substance of choice is crack. Nationwide, all forms of cocaine, including crack, are reportedly the most widely used illicit drugs by women of child-bearing age (Schutter and Briner 1992). For women attending Summit House, and national samples as well, crack use is especially prevalent in low socioeconomic, inner-city neighborhoods where toxic environments contribute to adult substance abuse, which in turn, has a detrimental impact on the child's home environment and, hence, the mother-child relationship.

Since its inception, 95 mothers and 141 children have resided at Summit House. In addition, nineteen babies have been born while their mothers were in the residential program. For many of these infants and children, their stay at Summit House constitutes a reprieve from the destructive effects of their mother's drug use. For many of the mothers, Summit House provides an opportunity to take a sobering look at the effects their drug use has had on themselves and their children. Many of the women at Summit House feel tremendous remorse over the impact their addiction has had on their children. They work hard in parenting classes and with their own behaviors to remedy the past. In many instances, their efforts are truly miraculous.

Future Directions

In the foreseeable future, Summit House will strive to stabilize the two new programs, while monitoring the continual gains in the established program. Recently, the agency hired a director for evaluation and training who is collaborating with program and management staff to design a comprehensive evaluation plan loosely following the five-tiered approach to program evaluation (Jacobs 1988). The intention is to measure not only program outcome, but also process gains to enhance services tailored to the special needs of women offenders and their children. As a pioneer in the field of rehabilitation and treatment for this population, Summit House is committed to maintaining excellence.

At present rates of incarceration, the need for rehabilitation and treatment services for women offenders and their children far exceeds established alternative programs to prison. To address this need, Summit House is developing a long-range plan for targeting regions throughout North Carolina to open new facilities, therefore enabling more women and children to be served. Concurrently, Summit House staff members are advocating for more programs and services for women offenders with children by giving presentations at professional meetings, community gatherings, and other events, and by providing consultation across the United States to those agencies developing similar programs.

Conclusion

Summit House remains committed to serving the needs of women offenders and their children through the provision of a comprehensive battery of services. The major long-term benefits that Summit House offers are: (1) assisting society to break the cycle of poverty and crime; (2) offering prenatal medical care for at-risk mothers with substance abuse problems, therefore potentiating the birth of healthy children; and (3) assisting mothers in modifying their behaviors, allowing them to become productive members of society in the future, and better parents to their children. The Summit House program provides a balance of treatment factors including those known to be effective with offenders in general (see Gendreau 1994), while simultaneously addressing the individual needs and dynamic characteristics of the women served. Their rehabilitation involves treatment of them as women and mothers within the larger systems of family and community.

The women who attend Summit House are a unique group, indeed. While they come with a lifetime of factors that have put them on a trajectory of crime and self-denigration, and come with a history of significant, nonviolent offenses, they are truly a testament of the human desire to rise above adversity. They come primarily for the sake of their children, who have paid the highest price for their mothers' addictions and criminal behaviors. These women come willing to live in the highly structured environment, and under the great demands placed on them, for self-enhancement and successful living. They come seeking better lives for and better relationships with their children. Often, they feel tempted to leave Summit House, but love for their children anchors their stay.

Our message is simple and strong—preserve the family, rehabilitate not merely habilitate, and look towards the future for these children by decreasing their likelihood toward criminal behavior. Summit House strives daily to accomplish these goals as it reaches out to preserve the outcomes of its clients—the women and their children. The significant investment in the people Summit House serves brings a return of self-sufficiency and empowerment, thus promoting a productive and prosocial future.

Endnote

1. MOTHEREAD, Inc. is a nationally acclaimed, North Carolina based nonprofit organization that targets educationally and economically disadvantaged families to promote self-sufficiency through literacy development of mothers, and it encourages mothers to read to their children.

References

Bloom, B. and D. Steinhart. 1993. *Why Punish the Children?* San Francisco: National Council on Crime and Delinquency.

Fritsch, T. A. and J. D. Burkhead. 1981. Behavioral Reactions of Children to Parental Absence Due to Imprisonment. *Family Relations*. 30: 83-88.

Gabel, K. and D. Johnston. 1994. *Children of Incarcerated Parents*. New York: Lexington Books.

Gaudin, J. M. and R. Stuphen. 1993. Foster Care vs. Extended Family Care for Children of Incarcerated Mothers. *Journal of Offender Rehabilitation*. 19(3/4): 129-147.

Gendreau, P. 1994. The Principles of Effective Intervention with Offenders. In A. Harland, ed. *What Works in Community Corrections*. Thousand Oaks, California: Sage.

Schutter, S. and R. Brinker. 1992. Conjuring a New Category of Disability from Prenatal Cocaine Exposure: Are the Infants Unique Biological or Caretaking Casualties? *Topics in Early Childhood Special Education*. 11: 84-111.

Spindler, S. and D. Key. 1994. *Children with Parents in Prison*. [Parent handout], Bethesda, Maryland: National Association of School Psychologists.

The Neil J. Houston House[*]: A Success Story

10

Phyllis Buccio-Notaro
Executive Director

Barbara Molla
Clinical Director

Carolyn Stevenson
Director, AIDS Services and Court-based Programs
Social Justice for Women, Boston, Massachusetts

Carolyn Diane Wood
Program Director
Neil J. Houston House, Roxbury, Massachusetts

Introduction

The Neil J. Houston House of Roxbury, Massachusetts, in its brief six-year history, has been the recipient of many local and national awards and has been privileged to enjoy the support of the criminal justice system, the health care system, the communities it serves, as well as the community in which it resides. The program began as a result of the progressive and compassionate thinking of its founder, Betsey Smith.

---

* A program of Social Justice for Women, Inc.

Background

Betsey Smith, founder of Boston's Social Justice for Women (SJW), had long been active as an advocate for women in conflict with the law when, in the early 1980s, she and others concerned about the conditions for women prisoners at MCI-Framingham, began to pursue the idea of providing gender-specific services for incarcerated women. At that time, MCI-Framingham was the only institution in the State of Massachusetts that housed women. While over 2,500 women were admitted yearly to the institution with a daily census approaching 500, corrections officials had not fully begun to address the complex and varied issues faced by women entering prison. In 1982, after convincing both the Department of Public Health and the Department of Correction of the critical need, Betsey Smith initiated the Women's Health and Learning Center (WHLC), the beginning of what would become the nonprofit corporation, Social Justice for Women.

The Women's Health and Learning Center

The Women's Health and Learning Center was the first program of Social Justice for Women. It addressed gender-specific issues with a gender-specific substance abuse treatment and health education curriculum. The program provided a holistic feminist approach to addressing the needs of the incarcerated women. The Women's Health and Learning Center was the first prison-based program of its type in the country and represented a unique collaboration between the Department of Correction, the Department of Public Health, and a community-based service provider. The Department of Correction provided space within the institution while the Department of Public Health provided the funding. Immediately, the Women's Health and Learning Center began to address the root causes of addiction and subsequent criminal behavior, including the impact of incest, sexual assault, family violence, poverty, homelessness, discrimination, and lack of education and job skills on this population.

As the Women's Health and Learning Center became a safe haven within the prison, more information was gathered about the complex needs of incarcerated women. Statistics showed that the majority of women participating in the Center were between the ages of twenty and thirty-five, and over 75 percent were mothers with sole responsibility for their children. The women were largely from urban areas, with limited education, and minimal job skills.

Many were polydrug users with histories of prostitution, needle use, and having sexual partners who also abused intravenous drugs. These factors placed the women in the second-highest risk group for HIV infection. Many of the women entered the prison with preexisting medical conditions and chronic illnesses that reflected some combination of poor preventative health care, substandard living conditions, inadequate diet, and long-term substance abuse.

Some suffered from mental illnesses, trauma-induced neurological disorders, and the emotional and physical effects of abuse. Some entered the system pregnant. These medical conditions were often compounded during incarceration by increased exposure to infectious diseases, poor diet, crowded living conditions, violence, and traumatic stress syndrome associated with prison life.

Program Expansion

As the decade passed, the Women's Health and Learning Center continued to provide daily substance abuse treatment and health education services to the women at MCI-Framingham. Yet, it became apparent that more extensive programming was needed. Social Justice for Women, now a nonprofit corporation with a board of directors, mission, and downtown Boston office space, proceeded to target the areas of most pronounced need: specific HIV services beyond those already provided, and medical care and treatment for pregnant women.

Social Justice for Women's response to the need for HIV services developed into the Women and AIDS Project, a first-in-the-nation program that advocated for medical care, proper diet, early medical parole, and provided pre- and post-test counseling, AIDS education, and discharge planning for women prisoners who were HIV positive. The response to the needs of pregnant women eventually became the Neil J. Houston House, a residential treatment facility for pregnant, addicted, incarcerated women and also a first-in-the-nation model program.

Both projects presented difficulties in terms of actual day-to-day operations. However, the need for expanded care for pregnant women was more problematic. Although increased awareness could address the medical implications of pregnancy, the protocol for delivery and subsequent separation of mother and baby provoked far-reaching sociological implications.

In 1985, approximately 150 pregnant women were incarcerated in Massachusetts. The majority of these women had high-risk pregnancies due to their drug abuse histories. The standard practice in the Massachusetts prisons was for the woman to deliver her baby at a designated medical facility, remain with the baby in the hospital for the standard recovery time (on average, two days), and then be returned to prison while the baby either went into the custody of relatives or the Department of Social Services.

As the situation was studied, certain realities appeared repeatedly. First, most women who delivered their babies while in prison eventually would have custody of the child. Often, the women received short sentences and would return to the community within a few months of the baby's birth. Yet, due to the policy of separating mother and infant, usually the mother was faced with trying to regain custody following her release from prison. Second, most of these women had committed nonviolent crimes stemming from addiction. Third, most lacked health care knowledge and parenting skills.

The Neil J. Houston House

In 1985, Social Justice for Women issued a report, "Expectant Mothers in the Massachusetts Criminal Justice System," which outlined the needs of pregnant, addicted, incarcerated women. The result was the creation of a task force that ultimately led to the development of what is now known as the Neil J. Houston House. After a year of thoughtful planning, task force recommendations called for the creation of a comprehensive residential treatment program at an alternative site, to benefit both the pregnant woman and her unborn fetus, and that would allow both mother and infant to remain together. The program's primary goals would be to provide comprehensive medical services, ensure optimal birth outcomes, and offer substance abuse treatment to women recovering from addiction. Medical care, substance abuse treatment, education, parenting, and community reintegration services would be the primary program components of the Neil J. Houston House. The program would address a preponderance of needs, to include: medical concerns of high-risk pregnancy, substance abuse precipitating criminality, a safe and clean living environment for mother and baby, education about parenting and other issues, and community reintegration support.

Community Collaborations

To ensure project success, Social Justice for Women worked to build collaborative relationships which would address each of the population's identified needs and provide for smooth operation of the program. Collaborative relationships were developed with the Department of Correction, the Department of Public Health, Dimock Community Health Center, Beth Israel Hospital, and Boston City Hospital Methadone Clinic. With these collaborations in place, the planners were able to create a program that provided a continuum of care that began at MCI-Framingham and continued after completion of the program.

At the prison, a program component called Project Catch the Hope was initiated by Social Justice for Women with federal funds. The program was staffed by a Dimock nurse and a case worker. The program's goal was to identify medically appropriate women for the Neil J. Houston House. For women who entered the Neil J. Houston House via Project Catch the Hope, medical care would be provided by Dimock, with delivery at Beth Israel Hospital. For women on methadone, Boston City Hospital Methadone Clinic would provide dosing with the intent to detoxify, in close medical collaboration with other Dimock obstetrics/gynecology staff.

Siting was next on the agenda. An appropriate building was available on the grounds of Dimock Community Health Center. It was leased from Dimock and renovated by Social Justice for Women with private funds. Siting the residence at Dimock Community Health also required that Social Justice for Women and Dimock conduct a neighborhood public relations campaign.

Treatment Philosophy

Once the working relationships were established and the site determined, Social Justice for Women turned to the actual service delivery methods. L. Ruth Smith was hired as director of the program. She had a long career in the substance abuse treatment field and was a well-respected member of Boston's treatment community. Second on the agenda was the treatment philosophy. The treatment philosophy used in the Women's Health and Learning Center was holistic, feminist, and empowering. Thus, the guiding theme of the new program at the Neil J. Houston House was, and is, its focus on a woman's strengths.

The program recognizes, in all activities, that women have the ability to change negative lifestyles. The program encourages each woman to look at her past and assists her in developing plans for a healthier future. Program services provide tools for a woman in her recovery process. By exploring feelings about womanhood, health, and parenting, each resident becomes able to make concrete choices as to the direction in her life. All services at the Neil J. Houston House are therapeutic and skill-building.

The delivery of medical and psychosocial services addressing maternal and infant health are integrated into the program. The services are delivered by an interdisciplinary treatment team and use the relational theory of service delivery being advanced by Dr. Jean Baker Miller of the Wellesley College Stone Center. This theory advances the idea that connections, through relationships, are central to a woman's psychological health. The desire for connectedness with others may lead to unhealthy relationships when the woman has limited and/or damaged ego strength. Eventually, this damage may lead to substance abuse and criminal behavior.

New positive connections are developed for the women while at the Neil J. Houston House. These positive connections provide support for constructive change within the woman, to improve her self-identity and allow her to see a different picture of herself. Thus, the cycle of negative thought and behavior is altered to allow for each woman's growth and development in ways that are appropriate for her.

Traditional male treatment approaches such as humiliation, breaking down the addict, forced confessions, and public punishment are not used at the Neil J. Houston House. Program staff believes that most women enter the residence having already been harshly judged by society and carrying their own deeply embedded sense of powerlessness and failure. The program's philosophy recognizes that women addicts have been victims themselves and need a positive treatment model focused on self-worth and self-respect. Women are encouraged to be introspective, creative, and self-loving.

The treatment is gender-specific and addresses such issues as guilt over past care of children, childhood sexual and physical abuse, battering, self-image, painful memories of drugging and drinking, employment, and educational experiences. Ethnic and racial pride, as well as gender pride, is fostered. Women are not labeled as "failures." Although self-examination of strengths and weaknesses is an integral part of treatment and recovery, this self-examination is focused on acknowledging past negative behavior and moving through the feelings to arrive at a different, hopeful frame of mind that is conducive to change and growth.

Finally, the program philosophy involves eligible women voluntarily deciding to enter the residence. For a woman to make a commitment to change, she must make the choice to become a resident.

Treatment Model

Treatment is delivered in a variety of formats, including individual and group counseling sessions, educational seminars, therapeutic "feelings" groups, and self-disclosure presentations. Within each format, a variety of treatment techniques are employed. These techniques are decided upon by the treatment team and are appropriate to the specific topic or issue. Techniques may include confrontation, but never with the humiliation that can occur in a more traditional "therapeutic community." Information is delivered in lecture format via peer-led group sharing, in 12-step commitment settings, and in "rap" sessions between staff and residents. Twelve-step program meetings are used both in-house and within the neighborhood, the latter provided as an adjunct to treatment and for building a support system upon which the women may rely after discharge.

Program Goals

The Neil J. Houston House program goals are as follows:

- To provide a structured, healthy, and supportive environment for addicted pregnant women, and for new mothers and their infants
- To strengthen the bonding between mother and infant, and to offer older children and significant others family services
- To decrease the number of addicted pregnant women incarcerated in the Massachusetts prison system
- To prevent the separation of infants and mothers forty-eight hours after birth
- To prevent drug-related pregnancy complications and birth defects
- To provide a community to assist women in their recovery from addiction
- To stop the cycle of addiction and criminality

Service Delivery

Service delivery (the day-to-day procedures, program plans and curricula) is designed to complement the philosophy, treatment model, and program goals of the Neil J. Houston House. The primary focus of the residential stay is to address each woman's needs with regard to medical treatment, substance abuse treatment, education, and community reintegration.

Medical Treatment

In planning day-to-day activities, the medical condition of the women and babies is of primary concern. The association of early and continuous prenatal care to positive birth outcomes has been well documented. Comprehensive medical care, which recognizes the broad range of issues affecting a healthy pregnancy, is essential to reducing the incidence of low birth weights and infant mortality at the residence. Early and ongoing risk assessment and risk management is of critical importance to successful clinical care for this particular group of women. Equally important is the inclusion of comprehensive psychosocial services that focus on the cultural, ethnic, and historical perspectives of pregnancy, childbirth, and motherhood.

A medical care provider is part of the interdisciplinary treatment team and participates in team meetings and case management decisions. This has been facilitated by locating the program on a health care campus where such collaborations are already in place. Following the initial evaluation, an obstetric database is established for each client including a comprehensive health history, a physical exam, and the following assessments: psychosocial, environmental, nutritional, and dental. The initial evaluation is scheduled for every resident to identify complications in the pregnancy which may require special planning and care. A comprehensive medical plan is developed for each woman based on individual need and her risk assessment.

Because the women in the program all are considered high-risk pregnancies, the traditional "six-week check-up" has been changed to a "two-week check-up" with an eight-week follow-up exam. This schedule promptly identifies areas of potential problems and allows for timely treatment of any medical complication.

Following the eight-week exam, women are seen on an "as needed" basis at the Adult Residence clinic at Dimock Community Health Center. A visit to the Family Planning Clinic for reproductive health matters and contraception information is routinely scheduled as part of a woman's discharge planning.

Newborn infant care is delivered in collaboration with specialists from both Dimock and Beth Israel and involves:

- Regular pediatric "well-baby" check-ups
- Early intervention services
- Comprehensive physical exams
- HIV monitoring
- Withdrawal management
- Physical development evaluations
- Nutritional assessments
- Appropriate immunizations

The importance of medical services for this population dictated that community partnerships be established with medical providers as an integral part of the program design. Locating the project on the Dimock Community Health Center grounds provides immediate access to prenatal and postnatal services, as well as services such as early intervention, dental, and pediatric clinics. Holistic nursing care is provided onsite for the women and infants. Included as part of the holistic nursing services is the application of stress reduction and relaxation therapy. Traditional education in women's health and baby care, as well as hands-on training, is provided as part of parenting education. These comprehensive nursing and educational services reinforce new and positive child management skills.

Another major concern for the medical providers are women with a history of opiate addiction. Traditionally, women who use opiates are placed on methadone during pregnancy. This is done (often, even if the woman has not used opiates recently) as a precaution to avoid fetal distress. The medical community historically has shied away from methadone detoxification for pregnant women. Concerns about fetal safety and the need for close medical supervision usually have precluded a detox with this unstable population.

However, at the inception of the Neil J. Houston House, Dr. Janet Mitchell had a record of success at Boston City Hospital in the 1980s with a methadone detox protocol for this population. Social Justice for Women examined this matter carefully. The agency wanted to provide services to the largest number of pregnant women possible; however, a woman on methadone maintenance was not clinically appropriate for the type of treatment program being planned for residents. Working in collaboration with the medical community within MCI-Framingham, the Beth Israel residents at Dimock's obstetrics/gynecology clinic, and the Boston City Hospital Methadone Clinic, a medical protocol was developed that now allows pregnant women on methadone to enter the Neil J. Houston House provided they agree to detoxification from the methadone prior to delivery.

This unprecedented collaboration involves highly orchestrated medical monitoring at Dimock, Beth Israel, and Boston City Hospital. Women who ordinarily might not participate in treatment have been more than willing to detoxify if it meant their babies would be born drug-free. Subsequently, of the eighteen women who entered the Neil J. Houston House on methadone, all but three were completely detoxified at the time of delivery. The other three women were down to such low dosages of methadone that the babies suffered minimal withdrawal and were placed at the Neil J. Houston House within one to three weeks after birth.

Substance Abuse Treatment

Equal in importance to the women's medical care are the substance abuse treatment services provided. The treatment model of the Neil J. Houston House is based on an integrated approach to comprehensive perinatal and substance abuse services. The residence offers a multidisciplinary substance abuse treatment program which includes an eclectic blend of therapies for high-risk pregnant women and new mothers. Based on setting concrete realistic goals specific to women's issues, the procedure combines several treatment modalities, which are delivered to the women "relationally." Alcohol and drug addiction are addressed in relation to family dynamics, experiences of victimization, health, socioeconomic forces, racism, and women's roles in society. The peer support of 12-step models, such as Alcoholics Anonymous, Narcotics Anonymous, and other self-help groups are also components of the treatment model.

Education

A third important focus of the program is education, more in-depth than simply education about addiction or General Equivalency Degree preparation. The educational component of the program consists of seminars and group discussions on the following topics: addiction/substance abuse, health, HIV, life skills, spirituality, violence against women, parenting, and nutrition, among others.

In our society, a child usually learns information and skills from within the home, extended family, neighborhood, and school. This process often is skewed when issues of substance abuse, poverty, incest and/or sexual assault exist within the family or the community at large. Thus, women enter treatment with a limited knowledge and information for adult survival in a complicated society. Counselors use a variety of teaching methods to engage women in the process. The goal is always to provide the woman with more information so she may improve her decision-making skills, make choices appropriate and meaningful for her, and ultimately, benefit society as a whole.

Also, as part of the weekly educational routine, women participate in a series of lectures by guest speakers drawn from the community, who speak on a variety of topics.

Community Reintegration

A fourth focus is community reintegration. The great emphasis placed on support after program completion helped to design the "resettlement" component. As each woman nears the completion of her stay at the Neil J. Houston House, she begins participation in the resettlement component. The resettlement component complements the reintegration of graduates and their infants into their home communities by providing access to needed community services, such as housing, continuing General Equivalency Degree programs, job placement, day care, continuing parenting education, counseling, and medical and substance abuse treatments. Connecting to community-based programs reinforces what the women have learned at the Neil J. Houston House. Also, resettlement involves one year of aftercare outpatient counseling services and support services. Resettlement is crucial to a woman's ongoing ability to combat substance abuse and to accept responsibility for a productive life for herself and her child.

Support during the early months of sobriety is vitally important for a woman to have following residential treatment. The resettlement component provides that support. The primary activities of the resettlement component include the following:

- Group counseling sessions

- Urinalysis

- Individual counseling sessions

- Aid with housing placement

- Peer support

- Vocational and educational referrals

- Community linkage

- Family reunification support

- Other miscellaneous social activities

As previously stated, a woman's success in maintaining recovery requires the consistent support provided by the resettlement counselor.

Admission Criteria

Pregnant women within eighteen months of parole eligibility meet the initial admission criteria. They then must have minimum—or prerelease—status and be classified to the residence from prison. The program also accepts women from the courts if they are clearly prison-bound. Admission into the residence is determined by a woman's:

- Pregnancy prior to sentencing

- Desire to parent

- Commitment to participate in treatment

- Medical clearance for participation

- Being within eighteen months of parole eligibility

- Having a willingness to detoxify from methadone during pregnancy if so advised by a physician

Prior to admission, every prospective resident must have:

1) a complete medical examination

2) a psychological assessment

3) a determination of her correctional status and resolution of any out-standing criminal matters

Pregnant women are examined by a physician at the prison to determine whether detoxification from methadone is warranted. Other assessments are conducted by the staff of the Neil J. Houston House.

The medical conduit between the prison and the Neil J. Houston House is Project Catch the Hope. Originally a federally funded program of Social Justice for Women, Project Catch the Hope proved so successful that the Massachusetts State Department of Correction incorporated the program as part of MCI-Framingham services when the federal funding ended.

Pregnant women are referred to Project Catch the Hope staff. The staff then work with each woman to access appropriate services for her, depending on her sentence structure and other circumstances. If she is referred to the Neil J. Houston House, the staff meet and interview each woman referred to assess her suitability for participation. The residence accepts women on a statewide basis and accepts women with medical complications as long as they are well enough to participate in the daily schedule of program activities.

Other than the methadone detoxification protocol, women entering the program must be drug-free. Women coming into the program from sites other than prison must be medically cleared and present proof of their drug-free status. If any woman enters the program on methadone, the program accepts the responsibility of her daily transportation to the dosing center. The Neil J. Houston House accepts pregnant women at any stage of pregnancy but attempts to receive referrals as early in pregnancy as possible. The residence does not discriminate against pregnant women who test positive for HIV infection. The residence is not able to admit women who are either severely retarded or actively psychotic or delusional and in need of hospitalization.

Clients

The client population of the Neil J. Houston House is roughly 50 percent white, 30 percent black, and 20 percent Latina. More than two-thirds of the women have other children. Most have prior involvement with the criminal justice system, but almost 30 percent are admitted during their first incarceration. The crimes for which the women have been incarcerated vary, though most are related to drug use. Typically, crimes identified against property of persons are also drug-related because substance use has led to the criminal behavior. The residents range in age between eighteen and midthirties, with most women in their late twenties.

Admission Procedures

At the time of admission, a client is given a *Client Policy Manual* as well as the *Client Orientation Package*. The *Client Policy Manual* lists clients' rights, the program's

HIV policy, the termination policy, the client grievance procedure, and includes the program consent form, and resident contract. Signed originals of these papers are placed in the client's file. Clients retain copies of signed forms along with the other materials included in the Orientation Manual. The Orientation Manual provides a written overview of the program, "Cardinal Rules," and general "House Rules." Cardinal Rules cite unacceptable behaviors which result in an automatic Return to Higher Custody. Cardinal Rules are:

1) No drugs/drug use

2) No sexual acts

3) No violence or threats of violence

House Rules and House Guidelines list general operating practices of the program to which the clients must adhere as well as general standards of behavior for all residents. Upon admission, residents sign a contract agreeing to the house rules and to their participation in the program. They also sign a release form at admission, authorizing the Neil J. Houston House to receive confidential documents and speak with individuals having a confidential relationship with the client. A "summary sheet," filled out during admission, is a permanent document in a woman's file. The summary sheet includes a range of vital information, including special medical notes and emergency information. The woman's "six-part folder" from the Department of Correction accompanies her to the program. The woman also signs forms that transfer her to Community Corrections, the Pre-Release branch of the Department of Correction.

Weekly Schedule

The primary focus of the residential stay is to address medical needs, substance abuse treatment, educational needs, and community reintegration needs. Meeting everyone's needs while maintaining the integrity of the services, the security needs of the Department of Correction, and effecting positive bonding between mother and infant has presented challenges to the Neil J. Houston House staff. To address all these concerns, the original program designers, along with the Program Director, Ruth Smith, had to be creative, practical, and security conscious. The following is a sample of a weekly schedule offered.

The Neil J. Houston House Sample Weekly Schedule

MONDAY

- Wake-up,* Breakfast
- Morning Connection group
- Appointments /Peer Discussion/ Individual Counseling
- Lunch
- Narcotics Anonymous (NA) meeting
- Parenting Class/ Child Development Seminar

- Weekly menu planning
- Appointments / Peer Discussion/ Individual Counseling
- Dinner
- AA Commitment

TUESDAY

- Wake-up, Breakfast
- Level II group (therapy group)
- Level I (written assignments)
- Lunch
- CODA Co-dependency meeting/Visiting Nurse (medical and educational)
- Appointments/ Peer Discussion/ Individual Counseling
- Dinner
- GED Tutoring

WEDNESDAY

- Wake-up, Breakfast
- Morning Connection group
- Nutrition Education/ Behavior Management Class
- Lunch
- Substance Abuse Education including Relapse Prevention/ Violence Against Women Series
- Dinner
- Life Skills Seminar/ Approved Visits
- Birthing Classes at Dimock Community Health Center

THURSDAY

- Wake-up, Breakfast
- Level I group (therapy group)
- Level II AA/NA Outside Meeting
- Lunch
- Spiritual Healing/ Health Education including HIV Education
- Mother-Baby Time/ Individual Counseling/ Peer Discussion
- Dinner

- Baby Care Seminar/ Exercise Class
- Grocery Shopping

FRIDAY

- Wake-up, Breakfast
- Morning Connection group
- House Meeting
- Individual Nursing Assessment/ Journal Writing
- Lunch
- AA/NA Outside Meeting
- Stress Management Seminar
- Dinner
- Recreational Activity such as reading, TV time or Mother-Baby time

SATURDAY

- Wake-up, Breakfast
- Morning Connection group
- House Cleaning
- Lunch
- Arts and Crafts/ Gardening
- Dinner
- NA Commitment

SUNDAY

- Wake-up, Breakfast
- Morning Connection group
- Lunch
- Approved Visits
- Dinner
- In-House activity, such as reading, TV time, Mother-Baby time

*Wake-up includes the woman being dressed, and having the bed made and baby prepared for the day.

Staffing

To provide this comprehensive weekly schedule and satisfy security concerns of the Department of Correction, the program is staffed twenty-four hours a day. Typical day staffing includes a program director, treatment supervisor, administrative assistant, resettlement coordinator, two residential counselors, and a part-time nurse. A minimum of two counselors are on duty during the evening, and two relief workers staff the midnight to 8:00 AM shifts. This staffing pattern is supported by a series of counselors and educators who each contract with Social Justice for Women for a prescribed period of time to provide addiction counseling and education services.

For example, violence prevention seminars are provided by a consultant who is scheduled for an hour and a half per week for eight weeks. This eight-week series is conducted six times annually. In addition, two nurse interns support nursing and health evaluation services for the women and infants, and law student interns provide educational seminars and support for legal matters for the women and assist staff with clearing outstanding warrants so that women may enter the residence. Also, program staff is supported by the administrative staff of Social Justice for Women.

The program can accommodate fifteen women and their infants at any time, and typically serves thirty to thirty-five women per year. The program is handicapped accessible and meets Department of Public Health regulations for residential treatment facilities in Massachusetts.

Length of Stay

The average length of stay for women is from six to nine months. Each woman makes a commitment to remain at the Neil J. Houston House during her pregnancy and for a minimum of eight weeks postpartum. A stay of nine months to one year of residential treatment, depending on the client, her sentencing structure, and her primary treatment needs is recommended and preferred.

Funding

Funding was of primary concern when designing the program and remains so today. Typically, in our six years of program operation, the budget has fluctuated from $690,000 to $750,000. Funding from the Department of Correction has varied from as high as $697,000 to the current low of $497,000. Social Justice for Women administration and board of directors have compensated for the contractual reductions by privately raising funds for the program from foundations, corporations, and individuals. In recent years, this has become an increasing burden and has placed the program in financial jeopardy.

Barriers to Program Implementation

Beyond the funding, several barriers have been encountered in implementing the program. A major barrier was security concerns. Since security is a major concern for the Department of Correction, it must be balanced with the clinical value of a woman's accepting increasing control of and responsibility for her own actions. In working with the

Department of Correction, several security measures were established that include daily "counts," which are either done by the Neil J. Houston House staff and called in, or conducted on-site by community corrections personnel; prior approval of visitors to the women and submission of the daily "Visitors Log" for review; weekly reports on program activities; submission for prior approval of client activities including community 12-step meetings, medical appointments, and shopping excursions; staff accompaniment on activities out of the house; and regular "house-runs" by staff during evening and overnight hours to ensure the presence and safety of all women. "House-runs" are built into the routine of the staff to further satisfy the security concerns of the Department of Correction.

Since the Department of Correction does not specialize in residential substance abuse treatment, the program has had to be responsive to the treatment and licensing regulations of the Department of Public Health and the building and code regulations of the Board of Health and Boston Housing Authority. Although the Department of Health does not fund the program, the Neil J. Houston House is a licensed treatment program and, as such, must adhere to its stringent guidelines for residential treatment facilities. Program managers must respond to four sets of regulations, those of the Department of Correction, Department of Public Health, Boston Housing Authority, and the Board of Health.

Beyond the funding and systematic barriers, barriers to a client's entering the residence may include any of the following: classification, outstanding charges, length of sentence, delivery date and methadone detox, and mental health issues.

The classification process occurs at the prison after a woman has been sentenced. It can take as long as two months which, in turn, slows down the transfer at a critical time if the client is pregnant. The classification board meets regularly and reviews each inmate within thirty days of her sentencing to an institution. Since the Neil J. Houston House is at prerelease level, women must be appropriate for transfer to lower custody. Factors considered include sentence structure and the woman's behavior within the institution. Sometimes women who may be appropriate for the program choose to remain in the institution and "wrap-up" their time, rather than make a longer commitment to a treatment program.

Outstanding legal matters also may prevent a speedy transfer and can slow the process by two to three months. Referral to the program is controlled by legal and Department of Correction protocols that can create a bottleneck for admission. Since the outstanding warrants are often for felony offenses, the cases must be addressed before the woman can be approved for the lower level of custody at the prerelease setting.

Length of sentence may also be a factor in transfer to the residence, since short sentences do not allow the client a length of stay consistent with program treatment recommendations and services. Longer sentences necessitate the return of the mother to prison and separation from the baby, which contradicts the philosophy of keeping mother and baby together.

Methadone maintenance also can prevent transfers. If a woman is receiving a high dose, the detoxification period may not be successful if the mother's gestational period does not match a decrease in methadone dosing. If a woman carries a mental health diagnosis, she cannot enter the Neil J. Houston House.

The fragmentation of systems is an historical problem. The transfer from a system whose primary agenda is public safety to one whose agenda includes medical care and substance abuse treatment is difficult. Valid concerns from each system must be addressed fully. Over the six years that the Neil J. Houston House has been operational, it has become clear that great benefits exist for the clients—and ultimately for society—if the barriers and obstacles can be overcome.

Program Benefits

The Neil J. Houston House program has demonstrated that positive outcomes for their clients are numerous. The provision of prenatal and postnatal care for mothers and infants results in the babies having improved birth weights. The benefits for mothers include:

- Connections into the community health care system
- Knowledge and practice of appropriate nutrition
- Interventions for any outstanding health issues

The education and life skills to support the beginning of a woman's life in recovery result in:

- Reduction or elimination of criminal activity
- Lower rates of recidivism
- Greater knowledge of addiction and its impact
- Relapse-prevention skills
- Increased lengths of sobriety
- Drug-free delivery
- Familiarity with 12-step programs

The environment for healthy mother/infant bonding occurs because:

- The mother and infant are not separated at birth as would happen in the prison setting
- The house provides a safe, homelike, drug-free environment
- The mothers are given the time, space, and support to be with their children mentally, physically, and spiritually

The assistance given to the mothers in developing parenting and other social/relational skills results in the women having:

- Improved parenting skills
- A richer knowledge of child development
- Increased ability to interact with peers and authority in a positive manner
- Greater recognition of their own feelings and ways to deal with them

The reintegration of clients back into the community results in each woman having:

- A discharge plan for needed medical, social, and other treatment services
- Reconnection with family members, when appropriate

- A transitional support system available for one full year after program completion
- Knowledge of alternatives to antisocial lifestyles

Conclusion

The Neil J. Houston House has been the recipient of many local and national awards. In 1991, the program was awarded the thirty-eighth Point of Light by President Bush. In 1992, the program was chosen by the Drucker Foundation for special recognition in the Peter F. Drucker Award for Nonprofit Innovation. In 1995, the Boston City Council and Massachusetts House of Representatives recognized the program. In May 1995, along with other Social Justice for Women programs, the Neil J. Houston House was named one of twenty-five pioneering models from across the United States. Additionally, the program has been recognized by the National Council on Crime and Delinquency as an innovative, effective response to needs of pregnant, addicted, incarcerated women.

Since the program began, 135 women have been admitted, 81 babies have been born drug-free, and 20 babies have been united with their mothers. The benefits of a compassionate response to pregnant women who are incarcerated are innumerable. Pregnancy provides an optimum time for intervention in the cycle of addiction. Most pregnant women want to do the "right thing," but their addiction and the negative lifestyle it creates prevents them from fully using their potential and making the changes necessary for a drug-free, crime-free life.

Substance abuse treatment, initiated during pregnancy, with the constraints of a criminal justice sanction in place, can help bring about these fundamental changes. A setting geared to women's special needs and issues can provide a foundation for the woman to continue with her life as a productive member of society. When a woman is in recovery, she is able to take care of herself and her family in ways which not only benefit her and her family, but also benefit society as a whole by saving jail costs, child custody costs, and other "placement" related costs. The Neil J. Houston House program, and programs like it, certainly provide a "win-win" situation for all concerned.

Las Comadres: A Parenting Education/Foster Parenting Program*

11

Gretchen Newby
Program Director, Friends Outside National Organization
San Jose, California

Introduction

Las Comadres is an innovative family reunification project that places babies born to incarcerated mothers with temporary volunteer foster mothers residing in the local communities. These unique and very special foster mothers take on the enormous responsibility of nurturing and caring for high-risk, often drug-affected babies, while simultaneously mentoring the birth mother.

The name of the program derives from the Spanish, *comadre*, the name given reciprocally to the mother and godmother of a baby. Together, they mother the child, commit to the child's well-being, and share the joys and responsibilities of motherhood. Literally, they are co-mothers.

Purpose

Research demonstrates that babies who fail to attach to their mother, or to a significant other in her place, will have serious difficulties as they move through childhood into adulthood. These children are at a greater risk for experiencing school failure, drug abuse, and delinquent behavior.

---

* A program of Friends Outside National Organization and the California Department of Corrections

The initial goal of the Las Comadres program was to provide for the well-being of inmates' babies by:

- Increasing the parenting skills and competence of the birth mother through education

- Reducing the likelihood of child abuse and neglect by building the mother's empathy for, and understanding and knowledge of, age-appropriate behaviors, and her ability to adjust her expectations accordingly

- Providing a family environment where the child could flourish and learn in safety, supporting the child's chances of becoming a capable adult who is able to function successfully in society

- Increasing the mother's motivation to continue to provide nurturing and skilled parenting in the family environment postrelease.

Mother-child attachment is encouraged through mentoring and role modeling, through nurturing and involving the parent by engaging her during pregnancy, and through providing regular mother-child contact beginning at birth. Research demonstrates that ex-offenders who are able to reunite and remain with their families have a higher probability of success on parole, and are less likely to reoffend. The curriculum includes family relationship skills that are designed to enhance parenting, but which also strengthen other family relationships, thereby enhancing the probability that the family will reunify successfully. In this way, the Las Comadres program provides opportunities for positive parole outcomes and a reduction in recidivism.

Institution Requirements

At the onset of the program, a Memorandum of Understanding is created by the host institution [1] and Friends Outside which specifies what will be provided by the program provider (Friends Outside) and the host institution. Typically, the host provides a suitable office and classroom location for the program. The host provides institutional clearances and identification for staff, staff training, custody support (if needed), access to inmates (to meet the needs of the program provider), staff support in the selection of participants, visitor clearances, photocopying, and a pool of inmates from which participants are selected. Access to inmate records may be provided, either directly or indirectly. The stipulation that program staff have the support and cooperation of institutional staff in preparing program evaluations may be made.

The program provider provides staff, curriculum, as-needed supervision of participants, and whatever else is agreed upon by both parties. Stipulations may be made regarding items which can be brought into the institution, or staff behavior, training, hiring, and supervision.

Friends Outside has an established model for program policies and procedures which is adapted to the needs of each host institution. Finally, this Memorandum of Understanding is signed by both parties and becomes the document which guides future decisions.

Program Overview

Before delivery, the pregnant inmate mother is paired with a volunteer mentor who nurtures and supports the mother-to-be. The volunteer serves as a teacher, mentor, role model, and guide—teaching nurturing by nurturing. After the baby's birth, the volunteer mentor's role is expanded to include foster mothering.

Las Comadres babies are brought weekly to see their biological mothers for extended visits. Parenting issues are discussed and stories swapped, as the "co-mothers" share the joys of nurturing new life.

In preparation for the day when they will assume their full role as mother/caregiver, inmate mothers participate in a twice-weekly parenting education program that uses a highly specialized curriculum developed by Friends Outside to meet the unique needs of incarcerated mothers. In preparation for the day when the foster mother will place the baby in the birth mother's arms and send them on their way, foster mothers are provided support, guidance, education, and nurturing by Las Comadres staff.

History

Las Comadres was started in 1992, in response to a pregnant inmate's request for assistance with finding a placement close to the prison from a Friends Outside caseworker. Typically, babies born to women in prison are placed with relatives or friends. If no one appropriate is available to take them in, authorities place the infants in state-subsidized foster homes in the county of the mother's residence. For women at the Central California Women's Facility (CCWF) in Madera, California—the largest women's prison in the world—this means their babies most often are placed a great distance away in Los Angeles County, which makes any contact extremely difficult, if not impossible.

Additionally, inmate mothers are fearful of "losing" their babies through county placement. Once authorities become involved, they likely will set a series of conditions which must be met by the mother upon her release before the child will be returned to her care. Often these conditions are overwhelming to a woman recently released from prison, who has no job, no place to live, and no support system.

The program began within the context of an existing, state-funded mentoring program for female inmates. In 1993, Las Comadres received a separate, three-year contract from the California Department of Corrections. Warden Teena Farmon supported the program from its onset and a collegial and collaborative environment quickly was established. Correctional staff at Central California Women's Facility consistently and enthusiastically have worked towards the program's success, as partners in the effort with Friends Outside.

The future of the Las Comadres program is uncertain. When the current contract expires at the end of calendar year 1996, the program will again be opened for contract bids, possibly at a greatly reduced funding level. Friends Outside, the originator and only provider of the program to date, will enter the competitive, low-bid process.

Issues Clients Bring

Attachment

When a woman is in prison, she has little cause for a joyful pregnancy. Instead of celebrating the beginnings of a new life, the mother-to-be often is filled with fear and dread. Sometimes she does not even understand what is happening to her body. Each day of her pregnancy is filled with anxiety and concern. Each special moment is kept inside. Each worrisome thought is left untended.

She listens to horrifying "birthing stories" from other inmates. She sometimes is embarrassed and anxious about "special treatment." She feels vulnerable in her bulbous condition, and unable to protect herself from aggression and violence.

It is no wonder that her anticipation of the approaching delivery may be filled with anxiety or dread. Indeed, she may not feel an attachment to the baby growing inside of her.

We notice that incarcerated women often refer to their unborn babies as "it," even when they know their baby's gender and their delivery date is near. The mentor's function is to encourage the birth mother to see her baby as a human being. She sows the seeds of attachment by speaking with terms of endearment. The joy she feels about the impending birth is "caught," and shared, by the birth mother. Mentors also strive to teach empathy by example. Herein lies the beginnings of the bond between "las comadres."

Recurrent Themes

The issues of substance abuse, family violence, dependency, and self-esteem are addressed throughout the Las Comadres program. Recognizing that inmate parents generally have a history of being poorly parented themselves, and that they are highly influenced in their parenting by this negative history, the program provides opportunities for re-parenting—recreating the inmate parent's experience of being parented in a nurturing, positive way.

Inmates are guided through re-parenting in a series of exercises which allow their "inner child" positive experiences with being parented. As they feel the joys of being read to, being praised, and hearing expressions of concern and caring, they "bank" the positive feelings. Old memories of rejection or neglect are replaced with their new experiences of acceptance and nurturance. As they heal through laughter, tenderness, and acceptance, they become increasingly capable of giving similar positive experiences to their own children.

The Parenting Program

Curriculum Design

The highly specialized parenting curriculum was developed in response to the need for programming addressing the special concerns, limitations, and learning difficulties of incarcerated, at-risk women. Originally developed for women in custody in Santa Clara County, California under court order for parenting education as a condition of family reunification, the program has since been adapted and used with incarcerated fathers, furlough facility inmates, and teen parents in Juvenile Hall.

Incarcerated women are likely to have a history of drug abuse. They are likely to have been abused and neglected during childhood. Their school experiences were probably unhappy. And, they are probably acquainted with violence, either as aggressors or as victims. Given these factors, the issues of substance abuse and family violence permeate the parenting program. The thirty-six-hour program is institution-friendly and flexible, depending on the needs of the host institution.

The curriculum is based on sound research regarding the behavior of abusing and neglectful parents. It addresses four observable and measurable types of parent-child relationship factors which are likely to result in abuse and/or neglect:

- Inappropriate developmental expectations of children

- Lack of empathic awareness of children's needs

- A strong parental belief in the use of corporal punishment

- The reversal of the parent-child roles

Acknowledging that inmates have certain characteristics that tend to interfere with the absorption of new information, this program is designed to reduce performance anxiety and open the participant to the possibility of change. The method is interactive rather than didactic, facilitated rather than taught. The atmosphere is accepting, welcoming, nonjudgmental, and supportive. Carefully chosen games and exercises are interspersed with discussion. Problem-solving skills are emphasized, and the group is encouraged to "find their own solutions."

The facilitator reads poetry and children's books aloud, demonstrating the value of children's literature for teaching moral lessons, learning to deal with life's problems, and encouraging shared experiences between the mother and child. Reading aloud also sets the stage for early literacy, and provides valuable preschool preparation. The experience of "reading aloud" is modeled by the facilitator for the program participants, who also experience this activity as part of their own re-parenting.

Videos and outside speakers are employed to maximize opportunities for learning and to provide diverse avenues for engaging this difficult-to-reach population. Subjects such as first aid for children, household safety, and prenatal development may be appropriately addressed through video presentations. Participants' successes are generously celebrated.

The parenting curriculum addresses the following components:

- Introduction to Parenting (this includes components regarding abuse and neglect)

- Communication Skills

- Self-esteem (of both parent and child)

- Childhood Growth and Development (covering pregnancy and prenatal development through adolescence)

- Nutrition

- Child Health and Safety

- Stress, Anger, and Parenting

- Sex, Drugs, and Outside Influences

- Special Concerns of Adolescence

- Guidance and Discipline

- Family Relationships

- Long-distance Parenting

- The Family Together: The family as a place of belonging

Children's Visiting Day

Participants in the Parenting Program are eligible to have their other children, not just the foster care babies, transported to the institution for a special visiting day. Warden Teena Farmon has designated a special visiting room for these participants and their visiting children.

Often, children have been unable to visit their incarcerated parents for reasons that are overcome very easily. The caregiver may not have reliable transportation, may not be able to drive the distance due to health or other reasons, or may not be able to get a clearance to visit due to extenuating circumstances (such as lack of proper identification, outstanding warrants, or inability to document citizenship). In some cases, the cost of the eight- or ten-hour trip may be prohibitive. Occasionally, caregivers simply cannot bring themselves to tell the child their mother is in prison, or they are too embarrassed to visit themselves.

On visiting day, volunteers and staff provide transportation from all over California. This allows inmate participants to visit at length and "try out" their new parenting skills and attitudes. Interactive toys and books are provided, and structured activities provide opportunities for mothers and children to have fun together.

Children range in age from one to nineteen years. The only criteria for their participation is that they have not had regular visits with their mother during her incarceration, that there is no court order or other restriction on visits, that the caregiver (and social worker, if appropriate) consents to the visit, and that they are able to be cleared to visit the institution under regular visiting regulations.

Friends Outside staff screen the applications, then contact the caregivers and other appropriate parties to obtain permission and make plans. Often, gaining permission involves much discussion during which Friends Outside staff provide ample reassurance, but few caregivers or social workers ultimately refuse to allow the visits. Staff supervise the paperwork until all appropriate forms are signed, visiting clearances are obtained, and a detailed history of the child is documented.

Staff also speak with the children by telephone. Using age-appropriate language, staff describe the visiting process to the child, and offer reassurance.

Each family has a volunteer or staff person assigned to help orchestrate the visit. Caregivers are contacted to discuss the child, the visiting day, and transportation details. With this information, age-appropriate snacks and books are arranged for each child's journey.

Recognizing that prison visiting is a difficult experience at best, volunteers and staff are trained to address the child's unique needs. En route to the visit, questions, apprehensions, and anxieties can be expected. After the visit, issues of loss, rejection, and sadness are common on the journey home.

Las Comadres staff prepare the inmate mothers for the visits, helping them to determine their expectations and work to make these realistic. Each mother may have a different goal she hopes to accomplish through the visit; staff help her plan for and achieve that goal. Staff also prepare mothers for the child's departure and for the accompanying sadness and grief.

Institutional staff are consulted about how best to handle the visit's close. They help to ease the stress of transitioning from the family visit back to institutional life.

Staff Qualifications and Training

The *Case Management Coordinator* is required to hold a master's degree in a related field, under state licensing requirements for foster care agencies. The *Parenting Program Facilitator* must hold a bachelor's degree in a related field, with course work in child development.

Both positions require multicultural competency, experience in working with at-risk parents, and the ability to work independently in an institutional setting. Each must be nonjudgmental and must model appropriate parenting skills.

Criteria are established and the hiring process completed through a collaboration between the institution and Friends Outside. Training includes regular staff institutional training provided by the host institution. The parenting program facilitator is given additional training by the program director in facilitation skills, the special issues of inmate parents, and use of the parenting program curriculum.

Participant Criteria

Inmate Participants

Inmate participants in both the Las Comadres and the parenting education programs are screened carefully according to criteria established by Friends Outside and the institution administration. These criteria reflect the needs and interests of the host institution and may vary between locations.

In an interview with the case management coordinator, each prospective participant completes a detailed application. The coordinator reviews each item and writes the answers; this allows for slight digressions, probing, and delving to obtain complete information. Application questions not only address the inmate's pregnancy and wishes for foster care placement, but also her education, employment, criminal history, drug use, support system, postrelease plans, and three things she would like to change about herself. Staff references are requested, and the correctional counselor must sign the application— verifying the information provided by the inmate and granting approval for participation.

Inmates must have a clean institutional disciplinary record and must clearly demonstrate motivation. They must agree to the following: drug tests on demand, complete participation in the parenting education program, strict adherence to all institutional rules, and full compliance with the case management plan established by Las Comadres staff. Those inmates reading below a seventh-grade level must be enrolled in a literacy program. They may be required to attend special programs, such as Alcoholics Anonymous, or to enroll in vocational training.

Participants sign a contract binding them to these stipulations. Violation of the contract results in expulsion from the program, and may result in the baby's transfer to Child Protective Services.

Las Comadres is devoted to meeting the best interests of each child. Thus, the parent's dedication to leading a clean and sober life is of the utmost importance. If the inmate mother appears to be uncommitted, at any time, to successful reunification, Child Protective Services is informed, and the voluntary placement is terminated.

Volunteer Participants

Volunteers are screened carefully prior to acceptance into the program. They must meet all requirements for state-licensed foster homes. In addition, they must possess certain qualities which set them apart from most foster parents.

They must agree to mentor the inmate during her pregnancy. Mentoring is accomplished through regular visiting at the institution which requires institutional clearance. Completion of a rigorous Friends Outside training is also required of all institutional volunteers. They must understand the unique characteristics of inmate mothers and accept them as human beings.

Volunteers also must be able to make their responsibility as the inmate mother's mentor take priority over their role as foster mother. *This relationship between the birth and foster mothers is what makes the program work.* This relationship enables the foster mother to return the baby to their birth mother upon her release, with the understanding that the child may well experience a lower standard of living than the foster family provided.

Volunteers must be able to cope during the first months, when high-risk babies can be incredibly needy and demanding. While much support is provided by staff and the other foster mothers, the cries of a baby in distress are difficult to bear. The foster mother's ability to accept these responsibilities willingly and with equanimity makes her a very special person.

Finally, foster mothers must participate in regular training sessions which are required of all foster participants as a condition of licensing. The Friends Outside foster parent training focuses on the special issues of incarcerated parents, their children, and reunification.

Support for Volunteers

Las Comadres staff provide ongoing support and guidance to foster parents, with frequent individual and group discussions regarding the impending separations. Foster fathers are included in this "prerelease preparation," since, as silent partners in the Las Comadres program, they often form strong attachments to their foster babies.

The foster mothers maintain an informal support network for each other. They babysit for other foster babies, getting to know each as a special person. They provide advice to and respite care for other foster mothers. When a foster mother must relinquish "her" baby to the birth mother, this informal network provides much-needed support.

Evaluation

No formal evaluation has yet been made of the Las Comadres program, which is still in the piloting phase. The California Department of Corrections is scheduled to measure recidivism among participants who successfully have completed the Las Comadres program. A sample of past participants will be tracked through their parole agents, to determine the incidence of abuse and neglect post program and the success of reunification.

Parenting program participants have pre- and post-tests administered which reliably measure their propensity for abuse and neglect. All participants have demonstrated a marked reduction in child abuse/neglect tendencies on the post-test.

Cost Benefits

Among the numerous cost benefits related to Las Comadres are expected future savings for successful program participants. They are less likely to recidivate, thereby reducing reincarceration costs to the state. For women, annual incarceration costs can exceed $25,000. Above this amount are costs for time spent in county jail prior to incarceration, law enforcement costs incidental to the investigation and arrest, court costs, and secondary costs for family support while the wage earner is incarcerated.

Further, children who are abused, neglected, or simply not attached to a functional family are likely to suffer school failure, drug abuse, and delinquency. The cost of foster care for a child whose parent is incarcerated can exceed $600 per month. These additional costs can be impacted by a successful Las Comadres program.

Our program provides comprehensive case management, foster care, and parenting education services to twenty-five women and their babies each year, resulting in over eighty months of placement annually. Eighty inmates are provided parenting education services. Both the parenting participants and the Las Comadres mothers are provided postrelease support through a toll-free number to their parenting educator and/or case management coordinator. The total annual cost per Las Comadres participant is less than $1,500.

Conclusion

Las Comadres is the only foster care program in the United States funded by a state Department of Corrections in partnership with a community-based organization whose foster mothers/mentors are volunteers. From the beginning, our plan has been to provide a program easily replicated. Program policies and procedures have been structured to facilitate such replication.

The potential impact of this program is impressive:

- An inmate who is attached to her child/ren is motivated to maintain the family unit postrelease; therefore, she has a greater chance for parole success.

- An informed, caring, attached mother, with well-developed parenting skills and positive parenting role models, has a decreased risk for child abuse or neglect.

- A child given the opportunity to bond with his or her mother, and attach to other caring adults, has a decreased risk of school failure, delinquency, and drug abuse.

The Friends Outside National Organization is located at 3031 Tisch Way, Suite 507, San Jose, California 95128.

Endnote

1. When describing a specific program, this chapter refers to the Las Comadres program in effect at the Central California Women's Facility; however, Friends Outside has designed a program to be replicable in other settings.

Camp Dismas

12

Raymond J. Weis
Executive Director
Dismas Charities, Inc., Louisville, Kentucky

Introduction

To address the unique needs of incarcerated mothers and their children, Dismas Charities, Inc., headquartered in Louisville, Kentucky, operates a program whereby the term "quality time" becomes reality. Known as Camp Dismas, the initiative is designed to provide an opportunity for children to have at least one twenty-four hour, on-site visit with their mothers at the Dismas Charities Owensboro facility in Western Kentucky. The purpose of the effort is threefold: to encourage inmate mothers in their parenting role, to improve the quality of parent-child interaction, and to provide an opportunity to continue the mother-child bond during incarceration. Offered overnight one month and as a day camp in the following month, on weekends, Camp Dismas has proven to be a natural extension of the Dismas Charities Owensboro Parenting Program.

The often overused term "quality time" adopts true meaning at Camp Dismas with the mother focusing all her attention on the child and thereby projecting a positive role model image. The program also provides the parent with the opportunity to interact in positive ways instead of complaining about her surroundings.

Louisville, Kentucky-based Dismas Charities, Inc. is one of the nation's largest nonprofit social service agencies specializing in community corrections. Dismas has programs in Georgia, Texas, Florida, Nevada, New Mexico, and California. The Owensboro program is a 100-bed, all female, minimum-security center. The typical resident is twenty-five to thirty-two years old; divorced; the mother of two to three children; has a tenth-grade education; was living with her mother when arrested on drug-related charges; and has a history of physical, emotional, or sexual abuse by her husband, boyfriend, or parents. The facility is approximately 40 percent white with the remainder made up of minorities.

The Parenting Program

The Parenting Program, a concept which focuses simultaneously on the needs of both parent and child, offers residents a practical and realistic means by which they can become effective and nurturing parents. As residents begin to perceive themselves as capable parents, they gain self-confidence which contributes significantly to their self-esteem.

The four focuses of the parenting initiative are (1) a basic eight-week parenting course, (2) individual parenting sessions, (3) small focus groups, and (4) Camp Dismas. The basic parenting program is offered several times a year at the Dismas facility to any female resident of the facility who qualifies by meeting very specific criteria.

The individual parenting sessions enable residents to request an appointment with the parenting program director to discuss personal issues and receive support and guidance in meeting particular challenges. Small groups are formed to address specific topics according to the interest and concerns of the residents.

During Camp Dismas, where transportation and housing are furnished by the Dismas organization, activities for the children and mothers encourage and stimulate conversation about deep-rooted family issues. Activities are considered a critical part of the bonding process between the mother and child. The goals of Camp Dismas also include:

- Providing an environment where incarcerated mothers and their children may strengthen their relationship in a focused one-on-one setting

- Emphasizing the importance of the women's impact as parents

- Addressing the emotional needs of both mother and child by providing an opportunity to maintain their mother-child bond

- Providing reassurance to the children that their mothers are living in a safe and humane environment

- Focusing the attention of incarcerated mothers on their children in anticipation of reentering their families

- Providing opportunities for mothers to practice new parenting attitudes and skills under the guidance of a skilled facilitator

- Assisting the mothers' re-adjustment to spending extended time periods with their children

- Providing mothers with an opportunity for self-evaluation to identify remaining concerns to be addressed in the Dismas Parenting Program

Stepping into the permanent role as a mother and not being relegated to being an occasional "visitor" who darts in, makes things "all better" and leaves again, is paramount among the goals established for every Camp Dismas participant.

Above all else during this period, mothers must remember and exercise the various aspects of restraint taught during the camp and in other areas covered in the parenting program. Mothers must understand clearly the value of compliance with their parole stipulations, so as not to be reincarcerated on further charges—if not for themselves then for the welfare of the child. The children of "graduates" must continue to work improving their relationship with their mother, offer support and try to understand Mom's "problem," whether it be drug addiction or some other issue. Parents and children alike must resolve their anger and resentment; both factors are discussed heavily during parenting sessions. If all factors are given consideration, the communication between both entities is improved and establishes a pattern for a lifetime.

Clientele

While participants are normally racially balanced, other internal research reveals the typical attendee mirrors the typical resident: low income, divorced mother of three, twenty-five to thirty-two years old, with a tenth-grade education. She was previously physically, emotionally, and sexually abused by her husband, boyfriend, or parents, was living with her mother when arrested, and was incarcerated on drug-related charges.

General Procedures

Mothers eligible to participate in Camp Dismas are notified in writing. If they intend to participate, they must notify the central monitoring office no later than five days prior to the weekend camp date. On Saturday, mothers pick up towels, washcloths, sheets, a blanket, and mattress for their child. They deliver the items, along with their own mattress, pillow, linens, and belongings, to the Dismas Charities Owensboro annex building between 11:00 AM and noon. Personal belongings are limited to night clothes, a change of clothes, and personal hygiene products.

Children arrive for camp about 2:00 PM but no later than 4:00 PM on Saturday. Any other arrival times must be approved in advance. The transporting adult must check the child in at the annex, where normal visiting procedures are followed, including inspection of person and items. The child may bring pajamas, robe, slippers, two changes of clothes, outer wear, toothbrush, a favorite (nonviolent) toy, and diapers, bottles, or other necessary care items. Other items, such as schoolwork or pictures may be brought, but must be approved specifically. Money may not be brought. Medications are not permitted except with the advance approval of a supervisor. The transporting adult must remain on the premises until the child has completed the check-in procedure. Following that, the adult must leave the grounds.

Upon arrival, the mother meets the child at the annex and is not allowed to return to the main building until Sunday afternoon. Meals are served exclusively to participants. Dinner is at 5:30 PM, breakfast at 8:30 AM, and brunch at 11:30 AM. Mothers and children must settle down in their bed areas at 10:00 PM. At that time, they may visit quietly, or watch television, unless this disturbs others. Participants begin cleanup of the facility immediately after brunch. At 2:00 PM on Sunday, the child is picked up at the annex.

If Sunday is the mother's normal visiting day and the adult transporting the child is an approved visitor and plans to visit with the mother at this time, the child may remain until the conclusion of visiting hours. Otherwise, all children are picked up promptly at 2:00 PM. Failure to comply may result in loss of future participation.

Emergency Procedures

Emergency procedures are clearly defined to provide for the safety of all participants while maintaining security within the facility. Prior to camp, all mothers must sign a waiver accepting all liability related to injuries or accidents which occur during the visit. Minor injuries requiring bandages, Tylenol, or creams may be treated by the child's mother. If a major injury occurs, a staff member accompanies the child to an appropriate facility; the child's mother contacts the legal custodian to ensure that this person meets them at the medical facility. A staff member certified in CPR remains at the main Dismas building throughout the Camp Dismas session. In the event of illness, the child will be sent home as soon as an "on call" adult can arrive.

In some instances, with prior approval, medication may be admitted into camp. Medication brought to camp is controlled by a staff member. Written instructions must be left by the transporting adult. The mother administers the medication to her child, supervised by a staff member.

Guidelines for Participation

A maximum of ten mothers may participate in any one camp session. Only mothers actively involved in the parenting program are eligible for participation.

Only one child of a participating mother may attend a particular session. Children invited to participate must be the natural, legally adopted, or stepchildren of a participating mother. Children may participate from eighteen months through seventeen years of age.

Eligibility for participation is based on the mother's degree of commitment to addressing parenting skills through the Dismas Parenting Program. Those mothers with the highest hours of involvement in the parenting program are given first priority. A mother must complete fifteen hours in the parenting program to be eligible. Hours can be achieved both through parenting classes and individual sessions with the program director, provided that mothers having a child under ten have accumulated at least ten hours in classes. For mothers whose youngest child is ten or older, at least five of these hours must be accumulated in class time.

Mothers with the highest accumulated hours receive priority until they have had an opportunity to participate with all of their eligible children. Those mothers wishing to attend consecutive camp sessions with different children must acquire five hours in parenting classes between the two camp sessions.

Mothers on medical restriction or bed rest may not participate. Mothers who have participated in a Camp Dismas session will become eligible to participate again after they have accumulated ten new hours in the parenting program; however, they must skip one camp session to allow newly eligible mothers to participate. If openings exist after new participants have been offered slots, past participants are invited to attend, with those who have accumulated the most "new" hours receiving first priority.

Policies

Each participating mother is responsible for the behavior, safety, and welfare of her child. If necessary, children may be given a "time out." Corporal punishment is prohibited. The supervising staff has the right to intervene in disciplinary matters, should they deem it necessary.

Participants are responsible for arranging the transportation to and from camp for their child. If the transporting adult wishes to remain in town during the camp, special rates may be available at certain motels. Dismas assists by providing transportation on a limited basis when necessary, which occurs most sessions. Children come from throughout the state.

Participants are responsible for adhering to all guidelines issued during the camp and for exhibiting cooperative behavior at all times. Participants' behavior, language and conversation must be appropriate for the presence of children. Any problematic behavior on the part of the mother could result in dismissal from the camp, and further disciplinary action.

Each mother must make arrangements for an "on call" adult to be available to pick up her child early in the event of illness or other unforeseen problems. Mothers are responsible for confirming their camp reservation at least five days prior to the camp date. Notice of cancellation must be given as soon as possible. Failure to give these notices can result in loss of eligibility. Mothers agree to refuse all other visits during camp.

Any mothers with weekend jobs must make arrangements in advance through their counselor to be excused from work, and/or to obtain coverage of their duties. Mothers are responsible for cleaning up at the conclusion of camp, and for laundering and returning all bedding items and linens.

Mothers must meet with the parenting program director for a follow-up session and agree to serve on a planning committee for future camp sessions. Mothers pay $2.00 per meal for the cost of their child's dinner and lunch. There is no breakfast charge.

A staff member will be present at all times to supervise Camp Dismas. Whenever possible, this will be the parenting program director. Community volunteers and Dismas residents serving on the camp committee also may assist.

General Policies

A committee comprised of at least three parenting program participants and led by the parenting director shall be responsible for organizing camp arrangements and activities, and for assisting with activities during the camp. Five program credit hours can be earned in this capacity. Dismas residents not participating in the camp are prohibited from the areas designated for camp activities.

Funding

The program has been funded for the past two years by a $30,000 grant through the Kentucky Justice Cabinet. An additional $10,000 comes from private sources, including the Owensboro Catholic Diocese, area banks, and the Owensboro Junior League. Because of Camp Dismas' success, permanent funding is now being sought.

Case Studies

The truly punishing aspect of incarceration for females can be the painful reality of being torn away from their children. Despite the fact that these women have broken a law, most are mothers, and their children suffer dire consequences for the "sins of their mothers." Specifically, the children often voice their concerns over embarrassment from their peers while lacking the skills required to deal with the trauma. Additionally, because their mothers are incarcerated, they have no one to talk with about daily events. They suffer grief while lacking a guiding force to help them deal with these feelings, and because they do not know when their mother will return, they are very insecure.

Alice: A Case Study

Alice was sent to prison at age forty-five as a result of four drug possession charges. Her criminal history spanned eleven years, and included arrests for disorderly conduct, prostitution, shoplifting, carrying a concealed deadly weapon, and trafficking in a controlled substance. At the time of her arrest, Alice was unemployed and her only source of income was the $196 in AFDC and $283 in food stamps that she was receiving monthly for her sole remaining dependent child. She had no particular job skills.

The sixth of ten children, Alice was reared by her parents for only a few years, until her father was sent to prison and she was sent to live with her grandmother. At the age of nine, she was shifted again, to live with an aunt and uncle. Alice reported that this was a good home environment; however, she quit attending school after the ninth grade and moved out on her own when she was sixteen years old. At this same age, Alice bore her first child. In the course of her relationship with the child's father, Alice had two more children in a two-year span, giving her three children by the age of eighteen. At twenty-five, she married her present husband and her fourth child was born two years later. Her last son, born five years later, was fathered by another man, now deceased. After twelve years of marriage, Alice and her husband separated, but they never divorced. Both the man who fathered her first three children and her husband were co-defendants in her drug possession case, as was her oldest daughter. One of her brothers already was serving time in prison. Prison became a family affair.

Entering the prison system at a more advanced age, Alice already had finished raising her four older children who had moved out on their own. Her youngest child, Tito, was not so lucky. At the vulnerable age of thirteen, both his mother and his stepfather were taken away from him. Tito's maternal aunt assumed responsibility for his care. This was a monumental change in his life.

Karen: A Case Study

Karen, thirty-six, currently is serving an eight-year sentence for trafficking in a controlled substance. Soft spoken and polite, she is an attractive woman, with striking green eyes. The eldest of three girls, Karen had a traumatic childhood. Her father, who never married her mother, left the family when she was three, and there ended any role in his daughter's life. Although her records indicate that she was abused as a child, Karen ironically reports a "happy" childhood. As a teenager, Karen was shot in the neck by her stepfather, who killed her mother in the same incident. She began using alcohol shortly after this tragic event, and began using other drugs by the age of eighteen. Karen did manage to complete her high school education. School records show that she was an average student and was regularly involved in sports.

Karen's first arrest came at age nineteen for shoplifting. She was given twelve months probation. For several years she worked at various jobs, including being a waitress, factory worker, model, receptionist, and cashier/bookkeeper. She received vocational training in commercial foods, and a certificate in word processing. At twenty-nine, she married, and her son and daughter were born in the first three years. At this time, Karen was arrested for possession of narcotics. She received a three-year sentence but was shock probated. The following year, her marriage ended. Karen cited her husband's jealousy as the reason for her divorce. Two years later, she attempted suicide, but was stopped by a friend. She violated her probation when she was convicted of trafficking in a controlled substance, leading to her current incarceration.

During her history of substance abuse, which included opiates, alcohol, and marijuana, Karen underwent five treatment programs. She also received extensive counseling due to emotional problems arising from witnessing her mother's violent death. She has been diagnosed as having major recurrent depression, post traumatic stress disorder, polysubstance dependency, and a personality disorder. When she began serving her prison sentence, she left behind her son, A. J., six, and her daughter Keisha, who was eight. The children were moved to another city to live with their father.

Camp Dismas Intervenes

These two moms became devoted participants in the parenting program offered at Dismas Charities Owensboro. Both missed their children tremendously and grieved over the pain they had created for them. Alice faithfully attended every program pertaining to her parenting role, and continued to focus on the welfare of her son. When Camp Dismas was inaugurated, she became a dedicated participant. The opportunity to spend special time with her son was truly a treasured event for Alice, and she participated every chance she got. During the camps, Alice could maintain her bond and share some meaningful time with her son. She supported this venture thoroughly, not only by using it to her own benefit, but also by serving as a camp committee member even when her own son could not attend.

Alice had a strong sense of family and commitment, and was old-fashioned in her parenting expectations. She commanded respect from her children, and they gave it. She was appalled if she ever witnessed an incident in which a child was disrespectful. For Alice, parenting her last child was her first priority. Having already raised four now-grown children, she worked at trying new approaches and skills learned in the 100 hours of parenting classes she attended. Her son attended Camp Dismas twice.

When Tito's mother left, his maternal aunt and a number of her foster children moved into his home. Tito had many adjustments to make while sharing his formerly quiet home with various strange children of all ages. Many of these children were taken from abusive homes and were difficult to manage. His mother met individually with the parenting counselor to address various problems and frustrations Tito was encountering at home. At one point, after conferring with the counselor, Alice decided to make a needed change in Tito's living arrangements. She asked her sister to move out and arranged for her twenty-seven-year-old son to move in and take care of his younger brother. This created a much healthier environment and relieved Tito from what had become chaotic and stressful surroundings.

Alice received parole after serving eighteen months of her sentence and was released last December. She is now working and living with her family in Louisville. Upon her release, Alice explained that Camp Dismas was instrumental in helping her establish and maintain a heretofore unexperienced closeness with Tito. She added that the encounters allowed her to fine tune her parenting skills by helping him deal with frustrations in his life, including peer pressure. Had she not been able to experience Camp Dismas, Alice said she would not have been able to keep that closeness, establish an open dialog, or reassure him that he was making the right decisions, that his mother was doing well and that, simply put, "everything would be okay."

Karen very rarely saw her children during her imprisonment. She did not receive furloughs for many months, so she was unable to visit home. Her children were in the care of her ex-husband, who lived two hours away and would not take a full day out of his weekends to bring the children for a visit. Further, Karen had no parents who might commit to take on this task.

When Dismas offered to transport children to and from the facility for a special "reunion" of families for the Easter holiday, Karen was ecstatic. For the first time in several months, she could see and hold her children. On that day, her children never left her side. Tears, restrained until the children were out of sight, streamed down her cheeks as she watched the bus carry them away. Karen emerged from Camp Dismas with a new focus on her role as a mother, and a renewed effort to strengthen herself in every way to become the mother her children needed. With an increased commitment, she has continued attending substance abuse, parenting education, and personal growth groups. When Dismas Charities Owensboro began to transport children to Camp Dismas with their van, Karen signed her children up for every possible camp. She has now had several opportunities to re-bond with her children, to show her concern for them, and to maintain her place in their lives. She awaits the day she can take them home.

Karen met with the parole board in October 1995. She was granted an early release. If she had been required to serve her full term, she would have remained imprisoned until the year 2001.

Program Evaluation

In two separate surveys, Camp Dismas was rated outstanding by participating residents. Specifically, from December 1994 to January 1995, the enrollees rated the program 4.34 on a maximum scale of 5. In another survey in late 1994, the program received perfect score ratings by all participants.

When asked to complete a questionnaire on the overall worth of the parenting program, of which Camp Dismas is an integral part, residents listed the following changes in their thinking and actions: understanding my child's behavior; talking to my children; knowing how to discipline my children and how to reward my child for small things; raising my next child; parenting, discipline, and praise; knowing how to talk effectively with my children about their problems; knowing how to correctly treat good and bad behavior; understanding time out and role reversal; not feeding into bad behavior; talking on eye level with children; spending more time with my child; learning how to be my child's friend; getting back in touch with my teen after being in here.

In addition, Dismas Charities Owensboro presently has a contract with a Kentucky Wesleyan College professor who has developed pre- and post-testing for those going into or coming out of the Parenting Program. While his tracking research is unfinished, early trends indicate the program is a success with changes in attitudes of residents dealing with their children. Preliminary information shows that of fifty-one randomly selected residents released in one year, only four, or 7.84 percent, have been reincarcerated. The state average is 23.9 percent.

One aspect of the Dismas Owensboro program which deals a heavy dose of reality is its vocational counseling. Often, counselors find, many of the women have a predetermined prescription for success that they want to follow once released, only to find later that it was not the best course of action. Consequently, counselors test them to determine their skills and other strengths and weaknesses. In the end, the women learn what they are realistically capable of doing and qualified to do rather than what they want to do but do not possess the skills to achieve.

The Future

Dismas Charities Owensboro Director William "Gus" Gesser, the creator of Camp Dismas, has an extensive background in law enforcement, having retired as Chief of the seventy-person Patrol Division of the Owensboro Police Department. Gesser's involvement with the department often included improving interpersonal skills between the department and the community, a quality he continues to use today. Included in his law enforcement efforts are lobbying for domestic violence legislation, starting the department's Crime Prevention and Officer Friendly programs, the latter a concept where police officers become more personable, especially in one-on-one contacts with children of the community. That same "bridge-building" is what has driven Gesser to add an additional element to his parenting program—an adult D.A.R.E. initiative.

D.A.R.E., an acronym for Drug Abuse Resistance Education, directly involved residents and their children with uniformed Owensboro law enforcement officers where no positive contact with police had ever existed. The concept has the enthusiastic endorsement of the Owensboro Police Department.

Another unique initiative at Dismas Charities Owensboro is Girl Scouts Beyond Bars (see Chapter 5), a program begun by the National Institute of Justice designed to have children of residents join the organization to promote an understanding of how to get along with their peers, learn self-discipline, and engage in productive activities. The Owensboro Dismas facility periodically hosts meetings of the troop, and mothers of the children are encouraged to take an active part.

Summary

Camp Dismas has been operational since September 1993 and has served over sixty-five incarcerated mothers and their children. An additional fifty-five residents also have been involved in the camps by serving on committees. Most of the committee members have been mothers whose children were unable to attend camp, yet the mother still benefitted by working with other children and interacting with them in a positive role.

This valuable time allowed for incarcerated mothers to act in their parenting roles served several unmet and critical needs. Being with her children reminded the mother of the important role she needs to resume upon release. This may have helped her remain focused on doing all she could to better herself and improve her skills before returning home. Such personal accountability often could be forgotten in the routines of an institutional setting. During Camp Dismas, mothers often became aware of previously unknown problems and issues. In some instances, mothers were alerted to abusive or neglectful situations. Mothers also identified and began to use available resources to address issues that they realized they were inadequately prepared to handle. For instance, they learned how to help their child process angry feelings or how to effectively handle a hyperactive child.

Although some mothers may visit their children during furloughs, Camp Dismas provides a totally different environment. While on furlough visits, the mother has many people making demands on her time and attention, children share their time with many other family members and friends, and mothers often report that these visits actually have had a negative effect on the parent-child relationship. The opportunity for a mother and child to spend an extended time period together, uninterrupted, allows both to discuss important concerns, to share honest feelings, to reestablish their bonds, and to enjoy each other. It is a chance to create positive happy memories, which are often sadly lacking. This is a very reassuring experience for children who may feel abandoned, and for mothers who are anxious and often grieving over the separation.

Dear Mom,

I love you. I miss you too. I hope you can come home soon.

I had fun at camp with you. I was scared to come but it was fun. If you don't come home soon can I come up there with you again. I hope so. Will you tell them people thanks for me. They were nice not like the T.V.

Mom I got to go to bed. I love you. I miss you a bunch.

Love, your son

(Letter written by a child following his stay at Camp Dismas.)

The Mother Offspring Life Development Program

13

Mary Alley

Coordinator

Mother Offspring Life Development Program, Nebraska Center for Women, York, Nebraska

Introduction

The Mother Offspring Life Development (MOLD) Program was started in 1974 at the Nebraska Center for Women, located in a rural setting outside the town of York. Developed by facility administrators seeking to preserve the bond between inmate mothers and their children, the program was funded initially by federal grant money. After this grant, the Nebraska Department of Corrections assumed financial responsibility for the program.

The MOLD Program was initiated when the population at the Nebraska Center for Women (NCW) was fewer than fifty women. As the population increased, the MOLD Program evolved. The current population is approximately 150 inmates.

The program has been studied by state judges and included in parole and rehabilitation plans for many of the inmate mothers sentenced here. The MOLD instructor works closely with the Department of Social Services, providing the supervised visits necessary for mother-child reunification. With parenting as the focus, the MOLD Program has expanded the number of classes available to all of the inmates; the MOLD instructor teaches these additional classes on a rotating basis. Our ultimate expansion was the 1994 addition of the nursery, which was modeled after the nursery in Bedford Hills, New York (see Chapter 7). The nursery is in a separate building but remains closely connected to the original program.

The 1974 grant provided a building of 853 square feet. The grant included funding for furniture, playground equipment, educational materials, a stove, a refrigerator, and a dishwasher. Ample room allows for a large play area, as well as classroom space. The building is situated on the outer edge of the main prison yard, enabling mothers and children to play in an area not authorized for the general population. Playground equipment and a small playhouse, constructed by inmates at the men's facility, establish the parklike atmosphere surrounding the MOLD building. A small storage shed houses bicycles, tricycles, Hot Wheels™, sleds, and other play equipment.

Community Support

York General Hospital provides a valuable resource for the Nebraska Center for Women. In addition to their working closely with MOLD on policy development, York General Hospital has a representative on MOLD's Community Advisory Board.

All of MOLD's toys, books, and games either have been purchased with donated funds or donated directly to Nebraska Center for Women. Donated items arrive regularly for both the MOLD and nursery programs, sent by any of the many resources interested in our programs. These resources include church groups, teacher's associations, and business organizations, among others. After the cost of salaries and building maintenance, the programs run almost exclusively on donated funds. Donations of money and materials are encouraged through public speaking and tours given by the MOLD and nursery instructors, the administrative assistants, and the warden.

Orientation

All new inmates participate in an orientation program led by the MOLD instructor, informing them of the classes available as well as the child visiting policy. The MOLD instructor also talks with new inmates about writing to their children, stressing that a letter provides children with tangible evidence that their mother is thinking of them. A handout provides ideas about reassuring statements mothers may wish to write to their children. Another handout for new inmates, "Talking to Your Child About Prison," is accompanied by discussion of how lying may affect the child, the caregiver, and the inmate. Additional materials are available to mothers in the MOLD area.

Educational Component

The position of MOLD instructor traditionally has been held by a certified teacher, although teachers have been hired with various backgrounds in education. The position's responsibilities include making the numerous classes available to inmates on a rotating basis, teaching the classes, and coordinating the children's visits on grounds. Before the nursery instructor was hired, the MOLD instructor also taught and coached the pregnant inmates in the Lamaze Method of Childbirth.

Classes

Classes available to all of the inmates at the Nebraska Center for Women now include:

Parenting I

The *Active Parenting Program* by Dr. Michael Popkins is used for this eight- to ten-session course. This video-based program discusses instilling responsibility and cooperation in children, as well as building self-esteem and developing communication skills. This course focuses on the parenting of two to twelve-year-olds.

Parenting II

Active Parenting for Teens is built on the foundations of the Parenting I course. The focus is on parenting adolescents. A unit on sex and drugs has been added to the original curriculum.

In addition to the Active Parenting Program, parts of another parenting program, *Parenting from a Distance*, are used. These lessons are incorporated into the course where most appropriate for our population of mothers.

Understanding Relationships

Discussion of and practice with communication skills may be used for improving all relationships, including those with our partners, parents, and children. Videos by Leo Buscaglia and John Bradshaw, two modern experts on relationships, are an integral part of this course.

Money Management

Basic skills in budgeting, using checking accounts, setting financial goals, and keeping household expense records are taught and practiced in this course.

Personal Growth and Development

Students examine their personal goals and values, with respect to all areas of their lives. Ways to build self-esteem, solve problems, manage stress, and care for one's self are studied.

Human Sexuality and How to Tell Your Child about Sex

After learning facts about human sexuality, inmate discussions focus on ways to discuss sexuality at different stages of childhood. Information about birth control and sexually transmitted diseases are included in the curriculum.

Social and Emotional Growth and Development

This course studies the stages of personality, communication, and social skills development. Outside influences, parenting skills, and building children's self-esteem are examined. Inmate students learn what children may be capable of at each stage of their growth.

Physical Growth and Development

All of the aspects examined in Social and Emotional Growth and Development are studied with emphasis on children's developing physical capabilities.

CPR/First Aid

Available to all inmates, cardiopulmonary resuscitation/First Aid is required of participants in the nursery program. Students must complete both written and practical exams in adult, infant, and child CPR, rescue breathing, and first aid procedures. Certification is given through the Lancaster County Red Cross.

Children with Special Needs

Many speakers from the community address such topics as Fetal Alcohol Syndrome, learning disabilities, behavioral impairments, and emotional and physical disabilities. Resources that provide support are introduced, and techniques for parenting children with special needs are discussed and practiced.

Courses for Pregnant Inmates

Women admitted to the Nebraska Center for Women while pregnant have the help and support of both the MOLD and nursery instructors. The entire staff works to ensure pregnant inmates receive adequate prenatal care. Pregnant inmates have access to the following classes:

Creating a Healthy Child

This course provides information about children's health needs prior to conception and birth. Each trimester of pregnancy is addressed. Good nutrition and health are encouraged throughout pregnancy, as are visits to the doctor. The course explains what information tests and examinations may reveal, and health risks. The mother-to-be is introduced to birthing procedures, the Lamaze Method of Childbirth, and breast-feeding.

Infant Growth and Development

In this course, pregnant inmates study the physical and emotional development of babies in their first year of life. Nutrition, daily care, clothing, self-esteem, and parenting are some of the topics covered.

Lamaze Method of Childbirth

A series of breathing exercises is taught to help minimize pain, increase the effectiveness of contractions, and relax mothers in labor. Women learn what to expect at each stage of labor. Hospital and individual doctor's procedures are discussed before an inmate goes to York General Hospital for delivery.

Child Visits

Inmate mothers interested in on-grounds child visits are required to take a class entitled "New Mother's Orientation." Interested inmates must pass a test covering all the rules and regulations of the program. Women who become involved also must enroll in at least one other MOLD Program class.

An inmate mother who qualifies may have her child stay with her up to five nights per month. If she has more than one child, the five nights must be divided among all her children. The policy of having each child visit separately evolved through staff observations that each child needs 100 percent of the mother's attention during a visit. Even so, children who live more than 200 miles away from the Nebraska Center for Women may visit in pairs; and their visits may be extended to ten days, but this only may occur once each quarter.

Daytime-only visits are an option for those mothers and children for whom overnight visits are precluded. Up to five daytime visits may be planned for mothers whose children do not meet the age requirements for overnight visits, whose visits require supervision, or who wish to have more than one child visiting at the same time. Day visits usually are scheduled for a specific day of the week and are held in the MOLD area.

Eligibility for Child Visits

An inmate mother is eligible for child visits when she has been in general population for thirty days. Permission, and verification of transportation, must be received by the child's guardian or social services caseworker before the child may come on grounds. A medical treatment permission form must be received before the child is allowed on grounds. Inmate mothers must plan each visit with the MOLD instructor and pay for meals and any special items fifteen days before the visit.

The inmate mother must make arrangements to be away from her assigned work area for the duration of the visit. A contract verifying the visit time, payment made, and rules must be signed by the inmate mother, MOLD instructor, educational/vocational coordinator, security, unit management, medical, and primary work supervisor.

The inmate mother requesting a visit must have a good institutional conduct record. Any visit can be canceled or denied at the discretion of the Nebraska Center for Women. All prerequisite classes must have been completed by the inmate mother before her child may visit.

On-grounds overnight visits may be made by boys ages one through eight, and girls ages one through twelve. These visits occur in designated MOLD rooms, in the halls, or in the nursery area. Assignments are made by the MOLD instructor.

Day visits in the MOLD area, under the supervision of the MOLD instructor, may be made by children between one month and sixteen years of age. These visits are planned by the mother in the same fashion as overnight visits.

Visits by children with medical conditions may be approved at the discretion of the medical department. Children with a chronic medical condition, such as asthma or hyperactivity, may come on-grounds after a letter of permission is received from their physician. Medication for chronic illnesses may come on grounds and be kept in the medical department, also accompanied by a complete letter of explanation from the child's doctor. No child requiring antibiotics for an acute illness is allowed on grounds.

Transportation must be arranged in advance of a child's visit. The family must approve any transporter. Children may leave the Nebraska Center for Women only with a driver whose name appears on the verifying forms.

During the child's visit, the mother must obey all Nebraska Center for Women rules and must stay with her child at all times. The child also must stay in assigned areas and obey the mother. No physical discipline is allowed while the child is on grounds. Mothers needing alternative methods of discipline may consult with the MOLD instructor. One hour of free time also is provided for the mother by the MOLD instructor.

Upon signing the child-visit contract, the mother will pay $1.20 per day for her child's meals. During visits, meals are eaten in the cafeteria at designated times before the general population, when the cafeteria atmosphere is more peaceful.

A few days before visits occur, the mother may check out toys, books, and games for her child. Items checked out are taken to the room where the visit is designated to occur and are returned after the visit.

Special items may be purchased to make while the child is on grounds. Items such as cookie dough, Rice Krispies bars, popcorn balls, and birthday cakes may be made by the mothers. These items are purchased by the MOLD instructor and are kept in the MOLD area. Popcorn, butter, oil, and eggs are donated and are provided at no charge to the inmate. Times for play, activities, and baking in the MOLD area are arranged between the MOLD instructor and the inmate mothers.

One inmate aide is assigned to assist the MOLD instructor. The inmate aide must have a good institutional record, and her crime cannot have involved a child. The inmate aide keeps the MOLD area clean, checks out items, disinfects items as they are checked back in, washes all laundry, and helps with filing, bulletin boards, and paperwork. She must possess a high school diploma or a General Equivalency Degree. This aide often is called on to help with the children's activities and to help the mothers prepare for their visits.

Eight overnight visits may be on grounds at one time. This number may vary occasionally due to population increases. Day visits are planned by the mother. If necessary, she completes an activities sheet and provides it to the MOLD instructor. The MOLD area lends itself so well to children that "what to do" has never been a problem.

Evaluation

Evaluations are completed following each child's visit. All visit evaluations consider completing of paperwork, cooperating with the MOLD instructor and other staff, being in assigned areas, arriving for meals on time, using appropriate discipline, and gauging the mother's attitude toward her child. Day visit evaluations are based on the observations that day of the MOLD instructor. Overnight visits also are observed by unit staff; a hall report from each shift is provided to the MOLD instructor.

Visit evaluations include suggestions for improvement, possibly to include shorter future visits. Evaluations also include encouragement for specific positive behaviors displayed by the mother during the visit, or for good planning of activities. Visit evaluations are read and signed by both the inmate mother and the MOLD instructor. Completed evaluations are kept in the inmate's file and are made available to the Department of Social Services, when necessary.

Conclusion

The MOLD Program has been examined by several other states as a model visiting program. The state of Minnesota has duplicated this program successfully, and others have adopted variations of it. The Nebraska Center for Women was the first in the nation to have such an overnight visiting program. This is now the only institution in the country to have both an overnight visiting program for children and a live-in nursery program.

Insightful administration certainly has played a major role in the twenty-two-year longevity of this program. However, of greatest significance are the positive aspects this program has demonstrated for administrators, past and present. The inmate-mothers at the Nebraska Center for Women have a vested interest in maintaining this program, intact. Not only does the program allow their children and grandchildren to visit, classes and inmates' participation have provided opportunities for learning. Having children on grounds provides incentive for good inmate behaviors: the women are carefully selective about their language and topics of conversation in the presence of children.

Inmate mothers whose children do not visit the Nebraska Center for Women still take some ownership of the program through their participation in special activities. Throughout this author's years here, the inmates have been very protective of this unique program, which allows them opportunities to be "normal" while in prison.

A Cross-national Perspective on Residential Programs for Incarcerated Mothers and Their Children

14

Kelsey Kauffman

Director
Putnam County Youth Development Commission and Putnam County
Court Appointed Special Advocates Program, Greencastle, Indiana

Introduction

For more than thirty years, Sister Elaine Roulet has held a lonely torch in the United States for the right of young children to remain in the care of their incarcerated mothers. While residential prison programs for mothers and babies were being abandoned in other states during the 1950s and 1960s, Sister Elaine assiduously protected her prison nursery at New York's Bedford Hills Correctional Facility for Women (see Chapter 7). Now, as interest in the plight of "prison orphans" reawakens in this country, we have few domestic models to which we can turn for guidance and inspiration. A look beyond our own borders, though, can provide useful insights and experience, for in much of the rest of the world incarceration of parents, especially mothers, does not automatically mean separation from children.

Social scientists have paid as little serious attention to women's prisons in other nations as they have in the United States. Reports on mother-child programs in prisons at home or abroad are scarce, and longitudinal studies addressing crucial questions regarding the long-term impact of such programs on children and mothers are strikingly absent. (Such research is reportedly in progress in Germany.) In the absence of published material on mother-child programs, this chapter relies primarily on the author's own visits to women's prisons in Asia, Australia, Europe, and North and South America, especially the well-integrated series of programs at Preungesheim Prison in Frankfurt, Germany.

Conditions of incarceration vary enormously from prison to prison and nation to nation. Children who share their mother's imprisonment on different continents and in different countries may do so under markedly different circumstances. Some experience life in "village-style" institutions in which adults and children, though restricted to a general area, have considerable freedom of movement and self-management. Other children are confined with their mothers in traditional cell blocks. Some become the catalyst for their mother's release into community-based programs. A few find themselves in prison settings specifically designed for mothers and children. In this chapter, we shall consider each of these models, in turn.

Village-style Institutions

Minimally secure prisons in developing countries sometimes take on the ambiance of a small village. Inmates' families may have relatively unrestricted access, with a conjugal visitation routine, and family members of varying ages residing within the institution. Amenities may be sparse; indeed, inmates' families may be saddled with the burden of providing food, bed, and clothing for their incarcerated loved ones. On the other hand, close family ties are maintained and resident children at least lack little in the way of adult attention. The village-style prison reflects a belief in the inviolability of family ties, regardless of criminal sanction. With freewheeling management, the village-style prison is unlikely to serve as a model for programs in the United States, although it may prompt questions about the wisdom of penal practices that divide rather than unite families.

Traditional Prisons

In the village-style prison, the presence of children seems unremarkable. Far more incongruous, at least to the outside observer, is the discovery of young children living amid the dreary expanses and regimented lifebeat of the traditional Western prison. New York's Bedford Hills is just such an institution: an old-style maximum-security prison housing approximately 750 women—and twenty-five pampered babies (see Chapter 7). The babies spend their evenings and nights with their mothers in an old wing of the prison and their days in the prison nursery, while their mothers work within the institution and take parenting classes. Babies can remain at Bedford Hills until they are one year old, with extensions possible if the mother's release date is within another six months. Most mothers in the program leave the institution at the same time as their children, although women with lengthy sentences and, thus, little prospect of being the permanent custodial parent, still may keep their infants until their first birthday. Under the determined leadership of Sister Elaine, the prison nursery has managed to thrive for decades despite its barren environs and periods of official hostility.

Nurseries exist under less daunting circumstances within the context of traditional prisons in other nations. The sizable women's prison just outside Buenos Aires, Argentina, for example, has an airy, dormitory-style wing for mothers and children up to age two. Mothers incarcerated in Queensland, Australia, may keep dependent children of any age with them, although in practice only the very young remain (and even they are more commonly found with their mothers in community-based programs). Three women's prisons in England have mother-baby units, as do prisons in Germany, France, Spain, and Austria. A comparison of the mother-baby unit at London's Holloway prison with the nursery at Bedford Hills may be instructive.

Like Bedford Hills, Holloway is a large, high-security women's prison serving a major metropolitan area. Within the prison is a small unit for mothers who are permitted to keep their babies until they are nine months old (mothers with release dates soon after their infant reaches that age can be transferred to the prison in York, England, where children up to eighteen months old are permitted).

Unlike Bedford Hills, the mother-baby unit at Holloway exists not because of the efforts of a single charismatic leader, but rather through official policy that emphasizes mother-child bonding. Not surprisingly, the program is better funded and operates under more favorable conditions. The mother-child unit is cheerful, with individual rooms for each mother and her child, a playroom, visiting room, and laundry. Mothers are expected to maintain the unit, and to attend classes with the general prison population during the day, taking their babies with them. Contact with extended family is encouraged, especially on Sundays when all-day visitation is permitted in the gym with lunch provided and many activities for the children including a "bouncy castle." In a further effort to maintain family ties, interprison visits are permitted at Holloway by fathers incarcerated elsewhere.

Pregnant inmates at Holloway live in their own unit at the prison awaiting delivery. If they want to keep their child with them after birth, they can apply to a committee consisting of the director, a staff member from the mother-child unit, a staff representative from the pregnancy unit, a member of the internal probation staff, and a social worker from outside the institution. Although mothers are not guaranteed a spot on the unit, the vast majority are accepted. As at Bedford Hills, mothers with lengthy sentences are not barred from participating even though their children will be required to leave the institution many years before the mother will do so. Newly sentenced mothers with babies outside the prison also may apply, although only after the mother has completed drug detoxification.

Despite different levels of funding, amenities, and official support, staff at both Holloway and Bedford Hills report very high motivation among participating mothers, and correspondingly low incidence of disciplinary problems—with a virtual absence of maternal abuse or neglect. Although reliable statistics do not exist, staff perceive favorable recidivism rates among those women released with their children in their arms.

Community-based Programs

As drug addiction and incarceration rates for women soar in the United States, whatever reluctance may have existed about sending mothers of young children to prison appears to have been lost.[1] These inhibitions remain in other cultures where women may be perceived as less of a threat, and greater emphasis is placed on the continuity of mother-child relationships. In Columbia, expectant mothers are reportedly released from prison during the seventh month of their pregnancy. Though in theory mothers are to return when their infants are two months old, in practice few do (Goetting, as reported in Boudouris 1996). In Queensland, Australia, mothers are placed with children in community correction programs whenever possible (when not possible, as noted above, the child may reside in the women's prison). Sweden has pioneered such approaches as community corrections and the day prison.

An experimental community program for convicted mothers was launched in California during the late 1970s. Legislation mandating expansion of the program was passed in the mid-1980s. Women convicted of nonviolent offenses who have children up to age six can reside with their children in one of seven community facilities in the state. Mothers are required to work or attend school, to participate in parenting classes and substance-abuse counseling, and to perform community service. The Family Unity Demonstration Project Act, passed by Congress in 1994 (but as yet, unfunded), owes much in its inception to the Mother-Infant Care Program in California.

The first three models discussed seek to maintain parent-child relations within quite different settings. In the village-style prison, children seem a natural if peripheral part of the scene. Prison life accommodates them but is not organized around them. In writing about liberal visitation policies in Central and South America, Goetting observed, "Family visitation is not something which the establishment uses to stimulate incentive for 'good behavior' or yields to under pressures of 'human rights.' Instead, it is viewed as a manifestation of life's natural order not to be interfered with because of incarceration" (Boudouris 1996).

Children may be present on prison grounds but not because authorities hope that inmates thereby may become better parents or be more likely to give up their criminal lifestyles. Nor are they present because of a belief in the primacy of the nuclear (as opposed to extended) family or the centrality of mother-child bonding.

Official rationales for mother-child units within the confines of traditional prisons may be very different. They often exist in cultures where neither extended families nor small, close-knit communities can be relied upon to raise children in the absence of their parents. Appropriate mother-child bonding is seen under these circumstances as central to healthy development of the child as well as a major mooring in the mother's life. Moreover, when parenting skills are seriously lacking (as they often appear to be for women who were themselves raised largely on the streets), a year of supervised parenting may seem advantageous for both mother and child. Because traditional prisons have high security, even mothers with violent records and long sentences can apply to keep their children through infancy. On the other hand, because the traditional prison is viewed as an inappropriate environment for children old enough to comprehend where they are, children usually are not allowed to remain beyond infancy.

Community-based programs also focus on the mother-child relationship, but do so in a more natural setting. Mothers commonly are accepted into such programs only when they have young children who will not reach school age prior to the expiration of their mother's sentence. The expectation is that the mother and child will remain in the program until the mother has finished serving her sentence, so there will be no period of separation after joining the program. These programs typically serve a limited clientele—mothers with very young children who have short sentences and who pose little security threat.

Mother-child Centered Approach

A fourth model seeks to respond to the variable and changing needs of convicted mothers and their children, and does so by combining elements from each of the first three models. The combination of programs for mothers and children at Preungesheim Prison in Germany exemplifies this approach.

The prison, located in Frankfurt, dates back more than a century. The old semicircular, radiating cellblocks are gradually being torn down and replaced with modern units having individual rooms and group lounges. Sentenced women can enroll in trade courses or work in a laundry serving all prisons in the German state of South Hessen. Reflecting Frankfurt's position as the international gateway to Germany, half of the several hundred inmates at Preungesheim are in prison for drug trafficking; a sizable minority are women from third-world countries who have been arrested as drug couriers.

Just inside the large outer wall that surrounds the prison is the "closed" Mutter-Kind-Heim or Mother-Child House. It is called a "closed" house because the mothers in it are deemed security risks (often due to their pretrial or foreign national status), and, thus, are not allowed to leave the institution. At the time of this author's visit in Spring, 1993, five women and their babies were in the unit—three from South America, one from the United States, and one from Ghana. Each woman and her child occupy a spacious room (nearly sixteen square meters), with a common kitchen, dining area, lounge, and small courtyard/play area. Babies remain with their mothers during the day; older children up to age three leave the grounds to go to the "open house" or to attend preschool.

Women who are not considered to be security risks are eligible to move to the "open" Mutter-Kind-Heim with their preschool-age children. The large wall that surrounds Preungesheim Prison has been indented on one side and in that space nestles the "open house," facing out toward the surrounding neighborhood rather than back toward the prison grounds. The "house" is a modern two-story building fronted by a wooden fence. Entrance to the building is through a security control room. On the downstairs level are staff offices and pleasant communal living, eating, and play areas that look out through large windows onto an attractive sunken courtyard complete with sandbox, tricycles, and sturdy playground equipment. Upstairs are individual rooms (approximately ten feet by fifteen feet) for up to eighteen mothers and their children.

During the daytime, mothers work in the house or at jobs in the community while certified child-care workers mind their children. Older children attend the neighborhood preschool while younger ones play at the house or local playground with their child workers. All the children take frequent supervised trips to visit the zoo, hike in the woods, or explore the surrounding community. When the mothers return to the unit after work, they resume responsibility for their children. Once household chores are completed, mothers are free to take their children out into the community up to thirty hours per week for shopping trips, doctor and dentist appointments, or visits to the local playground. (As is the custom in Germany, they even may take their children to the local pub!) A mother also may leave the unit for periods of time without her child but only after signing a form stating that another mother is caring for her child in her absence.

School-age children are not permitted to remain at the Mutter-Kind House. Yet, those who live in Frankfurt still need not be deprived of their mothers. On the assumption that parenting and housework is labor as valuable as working in a store or fast-food establishment, a mother who is eligible for work release may leave the prison daily to work for her own family outside the institution. She arises at the prison at 5:00AM, early enough to take public transportation to her children's home or apartment and roust them out of bed for school. Once the children are fed, clothed, and out the door, she is responsible for housework, shopping, and general household management. Whenever she must leave the house for more than an hour, she is required to call the prison. When her children return from school, she is responsible for their supervision, doctor's appointments, cooking, homework, and all the myriad tasks that consume a parent's time and energy. Once her children are tucked into bed, she leaves them in the care of another adult family member or caretaker, and returns to the prison to sleep.

Mothers who want to live in the open house or care for their children in the community must, of course, first be considered low-security risks. Those who are believed to have active drug habits are not accepted, and all women in the program are subject to monthly drug testing administered on randomly selected days. In the program's first decade, only one woman absconded (leaving her child behind), and only one had her child taken away for neglect or abuse. Beyond those two cases, staff report an absence of major disciplinary problems.

The progression of programs for mothers at Preungesheim—the closed house, open house, and home child care programs—combine elements of the three other types of programs discussed earlier. The closed house, like the prison nurseries at Bedford Hills and Holloway, is situated within the confines of a traditional prison. It serves to keep very young children with mothers who must remain in a secure facility. The open house has some of the same atmosphere as the village-style prison with its relaxed environment, communal living, and shared child raising. Both the open house and the home child care program share characteristics of community-based programs with participation by mothers in the outside work force and partial integration of mother and child into the surrounding neighborhood. Staff at the open house expressed interest in expanding their program to include a final period of supervised living in the community prior to completion of the mother's sentence.

The programs at Preungesheim are rooted in a belief in the centrality of the mother-child relationship to the well-being of the child. The combination of programs allows mothers the flexibility to nurture that relationship under the least-restrictive circumstances in each case. Mothers with poor security clearances are not automatically excluded as they must be in community-based programs. By the same token, unlike prison nurseries at other traditional prisons, the majority of mothers who are deemed good security risks can live with their children under controlled conditions that at least approximate those in the free world. And, with the option of home child care, the relationship between mother and child need not be attenuated solely because the child has reached school age.

Conclusion

Sixty thousand women are currently in state or federal prisons in the United States, triple the number a decade ago. When these women enter prison, 6 percent are pregnant; two out of three leave children under eighteen behind them. Despite their incarceration, most of these mothers regain legal custody of their children; on their release, many will resume their role as primary custodial parent.

Children left behind by incarcerated parents are among the most "at risk" of any in our society. They often were conceived unintentionally, exposed to drugs and alcohol prenatally, born prematurely, and/or subsequently subjected to considerable neglect and deprivation. During their mother's incarceration, they may change foster homes or placement with relatives frequently, visit their mothers only sporadically (half will never see their mothers at all), and bear considerable stigma of having an incarcerated parent. (Sister Elaine has established a home for children of imprisoned mothers which she named "My Mother's House." When these children are asked where they live, they can respond without shame or dishonesty, "I live at 'my mother's house.'").

Their mothers, while incarcerated, can take educational or occupational training courses and participate in drug therapy programs. Their activities may be more highly supervised and their access to drugs more constrained that at any other point in their lives. But they are unlikely to receive much preparation or training for what may be the most important activity they will perform once they are released from prison: parenting the children they left behind.

When a mother is released from prison, she frequently is reunited with a child whose problems have been compounded during her incarceration and who is, in part, a stranger to her. As the mother-child relationship falters, so, too, may the mother's resolve to alter her own lifestyle. The cycle perpetuates itself in two senses: first with the mother's return to addiction, crime, and incarceration; second, and more devastating from a societal perspective, with the child's eventual involvement in the same destructive patterns.

Societies throughout much of the rest of the world take care to maintain the mother-child bond despite the mother's criminal conviction and incarceration. They recognize the importance of continuity to the child and the powerful incentive for change that the child presents for the mother. Some prison systems go beyond mere continuity of that relationship to use the mother's time in prison to instill parenting skills and monitor mother-child interactions.

Assumptions underlying the most structured programs for incarcerated mothers and their children are that parenting is a critical activity for society, that parenting is a learned skill, and that parenting skills can and should be taught when they are seriously lacking. The question is not whether incarcerated women should be mothers; they already are. Nor is the question whether incarcerated mothers should retain custody of their children; most already do. The question is, rather, whether time together in a highly controlled and supervised setting can benefit both mother and child and reduce the prospects of future incarceration for either or both.

Reference

Boudouris, James. 1996. *Parents in Prisons: Addressing the Needs of Families.* Lanham, Maryland: American Correctional Association.

Endnote

1. Editor's Note: In New York City, the Office of Prosecution for Special Narcotics Courts, operates the PAIR+ (Pregnant and Addicted-Mothers Intervention and Rehabilitation/Plus) program, which offers a day-treatment alternative to incarceration for nonviolent defendants who are pregnant women, mothers, and women of child bearing age (over sixteen) with a substance abuse problem. Such programs are an attempt to address the soaring incarceration rates for women.

Index

A

Admission and orientation procedures
  Camp Dismas program, 145
  MOLD (Mother Offspring Life Development)
    Program, 152
  Neil J. Houston House, Roxbury, Massachusetts,
    122–123

Admission to programs, requirements for
  Bedford Hills (New York) Correctional Facility
    Nursery program, 75–76
  Camp Dismas program, 144–145
  Florida Department of Corrections SAPPORT
    program, 11
  Girl Scouts Beyond Bars program, 40–41
  Las Comadres foster mother and birth mother
    mentoring program, 137–138
  Neil J. Houston House, Roxbury, Massachusetts,
    121–123
  NEON (Norwalk Economic Opportunity Now)
    Women's and Children's Halfway House
    (WCHH) model, 91–94
  Summit House, 108–110

Aftercare, 10

AIDS and HIV
  New York State, percentage of HIV-positive
    women inmates in, 59
  perinatally acquired, 9
  PROGRAM for female offenders, 51
  Social Justice for Women (SJW), services
    provided by, 114

Alcohol abuse (See Substance abuse)

American Correctional Association (ACA)
  policy on baby placement, xii
  policy on Female Offender Services, vii–viii

Argentina
  residential programs for mothers and children,
    160

Arizona
  Girl Scouts Beyond Bars program, 36, 44, 45

Assessments
  NEON (Norwalk Economic Opportunity Now)
    Women's and Children's Halfway House
    (WCHH) model, 92–93
  parenting skills, 29

Australia
  residential programs for mothers and children,
    160, 161

B

Babies (See Residential programs)
  low birth weight, 9

Bedford Hills Correctional Facility Children's
  Center Programs, Bedford Hills, New York, xi,
  55–86, 159, 160, 161

Behavior modification programs
  Bring It All Back Home agency (Morganton,
    North Carolina) Teaching Family Model used
    at Summit House, 101, 107

Bibliographies (See Reference materials)

Bonding between parent and child (See Early child
  development and parental bonding)

Books on tape
  Bedford Hills Children's Center program, 65

Boston, Massachusetts
  Social Justice for Women (SJW), 114

Bring It All Back Home agency, Morganton, North
  Carolina
    Teaching Family Model, 101

Budget management, 13

C

California
  Center for Children of Incarcerated Parents,
  Pasadena, 15–23

first-term for women, 2
Girl Scouts Beyond Bars, 36, 45
Las Comadres foster mother and birth mother
    mentoring program, 131–140
residential program, 162

Card Shop program
    Bedford Hills Children's Center program, 65

Caregivers, training for, 17

Case management
    NEON (Norwalk Economic Opportunity Now)
    Women's and Children's Halfway House
    (WCHH) model, 94–96

Center for Children of Incarcerated Parents,
    Pasadena, California, 2, 15–23

Child abuse
    corporal punishment (See Corporal punishment of
        children)
    Girl Scouts Beyond Bars program, mothers
        convicted of child abuse not eligible for, 40–41
    Las Comadres educational program, issues of
        abuse and family violence raised in, 135

Childbirth, 54

Child Custody Advocacy Services (CHICAS)
    Project, 21

Child custody and family reunification
    Bedford Hills (New York) Correctional Facility
        Children's Center workshops, 72
    Center for Children of Incarcerated Parents,
        Pasadena, California, 21–22
    counseling, 31
    legal rights, 29
    male versus female offenders, 1, 2
    Neil J. Houston House, Roxbury, Massachusetts,
        115–129
    pregnant offenders, 115
    recidivism, effect of, 2–3
    reunification services, 4
    Rhode Island Women's Prison, 29

Child welfare system, 4

Children of incarcerated mothers
    alternative adult role models, need for, 37
    Bedford Hills (New York) Correctional Facility
        Children's Center Programs, 55–86
    Center for Children of Incarcerated Parents,
        Pasadena, California, 15–23
    Children's Advocacy Program, 69–71
    community programs, 37–38
    correctional facility, residence in (See Residential
        programs)
    criminal involvement, likelihood of, 37, 51, 53,
        82, 100
    educational programs for, 53–54
    Fetal Alcohol Syndrome and Fetal Alcohol
        Effects, 9
    generational cycle of crime, program to intercept,
        51
    LINK (Life Is Nurturing Kids) program, Harrisburg,
        Pennsylvania, 53
    mental health programs, Girl Scouts Beyond Bars
        Program, 40, 43

mentoring program for, 53
needs of child, encouraging mothers to consider,
    70–71
newborns, Bedford Hills (New York) Correctional
    Facility Nursery program for, 74–78
placement, 3
psycho-social damage sustained by, 164–165
services for incarcerated mothers, involvement in
    designing and implementing, 5
special needs of, 56
statistics on problems faced by, 36–37
therapeutic intervention programs for, 22

Classification of offenders
    Bedford Hills (New York) maximum-security
        facility, Children's Center programs, 55–86
    Girl Scouts Beyond Bars program, Maryland, 40
    Neil J. Houston House, Roxbury, Massachusetts,
        127
    residential programs, 163
    Rhode Island Women's Prison children's center
        for minimum-custody and work-release
        inmates, 28
    Summit House program for nonviolent offenders,
        100, 101
    village-style institutions for minimum-security
        prisoners, 160

CODAC
    Rhode Island Women's Prison program, 28

Columbia
    pregnant offenders, 161

Communication skills
    PATCH (Parents and Their Children at Home)
        program, Harrisburg, Pennsylvania, 52
    substance abuse programs, 13

Community involvement and programs
    Australia, 162
    Bedford Hills (New York) Correctional Facility
        Children's Center programs, 80–81
    children of incarcerated mothers, special
        community needs of, 37–38
    Girl Scouts Beyond Bars Program, 37–38
        Arizona, 44
        chart of, 45
        Fort Lauderdale, Florida, 43
        Tallahassee, Florida, 42
    incarcerated mother's involvement in child care,
        69
    incarceration, alternative, xiii
    LINK (Life Is Nurturing Kids) program, Harrisburg,
        Pennsylvania, 53
    MOLD (Mother Offspring Life Development)
        Program, 152
    Neil J. Houston House, Roxbury, Massachusetts,
        116, 120–121
    residential programs for mothers and children,
        161–162
    Rhode Island Women's Prison, 29, 31–32
    services for incarcerated mothers, designing and
        implementing, xii, 5
    staffing, 5
    Summit House, 100, 104

Sweden, 162
verification of programs provided by, 96

Connecticut
NEON (Norwalk Economic Opportunity Now)
Women's and Children's Halfway House
(WCHH) model, 87–98

Contact between mother and child, 2
between-visit contact and communication,
programs providing, 65
visitation programs (See Visitation programs)

Contraband
Girl Scouts Beyond Bars program, 41
searches, children disturbed by, 27, 52

Corporal punishment of children
Camp Dismas program, 145
maternal offender's opposition to custodial adult's
use of, 69–70
NEON (Norwalk Economic Opportunity Now)
Women's and Children's Halfway House
(WCHH) model, 96

Correctional population, persons working with
Bedford Hills (New York) Correctional Facility
Children's Center programs, 79–80
Center for Children of Incarcerated Parents,
Pasadena, California, 16–17
community programs (See Community programs)
expertise in dealing with parents and children,
need for, 28
Girl Scouts Beyond Bars program, 41
group supervision and debriefing, importance
of, 32
inmate-centered programs, 18, 57, 58, 78–79
Las Comadres foster mother and birth mother
mentoring program, 137
Neil J. Houston House, Roxbury, Massachusetts,
126
NEON (Norwalk Economic Opportunity Now)
Women's and Children's Halfway House
(WCHH) model, 94
Rhode Island Women's Prison, 28, 32
services for incarcerated mothers, designing and
implementing, 5–6
staffing resources, 5, 6
Summit House, 104, 105
therapeutic intervention training, 20

Counseling
child custody and family reunification, 30–31
Neil J. Houston House, Roxbury, Massachusetts,
117

Crime prevention
generational cycle of crime, programs to
intercept, 37, 51, 53, 82, 100

D

DARE (Drug Abuse Resistance Education)
Dismas Charities initiative, 149

Day-reporting programs
nonviolent maternal offenders, 99–112

Delaware
Girl Scouts Beyond Bars, 36, 45

Discharge planning, 97

Dismas Charities, Inc., Louisville, Kentucky
Camp Dismas program, 141–150
Girl Scouts Beyond Bars, 36

Diversity training
substance abuse program, as part of, 12–13

Domestic violence, 4
Girl Scouts Beyond Bars program, mothers
convicted of child abuse not eligible for, 40–41
Las Comadres educational program, issues of
abuse and family violence raised in, 135

Drug abuse (See Substance abuse)

Drug Abuse Resistance Education (DARE)
Dismas Charities initiative, 149

E

Early child development and parental bonding
Bedford Hills (New York) Correctional Facility
Nursery program, 74–78
incarceration of mother, effect of, 100
Las Comadres foster mother and birth mother
mentoring program, 131–132, 134
MOLD courses, 153–154
Neil J. Houston House, Roxbury, Massachusetts,
128
NEON (Norwalk Economic Opportunity Now)
Women's and Children's Halfway House
(WCHH) model, 90–91

Early Therapeutic Intervention Project (ETIP), 22

Education and information services
adolescent inmates, 73
Bedford Hills Correctional Facility Children's
Center Programs, Bedford Hills, New York,
72–74
bibliographies (See Reference materials)
Center for Children of Incarcerated Parents,
Pasadena, California, 17–20
children of incarcerated mothers, educational
programs for, 53–54
Clearinghouse at Pacific Oaks, 17
communication skills
PATCH (Parents and Their Children at Home)
program, Harrisburg, Pennsylvania, 52
substance abuse programs, 13
court requirements, 4
Ex-Offenders' Parent Education Project
(EPEP), 19
Family Life Education Project (FLEP), 20
Jail Health Education Project, 20
life skills (See Life skills)
literacy program, Bedford Hills (New York)
Correctional Facility Children's Center, 83
maternal offenders' self-examination programs,
73–74
MOLD (Mother Offspring Life Development)
Program, 152–154
Neil J. Houston House, Roxbury, Massachusetts,
120, 128
NEON (Norwalk Economic Opportunity Now)
Women's and Children's Halfway House
(WCHH) model, 96
parenting skills (See Parenting skills)

pregnant women and mothers of newborns,
Bedford Hills (New York) Correctional
Facility Nursery program, 76
Prison Parents' Education Project (PPEP), 18–19
Reclaiming Parenthood Project (REPP), 20
reference materials (See Reference materials)
substance abuse programs, 12
Summit House, 104
Therapeutic Intervention Project (TIP) Training
Project, 20
England
residential programs for mothers and children,
161
EPEP (Ex-Offenders' Parent Education Project), 19
Ethnicity
children of incarcerated mothers, LINK program
volunteers ethnically matched with, 53
diversity training as part of substance abuse
program, 12–13
Evaluation of program and inmate performance
Camp Dismas program, 148–149
Florida Department of Corrections SAPPORT
program, 14
Las Comadres foster mother and birth mother
mentoring program, 139
LINK (Life Is Nurturing Kids) program,
Harrisburg, Pennsylvania, 54
MOLD (Mother Offspring Life Development)
Program, 156–157
NEON (Norwalk Economic Opportunity Now)
Women's and Children's Halfway House
(WCHH) model, 97
Summit House
funding provisions, 103
goals for clients, 105
program evaluation, 110
Ex-offenders, programs for
Center for Children of Incarcerated Parents,
Pasadena, California, 19
discharge plans, 97
Girl Scouts Beyond Bars program, 40
Fort Lauderdale, Florida program, 43
Tallahassee, Florida program, 42
halfway houses
NEON (Norwalk Economic Opportunity Now)
Women's and Children's Halfway House
(WCHH) model, 87–98
Summit House, 99–112
Neil J. Houston House, Roxbury, Massachusetts,
121
NEON (Norwalk Economic Opportunity Now)
Women's and Children's Halfway House
(WCHH) model, 87–98
verification requirements, 96

F

Family court, 68
Family Life Education Project (FLEP), 20
Family reunification (See Child custody and family
reunification)
Fathers, incarcerated (See Paternal offenders)

Female offenders and female offender programs
ACA policy on, vii–viii
growth in, xii
history of, xi–xiii, 26–27
male offenders, female offenders versus
different needs of, xi, 1
substance abuse statistics, Florida, 10
mothers (See Maternal offenders, Maternal
offender programs, See also more specific topics)
programming for, 4
Fetal Alcohol Syndrome and Fetal Alcohol
Effects, 9
Figures
Bedford Hills (New York) Correctional Facility
Children's Center programs, timeline, 83–85
Girl Scouts Beyond Bars community
partnerships, 45
Johari's Window, 13
Maryland, statistics for maternal offenders, 39
FLEP (Family Life Education Project), 20
Florida
Department of Corrections
male versus female offenders, substance abuse
statistics, 10
Substance Abusing Pregnant and Post-Partum
Offenders Receiving Treatment (SAPPORT)
program, 10–14
Girl Scouts Beyond Bars Program, 45
Broward County, 36
Fort Lauderdale, 42–44
Tallahassee, 41–42
Foster care
Bedford Hills (New York) Correctional Facility
Children's Center workshops, 68, 73
group homes connected to correctional
facilities, 70
historically, xii
incarcerated mother's involvement in child care,
68–69
Las Comadres program, 131–140
visitation, custodial adults' resistance to, 66, 67
Friends Outside
Las Comadres foster mother and birth mother
mentoring program, 132–140
Funding
Bedford Hills (New York) Correctional Facility
Children's Center programs, 81
Camp Dismas program, 145
Center for Children of Incarcerated Parents,
Pasadena, California, 15
Florida Department of Corrections SAPPORT
program, 10
Girl Scouts Beyond Bars program, 41, 45, 46
Fort Lauderdale, Florida program, 44
Ohio program, 44
Tallahassee, Florida program, 42
MOLD (Mother Offspring Life Development)
Program, 152
Neil J. Houston House, Roxbury, Massachusetts,
126

NEON (Norwalk Economic Opportunity Now) Women's and Children's Halfway House (WCHH) model, 89

Rhode Island Women's Prison visitation and parenting education program, 28

Summit House, 101–103

G

Gender differences, 1

Generational cycle of crime
programs to intercept, 37, 51, 53, 82, 100

Germany
Preungesheim Prison residential program, 163–164

Girl Scouts Beyond Bars program, 35–49, 149

Goals and objectives
Camp Dismas program, 142
Florida Department of Corrections SAPPORT program, 10–11
Las Comadres foster mother and birth mother mentoring program, 131–132
Neil J. Houston House, Roxbury, Massachusetts, 118
NEON (Norwalk Economic Opportunity Now) Women's and Children's Halfway House (WCHH) model, 90–91
PATCH (Parents and Their Children at Home) program, Harrisburg, Pennsylvania, 52–53
Summit House, 104–105

Greensboro, North Carolina
Commission on the Status of Women, 100
Women's Learning and Resource Center, 101

Guilford County, North Carolina
Women's Residential and Day Center, 100

H

Halfway houses
NEON (Norwalk Economic Opportunity Now) Women's and Children's Halfway House (WCHH) model, 87–98
Summit House, 99–112

Harrisburg, Pennsylvania
PROGRAM for Female Offenders, Inc., 51–54

Health services
emergency procedures, Camp Dismas program, 144
Jail Health Education Project, 20
MOLD (Mother Offspring Life Development) Program, 153–154
Neil J. Houston House, Roxbury, Massachusetts, 118–120
NEON (Norwalk Economic Opportunity Now) Women's and Children's Halfway House (WCHH) model, 95–96
pregnant offenders, 118–120

HIV (See AIDS and HIV)

Holloway Prison, London, England
residential programs for mothers and children, 161

Home child care programs
Preungesheim Prison, Germany, 163–164

I

Incarcerated fathers (See Paternal offenders)

Incarcerated mothers (See Maternal offenders)

Incarcerated parents (See Parental offenders)

Information services (See Education and information services)

Interagency relationships, 31

Interviews
NEON (Norwalk Economic Opportunity Now) Women's and Children's Halfway House (WCHH) model, 92–93

J

Jail Health Education Project, 20

Jails, Girl Scouts Beyond Bars, 47

Johari's Window
substance abuse programs, 13

K

Kentucky
Dismas Charities, Inc., Louisville, 141–150
Girl Scouts Beyond Bars, 36, 45

L

Las Comadres, 131–140

Life Is Nurturing Kids (LINK) program, Harrisburg, Pennsylvania, 53

Life skills
MOLD (Mother Offspring Life Development) Program, 153–154
Neil J. Houston House, Roxbury, Massachusetts, 128
substance abuse programs, 13–14
Summit House programs, 106–108

LINK (Life Is Nurturing Kids) program, Harrisburg, Pennsylvania, 53

Literacy programs
Bedford Hills (New York) Correctional Facility Children's Center programs, 83

Louisville, Kentucky
Dismas Charities, Inc., 141–150

M

Male versus female offenders
different needs of, xi, 1
substance abuse statistics, Florida, 10

Maryland Correctional Institution for Women (MCIW)
Girl Scouts Beyond Bars program, 35–49

Massachusetts
Neil J. Houston House, Roxbury, 113–129
Reformatory for Women, xi
Social Justice for Women (SJW), Boston, 114

Maternal authority and responsibility (See Parental authority and responsibility)

Maternal bonding (See Early child development and parental bonding)
Maternal offender programs (See also more specific topics)
  ACA policy on, vii–viii
  history of, xi–xiii, 26–27
  inmate-centered, 18, 57, 58, 78–79
Maternal offenders (See also Parental offenders)
  admission to programs, requirements for (See Admission to programs, requirements for)
  aftercare, 10
  adolescent inmates, educational program for, 73
  children's needs, focusing on, 70–71, 153
  classification of (See Classification of offenders)
  cooperation between, 96–97, 104
  educational programs focusing on self-examination and self-knowledge, 73–74
  inmate-centered programs, 18, 57, 58, 78–79
  in jails, 1
  mental health programs
    NEON (Norwalk Economic Opportunity Now) Women's and Children's Halfway House (WCHH) model, 95
    Summit House, 107
  parental rights, 68
  parenting skills of, 2
  pregnant women (See Pregnant offenders)
  primary care, Summit House residential and day-reporting programs allowing mothers to provide, 99–112
  in prisons, 1, 3
  services for incarcerated mothers, involvement in designing and implementing, 5
  special needs of, 56
  special problems of, 32
  statistics (See Statistics)
Maternal rights
  custody issues (See Child custody and family reunification)
  incarcerated parents, rights of, 68
Maximum-security facilities
  Bedford Hills (New York) Correctional Facility Children's Center programs, 55–86
MCIW (Maryland Correctional Institution for Women)
  Girl Scouts Beyond Bars program, 35–49
Medical treatment (See Health services)
Mental health programs, children of incarcerated mothers
  Girl Scouts Beyond Bars Program, 40, 43
Mental health programs, maternal offenders
  NEON (Norwalk Economic Opportunity Now) Women's and Children's Halfway House (WCHH) model, 95
  Summit House, 107
Mentoring programs
  children of incarcerated mothers, 53
  Las Comadres foster mother and birth mother mentoring program, 131–140

Methadone maintenance
  substance abuse, 119, 127
Money management (See Budget management, Life skills)
Mother Offspring Life Development (MOLD) Program, 151–157
Mother/child relationship (See Parent/child relationship)
MotherRight Project, 21–22
Mutter-Kind-Heim, Preungesheim Prison, Germany
  residential program, 163–164

N
National Committee on Prison, xii
National Institute of Corrections, 10, 11
National Institute of Justice (NIJ), 36
Nebraska Center for Women
  MOLD (Mother Offspring Life Development) Program, 151–157
Needs assessment
  parenting skills, 29
Neil J. Houston House, Roxbury, Massachusetts, 113–129
NEON (Norwalk Economic Opportunity Now) Women's and Children's Halfway House (WCHH) model, 87–98
New Jersey
  Girl Scouts Beyond Bars, 36, 45
New York
  Bedford Hills Correctional Facility Children's Center Programs, 55–86
Newborns
  Bedford Hills (New York) Correctional Facility Nursery program, 74–78
  Las Comadres foster mother and birth mother mentoring program, 131–140
  MOLD (Mother Offspring Life Development) Program, 151
North Carolina
  Greensboro Commission on the Status of Women, 100
  Women's Learning and Resource Center (WLRC), 101
  Guilford County Women's Residential and Day Center, 100
  Summit House, 99–112
Norwalk Economic Opportunity Now (NEON) Women's and Children's Halfway House (WCHH) model, 87–98
Nursery facilities (See Residential programs)

O
Objectives (See Goals and objectives)
Ohio
  Girl Scouts Beyond Bars program, 36, 44, 45
Orientation (See Admission and orientation procedures)

P

Parental authority and responsibility
  initiative and involvement, encouraging, 69–70
  need to maintain, 3
  NEON (Norwalk Economic Opportunity Now)
    Women's and Children's Halfway House
    (WCHH) model, 96
  pregnant women and mothers of newborns,
    Bedford Hills (New York) Correctional Facility
    Nursery program, 77
  support programs, 66
  visitation programs, 64

Parental bonding (See Early child development and
  parental bonding)

Parental offenders
  Center for Children of Incarcerated Parents,
    Pasadena, California, 16
  fathers specifically (See Paternal offenders)
  male versus female
    different needs of, xi, 1
    substance abuse statistics, Florida, 10
  mothers specifically (See Maternal offenders)
  parental rights, 68
  tatistics regarding, 1

Parental rights
  black families, 2
  custody issues (See Child custody and family
    reunification)
  incarcerated parents, rights of, 68

Parent/child relationship
  child's understanding of mother's problem,
    attempts to foster, 143
  damage caused by incarceration, 165
  early child development and parental bonding
    (See Early child development and parental
    bonding)
  needs of child, helping mother to focus on, 70–71
  permanent role, attempt to establish, 142
  problems in maintaining, 3–4
  socialization goals, 52
  strengthening, programs aimed at, 56–57, 100
  visitation programs and, 62–64

Parenting skills
  baby hygiene, xii
  Bedford Hills Correctional Facility Children's
    Center Programs, Bedford Hills, New York, 72
  Center for Children of Incarcerated Parents,
    Pasadena, California, 21–22
  court requirement, 4
  Dismas program, 142–143
  expectation, 4
  Girl Scouts Beyond Bars program, 39–40
    Tallahassee, Florida program, 41–42
  MOLD (Mother Offspring Life Development)
    Program, 153–154
  needs assessment, 29
  needs of child, encouraging mothers to focus
    on, 70–71
  Neil J. Houston House, Roxbury, Massachusetts,
    128

NEON (Norwalk Economic Opportunity Now)
  Women's and Children's Halfway House
  (WCHH) model, 95
PATCH (Parents and Their Children at Home)
  program, Harrisburg, Pennsylvania, 51–53
reading to children, 30, 65
residential program, demonstration of learned
  skills in, 107
Rhode Island Women's Prison, 28, 29–30
studies of incarcerated mothers, 2
substance abuse programs, 13–14, 20
Summit House programs, 106–108
visitation program, combined with, 30–31, 52
women other than mothers in caretaking roles, 30

Parents and Their Children at Home (PATCH)
  program, Harrisburg, Pennsylvania, 51–53

Pasadena, California
  Center for Children of Incarcerated Parents,
    15–23

PATCH (Parents and Their Children at Home)
  program, Harrisburg, Pennsylvania, 51–53

Paternal offenders
  Center for Children of Incarcerated Parents,
    Pasadena, California, 20
  Family Life Education Project (FLEP) and Young
    Father's Project, 20
  Rhode Island prison system, 28

Pennsylvania
  PROGRAM for Female Offenders, Inc.,
    Harrisburg, 51–54

Performance evaluations (See Evaluation of
  program and inmate performance)

Philosophy of programs
  assumptions generally underlying most
    programs, 165
  Bedford Hills Correctional Facility Children's
    Center Programs, Bedford Hills, New York, 57
  Girl Scouts Beyond Bars Program, 36–38
  Neil J. Houston House, Roxbury, Massachusetts,
    116–117
  NEON (Norwalk Economic Opportunity Now)
    Women's and Children's Halfway House
    (WCHH) model, 90–91
  residential programs, 162
  Summit House, 104

PPEP (Prison Parents' Education Project), 18–19

Pregnant offenders
  Bedford Hills (New York) Correctional Facility
    Nursery program, 74–78
  Columbia, 161
  custody and separation issues, 115
  health services, 118–120
  high-risk, 14
  Holloway Prison, London, England, 161
  Las Comadres foster mother and birth mother
    mentoring program, 131–140
  MOLD (Mother Offspring Life Development)
    Program, 153–154
  Neil J. Houston House, Roxbury, Massachusetts,
    115–129

substance abuse, treatment of, 10, 119

Preungesheim Prison, Germany
residential program, 163–164

Prison Parents' Education Project (PPEP), 18–19

PROGRAM for Female Offenders, Inc., Harrisburg,
Pennsylvania, 51–54

Q

Quakers, reformatories for women, xi

Quality time
Camp Dismas program, 141–150

R

Recidivism
child custody, effect on, 2–3
substance abuse program aimed at preventing, 12
Summit House program for high-risk maternal
offenders, 108
welfare of child, parental understanding of effect
on, 143

Reclaiming Parenthood Project (REPP), 20

Reference materials
Bedford Hills (New York) Correctional Facility
Children's Center programs, 85–86
Center for Children of Incarcerated Parents,
Pasadena, California, 17
Clearinghouse at Pacific Oaks, 17
services for incarcerated mothers, designing and
implementing, 6–8
Summit House (North Carolina) residential and
day-reporting programs, 111–112

Reformatories for women, xi–xii

Rehabilitation
Bedford Hills (New York) Correctional Facility
Children's Center programs, 82
Neil J. Houston House, Roxbury, Massachusetts,
reintegration and resettlement programs,
120–121, 128
Summit House, 104, 107

Reinforcement techniques
Summit House behavior modification program,
108

Relapse prevention (See Substance abuse, relapse
prevention)

Release from prison, treatment following (See
Ex-offenders, programs for)

Re-parenting of maternal offenders
Las Comadres foster mother and birth mother
mentoring program, 134

Repeat offenders (See Recidivism)

REPP (Reclaiming Parenthood Project), 20

Research projects
Center for Children of Incarcerated Parents,
Pasadena, California, 18

Residential programs
Argentina, 160
Australia, 160, 161
Bedford Hills (New York) Correctional Facility
Nursery program, 74–78, 159, 160, 161

California, 162
classification of offenders, 163
community programs, 161–162
England, 161
Germany, 163–164
historical background, xi–xii, 26
Holloway Prison, London, England, 161
international trends, 159–165
mother-child centered approach, 162–164
Neil J. Houston House, Roxbury, Massachusetts,
113–129
NEON (Norwalk Economic Opportunity Now)
Women's and Children's Halfway House
(WCHH) model, 87–98
nonviolent maternal offenders, 99–112, 100
philosophy of program, 162
security issues, 163
Summit House, 99–112
traditional institutions, 160–161
United Kingdom, 161
village-style institutions, 160

Reunification with child (See Child custody and
family reunification)

Rhode Island Women's Prison, 25–33

Roulet, Sister Elaine
Bedford Hills (New York) Correctional Facility
Children's Center Programs, 58, 70, 80, 81, 83,
159

Roxbury, Massachusetts
Neil J. Houston House, 113–129

S

Scheduling practices
Camp Dismas program, 143–144
Neil J. Houston House, Roxbury, Massachusetts,
123–125

School system, involvement of
Girl Scouts Beyond Bars Program, Tallahassee,
Florida, 42

Screening and referral of maternal offenders (See
Admission to programs, requirements for)

Security issues
classification of offenders (See Classification of
offenders)
contraband, detecting
Girl Scouts Beyond Bars program, 41
searches, children disturbed by, 27, 52
Neil J. Houston House, Roxbury, Massachusetts,
126–127
residential programs, 163

Self-esteem
Florida Department of Corrections SAPPORT
program, 12–13
Las Comadres foster mother and birth mother
mentoring program, 135
LINK (Life Is Nurturing Kids) program,
Harrisburg, Pennsylvania, 54

Services for incarcerated mothers (See also more
specific topics)
designing and implementing, 4–6
multiple needs, necessity of meeting, 94–95

types required, 3–4

Sex education, 12, 153

SJW (Social Justice for Women), 114

Smith, Betsey
  Neil J. Houston House, Roxbury, Massachusetts, and Boston's Social Justice for Women (SJW), 113, 114

Social Justice for Women (SJW), 114

Staffing (See Correctional population, persons working with)

Statistics
  children of incarcerated mothers, problems faced by, 36–37
  maternal offenders
    Bedford Hills, New York, 59
    Camp Dismas program, 143
    Maryland, 39
    Massachusetts, 114
    Neil J. Houston House, Roxbury, Massachusetts, 122
    North Carolina, 99
    U.S., generally, 164
  parental offenders, 1
  Rhode Island women prisoners, 25
  substance abuse
    childbearing age, female users of, 9
    male versus female offenders, Florida Department of Corrections, 10

Stress management, 12

Substance abuse, 9–11
  Center for Children of Incarcerated Parents, Pasadena, California, 16, 20
  communication skills, 13
  Dismas Charities DARE initiative, 149
  education and information, providing, 12
  ethnic diversity training, role of, 12–13
  Florida Department of Corrections SAPPORT program, 10–14
  Johari's Window, 13
  methadone maintenance, 119, 127
  Neil J. Houston House, Roxbury, Massachusetts, 119, 120, 127, 129
  MOLD courses, 154
  NEON (Norwalk Economic Opportunity Now) Women's and Children's Halfway House (WCHH) model, 95
  parenting skills...13–14, 20
  pregnant offenders, treatment of, 119
  PROGRAM for female offenders, 51
  Reclaiming Parenthood Project (REPP), 20
  recovery, introducing concept of, 12–13
  relapse prevention, 12, 13
  statistics
    childbearing age, female users of, 9
    male versus female offenders in Florida, 10
  Summit House programs, 104
  treatment requirements, 4
  Women's Health and Learning Center, Massachusetts, 114–115

Summit House, 99–112

Support programs
  Las Comadres foster mother volunteers, 138–139
  parental authority and responsibility, encouraging, 66
  visitation program, as part of, 65, 67

Sweden
  community programs, 162

T
Technical assistance
  Center for Children of Incarcerated Parents, Pasadena, California, 17–18

Telephone contact for maternal offenders, 3

Therapeutic intervention
  children of incarcerated mothers, programs for, 22
  Summit House, 100, 104
  training for correctional workers, 20

Transportation issues, 1, 27, 81, 148

Treatment techniques
  Las Comadres foster mother and birth mother mentoring program, 134–135
  Neil J. Houston House, Roxbury, Massachusetts, 117
  NEON (Norwalk Economic Opportunity Now) Women's and Children's Halfway House (WCHH) model, 95

Twelve-step programs
  Neil J. Houston House, Roxbury, Massachusetts, 117
  NEON (Norwalk Economic Opportunity Now) Women's and Children's Halfway House (WCHH) model, 95

U
United Kingdom
  residential programs for mothers and children, 161

V
Visitation programs
  Bedford Hills, 61–65
  Camp Dismas program, 141–150
  contact between visits, programs providing, 65
  contraband searches, problems with, 27, 52
  custodial adults' resistance to, 66, 67
  distance and, 1
  extended visits, 28, 30, 61–62, 141–150, 155–156
  Girl Scouts Beyond Bars program, 35–49
  importance of, 3–4
  importance to children and mothers, 62–64
  Las Comadres foster mother and birth mother mentoring program, 133, 136–137
  MOLD (Mother Offspring Life Development) Program, 155–156
  obstacles to, 3–4
  on-site childcare, 3
  parental authority and responsibility, 64
  parental instruction, combined with, 30–31, 52
  play as part of, 60–61
  preparation and planning for visits, 30–31

Rhode Island Women's Prison, 26, 27–28, 30–31
  separate children's centers, value of, 28, 60–61
  supervision of visits, problems with, 27, 52
  support program as part of, 65, 67
  transportation issues, 1, 27, 81, 148

Visiting rooms, xiii, 52, 60

Vocational training and counseling
  Dismas Owensboro program, 149
  NEON (Norwalk Economic Opportunity Now)
    Women's and Children's Halfway House
    (WCHH) model, 96

W

WCHH (Women's and Children's Halfway House)
  model
  NEON (Norwalk Economic Opportunity Now),
  87–98

Women offenders (See Female offenders and
  female offender programs)

Women other than mothers in caretaking roles
  parenting skills, 30

Women's and Children's Halfway House (WCHH)
  model
  NEON (Norwalk Economic Opportunity Now),
  87–98

Women's Education and Empowerment Series,
  20

Women's Health and Learning Center
  Social Justice for Women (SJW), 114

Women's reformatory (See Reformatory for
women)

Work-release programs, offenders in
  Preungesheim Prison, Germany, 163–164
  Rhode Island Women's Prison children's center,
  28

Y

Young Father's Project, 20

About the Editor

Cynthia L. Blinn is an author and educator who entered corrections in 1993 as an independent program consultant to the Massachusetts Department of Correction. She developed and implemented educational curricula for the Massachusetts Department of Correction designed to teach cognitive skills through writing and literature. *THINK FIRST*, her step-by-step model for problem solving, incorporated in both the *Writing for Our Lives* program as well as in the literature-based discussion program *ABLE MINDS: Using Literature to Transform Behavior*, has been used effectively with offenders in correctional facilities and work release programs across the country. Also a public school educator, Cynthia Blinn has an interest in the welfare and education of all children, and a special interest in the high-risk populations served by the programs described in *Maternal Ties*.